The Unsearchable
Riches of Christ

The Unsearchable Riches of Christ

An Exposition of Ephesians 3:1 to 21

D. M. LLOYD-JONES

BAKER BOOK HOUSE
Grand Rapids, Michigan

PHOTOLITHOPRINTED BY CUSHING - MALLOY, INC.
ANN ARBOR, MICHIGAN, UNITED STATES OF AMERICA

Preface

Each chapter of this book records a sermon preached by me on a Sunday morning during my regular ministry in Westminster Chapel, London, during the year 1956.

The title suggests immediately that we have here the Apostle Paul's profoundest or highest teaching. At the same time it is, possibly, the most experimental chapter in all his epistles, and one in which the fervour of his great pastoral spirit is most evident. This with the references to himself and to his calling, together with his recording of his fervent prayers for these Ephesian Christians, leads to one of the sublimest and most eloquent and moving statements the Apostle ever wrote.

Its intrinsic value demands attention at all times, but it is particularly relevant to the condition of the church today. Its experimental or experiential emphasis is needed urgently in view of certain alarming tendencies.

One tendency is what is described as fideism or 'easy-believism'. This, in its crudest form, teaches that in the light of Romans 10:9 if we but say that we believe, then we are saved. But still more dangerous, perhaps, is the highly intellectualist attitude which argues that in the light of the third verse of the first chapter of the Epistle to the Ephesians, all believers have already received everything possible to the Christian, and should never be seeking any further blessing. This erroneous teaching, which dislikes any emphasis on experience, is but a modern version of what was propagated in Scotland by the Glassites, and in England by the Sandemanians, of the eighteenth century, and which led to much spiritual dryness, hardness and barrenness.

The simple answer to such teaching is found in this third chapter of Ephesians, where Paul tells us that he prayed constantly that the Ephesians, who had already believed and received so much, should receive so much more – even to being filled with 'all the fulness of God'! The Puritans of the seventeenth century likewise drew, and emphasized, the vital distinction between believing in what is possible for the Christian, and the appropriating of that possibility. This common modern attitude which is so afraid of experiencing the love of God, because of the excesses of certain people who put experiences before truth, is virtually a defence of the attitude of the members of the church of Laodicea who said: 'I have need of nothing'.

If I were asked to name the greatest trouble among Christians today, including those who are evangelical, I would say that it is our lack of spirituality and of a true knowledge of God. We have a certain knowledge about God, and we are expert in the 'Christian attitude' towards politics, social affairs, drama, art, literature, etc. but do we, with Paul, say that our deepest desire is to 'know Him'?

No man had a greater theological and intellectual understanding than the Apostle Paul, but, at the same time, no man had a deeper, personal and experimental knowledge of 'the love of Christ which passeth knowledge'. To put our entire emphasis on the one or the other, or to over-emphasize either is the prevailing danger today. We should be concerned about both. We are to 'grow in grace and in the knowledge of the Lord'. We can never know too much concerning the great doctrines of the Faith, but if that knowledge does not lead to an ever deeper experience of the love of Christ, it is merely the knowledge that 'puffeth up'.

Thank God, both are possible for us, and it is my prayer and my trust that the reading of this book will help many to attain unto both increasingly. What do we really know?

As ever, I am deeply grateful for the invaluable help and assistance of Mrs E. Burney, who has laboured with the typing, Mr S. M. Houghton and my wife.

D. M. Lloyd-Jones

London
July 1979

[6]

Contents

THE UNSEARCHABLE RICHES OF CHRIST

Ephesians 3:1-21

1 *For this cause I Paul, the prisoner of Jesus Christ for you Gentiles,*

2 *If ye have heard of the dispensation of the grace of God which is given me to you-ward:*

3 *How that by revelation he made known unto me the mystery; (as I wrote afore in few words,*

4 *Whereby, when ye read, ye may understand my knowledge in the mystery of Christ)*

5 *Which in other ages was not made known unto the sons of men, as it is now revealed unto his holy apostles and prophets by the Spirit;*

6 *That the Gentiles should be fellow-heirs, and of the same body, and partakers of his promise in Christ by the gospel:*

7 *Whereof I was made a minister, according to the gift of the grace of God given unto me by the effectual working of his power.*

8 *Unto me, who am less than the least of all saints, is this grace given, that I should preach among the Gentiles the unsearchable riches of Christ;*

9 *And to make all men see what is the fellowship of the mystery, which from the beginning of the world hath been hid in God, who created all things by Jesus Christ:*

10 *To the intent that now unto the principalities and*

powers in heavenly places *might be known by the church the manifold wisdom of God,*

11 *According to the eternal purpose which he purposed in Christ Jesus our Lord:*

12 *In whom we have boldness and access with confidence by the faith of him.*

13 *Wherefore I desire that ye faint not at my tribulations for you, which is your glory.*

14 *For this cause I bow my knees unto the Father of our Lord Jesus Christ.*

15 *Of whom the whole family in heaven and earth is named,*

16 *That he would grant you, according to the riches of his glory, to be strengthened with might by his Spirit in the inner man;*

17 *That Christ may dwell in your hearts by faith; that ye, being rooted and grounded in love,*

18 *May be able to comprehend with all saints what* is *the breadth, and length, and depth, and height;*

19 *And to know the love of Christ, which passeth knowledge, that ye might be filled with all the fulness of God.*

20 *Now unto him that is able to do exceeding abundantly above all that we ask or think, according to the power that worketh in us,*

21 *Unto him* be *glory in the church by Christ Jesus throughout all ages, world without end. Amen.*

I
'The Prisoner of Jesus Christ'

'For this cause I Paul, the prisoner of Jesus Christ for you Gentiles.'

Ephesians 3:1

As we begin to consider the third chapter of this Epistle to the Ephesians it is most important that we should remind ourselves of its context and setting. The mind of the great Apostle always worked very logically. He was not an intuitive thinker; he was a logical thinker. He does not simply throw out ideas, he always has a plan and a scheme. However much he may depart from it here and there, fundamentally he always comes back to it. The very word 'For' at the beginning of the chapter reminds us of the connection. It is to our advantage that these New Testament epistles were divided up into chapters; but we must never forget that originally they were not thus divided. I doubt whether there was even an indication of a new paragraph at this point, but the authorities who divided it into chapters felt that they should divide it up in this way; and on the whole the divisions are valuable. Sometimes it can be a real hindrance, because it gives the impression that a new chapter introduces a new subject.

Here, clearly and obviously, it does not do so. 'For this cause', or 'because of this', says the Apostle; but to what is he referring? Clearly, to what he has just been saying, namely, that the astounding truth which has come to light in the gospel of Jesus Christ is that the Gentiles who have believed the gospel have been made one body with the Jews in Christ Jesus. That is the message of the second chapter. These Gentile Ephesians who had been 'dead in trespasses and sins', who were 'strangers from the covenants of promise and aliens from the commonwealth of Israel, without hope and without God in the world', had been 'made nigh'. Not

[11]

only so, but of these twain 'one new man' had been made, 'so making peace'. This had led on to the doctrine of the nature of the Christian Church, showing that Gentile Christians are now 'fellow citizens with the saints, and (members) of the household of God', 'built upon the foundation of the apostles and prophets', and are made 'a holy temple' for the Lord to dwell in. This is true of both Gentiles and Jews; all middle walls of partition have been broken down and abolished; all the enmity has gone. This amazing unity and peace has been brought to pass through the blood of our Lord and Saviour Jesus Christ (2:13).

Having expounded those truths to the Ephesians, the Apostle says: Now then, because of that, I Paul the prisoner of Jesus Christ for you Gentiles, . . .' Suddenly, however, he seems to stop. He was obviously going to say something further, but he pauses, he hesitates, and he does not say it until he gets to verse 14, where we find exactly the same formula again – 'For this cause I' – and then he goes on to tell them that he is praying for them, and what he is praying for them. In other words, from verse 2 to the end of verse 13 we have a long digression, and the punctuation should have given indications of this at the end of verses 1 and 13.

In this digression the Apostle gives the Ephesians an account of his own ministry – his calling, his office – and its great object and purpose. Then, having done so, he comes back again to his theme and says what he was setting out to say in the first verse.

*   *   *

Bearing this in mind we must consider why the Apostle suddenly interrupted his own thought, and introduced this digression. Why did he for the time being interrupt the flow of his argument and thus become guilty of what the purists and the pedants call a blemish in his style? The criticism that is brought against Paul as a stylist is that he is constantly guilty of what they call anacoluthia, that is to say, interruptions in which the writer suddenly breaks off from what he is saying and goes off on to something else, and perhaps never comes back to what he had intended saying. In other words, instead of the style flowing on steadily and easily and quietly, suddenly there comes an interruption, an interjection, a digression, a parenthesis. It is bad style, say the pedants, thoroughly bad style. The Apostle is certainly guilty of that at this particular point, so we must ask ourselves why he did so. What was it that suddenly gripped him and moved him to introduce the digression? There is no real difficulty about answering the question. He gives the answer himself in verse 13, which must be taken with verses 1 and 2 if we are really to understand this matter, for he says: 'Wherefore, I desire that ye faint not at my tribulations for you, which is your glory'. This links with his description of himself in verse 1 – 'the prisoner of Jesus Christ for you Gentiles'. He is urging the Ephesian Christians not to faint at his tribulations for them, but rather to regard them as their own glory. In other words, what accounts for the digression is one of the most wonderful and moving things about the Apostle. We see here his great pastoral heart. His concern for others was his most outstanding characteristic.

We must understand that Paul was not setting out here to write a theological treatise or a literary masterpiece. None of Paul's epistles, perhaps, has more theology and doctrine in it than this Epistle to the Ephesians, yet he was writing with a purely pastoral motive. He was writing in order to help these Ephesian Christians, to encourage them in the faith, to establish them, to lead them into the higher heights and the deeper depths of this great salvation. Because that was his objective and his real motive these questions of style and form were mere irrelevancies to him. He paid no attention to them. What does the style matter in comparison with the desire that these people should really come to understand the truth? What is the point even of teaching them theology if they are going to break down on some practical matter? So all these things must be taken together; and the Apostle invariably keeps them in mind.

We might very well spend much time with this matter, but I do not propose to do so. I content myself with a passing word to any preacher, or to anyone who hopes to be a preacher, or who is training to be a preacher. I often think that what accounts very largely for the present state of the Christian Church is that those of us who are privileged to preach have somehow forgotten the apostolic method and have departed from the apostolic pattern. It was probably about the second quarter of the last century that a subtle change took place in our pulpits. Preaching began to become scholarly. Preachers began to pay great attention to literary style and literary form. It may well be that the publication of books was responsible for this, for as a result of it more and more attention has been given to form and to style, to diction and to language, to literary and historical quotations and allusions.

This is a fascinating study. The long history of the Christian Church shows that every new revival and reformation has had to break through this tendency. It happened, for example, at the Protestant Reformation. The Roman Catholic method of preaching, with its marshalling and considering of philosophical arguments and its subtle distinctions, had become utterly arid and barren spiritually. It may have been stimulating from the intellectual standpoint but it conveyed no spiritual truth and life to the people. So Luther and Calvin and others had to bring in an entirely new style of preaching based on an expository method.

By the beginning of the seventeenth century, however, Anglican preaching had become mainly literary in form. This is seen in the writings of such men as Bishop Launcelot Andrewes, Jeremy Taylor and others. Wonderful style, marvellous prose! Some people would argue that Jeremy Taylor is the finest English stylist this country has ever produced. It was marvellous from the standpoint of form and diction and balance; never any ana-coluthia, never any disgressions or parentheses. And the classical quotations in Latin and in Greek were always perfectly set forth. But such preaching produced no spiritual life. It was given to the Puritans to see that what was needed was a living presentation of truth at the expense of style and all these ornate embellishments. The eighteenth century shows a repetition of the same weaknesses in the church, both in this country and in America, but the Lord raised up men to counteract them. Certain scholars criticize the great Jonathan Edwards for his appalling literary style. I grant that his style is not good; but the truth and the life and power are present. His preaching was under the unction of the Spirit and led to glorious revival.

Similarly the Apostle Paul, with his heart of love and his pastoral interest, is concerned that men and women should be built up in the faith. So he does not hesitate to go off into a digression; but he always returns and takes up his former theme.

But again I ask, why did he do this, why the digression? The answer is that he knew that these Ephesians would be troubled at the fact that he was a prisoner in Rome. He knew that they would be anxious concerning his health and his future. Not only so, but he knew something else which is much more important, namely, that his sufferings and his tribulations as a prisoner might very well become a stumbling block to them. He knew that there was a danger of their arguing and saying to themselves: Well now, when Paul was with us, and preached to us, he told us about the blessings of the Christian life, and how as a child of God he was always safe, and that nothing could ever harm him; indeed, that Christ had said that 'the hairs of our head are all numbered'. He emphasized these glorious aspects of the Christian life; but now he is a prisoner, and suffering as a prisoner. Does this fit with Christianity? Does God allow His own people to suffer in this way? Paul knew that they might well be thinking and arguing in that manner, as Christian people have always tended to do, and that this might really cause them to stumble in their faith. So while his purpose is to set out the glorious possibilities of the Christian life, which we find from verse 14 to the end of the chapter, he was sufficiently wise as a teacher to realize that it would avail him nothing to show them the spiritual riches of the Christian life if they were made to doubt the gospel itself by reason of the fact that he was at that moment suffering in Rome.

Nothing has so frequently perplexed God's people as the question of suffering. Why does God allow His own people to endure trials and tribulations? Why should a distinguished servant like Paul of all others ever be allowed to be a prisoner? That is why this theme is so often dealt with in the Scriptures, and particularly by this Apostle Paul. It is found in his Epistle to the Philippians, where in the first two chapters he deals with it in a most extraordinary manner. He does it particularly in writing to Timothy because this seems to have been Timothy's perpetual problem. He was perplexed by the fact that the Apostle Paul is being allowed to suffer, and that he is going to be put to death. Timothy cannot understand it, and it always depresses him. That is why Paul has to write his letters to him. Here at the beginning of the third chapter of his letter to the Ephesians the Apostle takes up this very theme. That is the purpose of this digression. It deals with this particular problem of the suffering of the godly and the righteous, and why it is that Christian people have to endure trials and tribulations in this world.

* * *

Turning now to the Apostle's method of helping his readers and hearers we notice negatively that he does not write to them a mere general statement or send them a general word of comfort. He does not write to them and say: Well, this is most unfortunate. I have my plans and proposals, but, you know, in a world and a life like this, these things will happen. But do not be too greatly troubled, for I am sure that, eventually, everything is going to turn out well. That is not his method. What he does, you notice, is to tell them how he himself looks at it; he shows them his own attitude and reaction to events. And then he urges them to look at the problem in a like manner. He teaches them and enables them to reason it out even as he himself is reasoning it out. And I call attention to it, not only because it is an essential part of the exposition of this Epistle, but because we have here once and for ever the great principles which should always govern our thinking as we face this vexed and difficult problem. This is the message for anyone who is undergoing trials and tribulations, and who may be so much troubled as to ask, Why does God allow this? Or it may be someone who is very dear to you who is suffering. Or it may be something in the Church which is shaking your faith. Here is a great statement on this whole question. Whatever persecution you may be suffering, whatever illness or pain you may be enduring, or whatever disappointment – I do not care what it is – here is the way in which it has to be faced.

As we examine the way in which the Apostle himself looks at the problem we find that he does not utter a single word of complaint. There is not a suspicion of a grumble. He does not for a second allow the question to enter into his mind or heart, Is this fair? I have served God for years, I have travelled, I have been indefatigable, I have suffered, I have become an old man before my time in God's service – why has this come to me? There is never a suspicion of that! Not a word! No complaints, no grumbles!

Secondly, we note that Paul does not simply resign himself to trouble with a kind of stoical fortitude. Many do so! But there is nothing of that here. He does not write and say: Well, you know, you have to take the bad with the good in a world like this; you cannot have a rose without a thorn; you have to reconcile yourself to the fact that life is a mixture of good and bad, pleasure and pain, and because it is so you must not grumble and complain. You have had a good time, so do not whimper if things are beginning to go wrong. Be balanced, be steady, pull yourself together, be a man, put a little courage into your life, maintain a stiff upper lip. There is not a suspicion of such teaching! That is Stoicism, that is paganism, that is the world's so-called courage! It has nothing to do with Christianity; indeed it is almost the very antithesis of it.

The fact is that if you read this chapter quietly you must come to the conclusion that the Apostle seems to be rejoicing in the midst of his trials. There is a note of exultation here, a note of triumph. At the end in verse 13 he says, 'Wherefore, I desire that ye faint not at my tribulations for you, which is your glory'. He wants the Ephesian Christians to be 'more than conquerors' as he is 'more than conqueror'. He is not merely putting up with his circumstances, he is going beyond that, he is exulting in his suffering. He is triumphant, he is jubilant. There is a marvellous element in this, he tells them, if they can but see it. This is characteristic New Testament teaching. I have already stated that the Apostle gives the same teaching in the Epistle to the Philippians in verse 12 of the first chapter. There, too, he is writing as a prisoner and he says, 'But I would ye should understand, brethren, that the things which happened unto me have fallen out rather unto the furtherance of the gospel'. Do not waste your tears on me or on my condition, says the Apostle. I want you to look at these things in such a way, that you will see, as I see, that all these things that have come about have happened rather 'unto the furtherance of the gospel'. He virtually says, Thank God for it. In writing to Timothy he has the same note in the Second Epistle, chapter 1: 'God', he says, 'hath not given us the spirit of fear; but of power and of love and of a sound mind' (v. 7). Again in chapter 2, 'Thou therefore endure hardness as a good soldier of Jesus Christ' (v. 3). 'If we suffer, we shall also reign with him' (v. 12). And going beyond that in chapter 3 he

[17]

says, 'Yea, and all that will live godly in Christ Jesus shall suffer persecution' (v. 12). That is the doctrine.

But this doctrine is not confined to the Apostle Paul. We find the same teaching in the First Epistle of Peter: 'Beloved, think it not strange concerning the fiery trial which is to try you, as though some strange thing happened unto you: but rejoice, inasmuch as ye are partakers of Christ's sufferings; that, when his glory shall be revealed, ye may be glad also with exceeding joy. If ye be reproached for the name of Christ, happy are ye; for the spirit of glory and of God resteth upon you: on their part he is evil spoken of, but on your part he is glorified' (4:12–14). There, then, is the essence of the teaching. The Apostle wants these Ephesians to look at his imprisonment and his sufferings in such a way that they will really see the glory shining through it all, and will glorify God in it.

But how do Christians arrive at this position? How does the Apostle bring himself and the Ephesians to it? This is the most practical question of all. He does so not because he happens to have been born with a placid kind of temperament. His temperament was the exact opposite. Paul was a man who by nature could be easily depressed. He was naturally morbid and introspective and sensitive. His peace of mind when in tribulation was not merely a matter of temperament, but rather the end-product of a method which he employs. He asks questions, and then, having noted the answers, he works out an argument. This is his invariable method. It is precisely what he does here in this digression. The first thing you and I have to do in this Christian life is to learn that secret. Instead of allowing things to overwhelm us and to depress us, and to make us sit down and commiserate with ourselves, we must stop and look at the circumstances, and ask questions about the thing itself, not about God. Having done so we must note the answers and then work out an argument. We must put the whole matter into its context, into its setting, and relate it to the whole of the Christian faith and life. As we do so we shall find that an argument will emerge. Let us consider what it is.

* * *

Here is Paul a prisoner. He is aware of that fact; and the Ephesians are also aware of it. Now here are the questions: How and why is he a prisoner? What is the cause of his imprisonment? Instead of commiserating with himself in the cell as he is chained to a soldier on each side, he says: I must enquire into this and ask why I am here at all; why am I a prisoner? How has it come to pass, what is the explanation, what is the reason? Then he begins to give the answers to himself and to the Ephesians. So we start by looking at the answers that are given in the first verse.

The first thing he tells us is that he is not an ordinary prisoner. His way of putting the matter is this – 'For this cause I Paul, the prisoner of Jesus Christ'. In a sense, by speaking thus he has already solved his problem. He is not Rome's prisoner. He is not in prison because of the mighty Roman Empire. He is not really Nero's prisoner. Nero is the Emperor, incidentally; but Paul is not Nero's prisoner. He is not in the prison because of Roman law; he is not in prison as all the other prisoners presumably are because of some misdemeanour or crime. Well, if not, why is he in prison?

His answer is: I am the prisoner of Christ, the Christ Jesus. What a staggering statement! Have you noticed how, with this Apostle, everything that is true of him is always expressed in terms of Christ? He is 'the apostle of Christ', 'the servant of Christ', he is 'the minister of Christ', 'the bondslave of Christ'. Watch his terms always and especially in the introductions to his Epistles. Everything is in relation to Christ, and because of Christ. And here he does not hesitate to say that he is in prison for one reason only, namely, because he is 'in Christ'. He is Christ's prisoner.

This is probably what he said to himself: If I were still the man I once was, if I were still Saul of Tarsus, if I were still that Pharisee, that blasphemous, injurious person that I once was, if I were still a teacher of the Jewish law and of all the comments of the scribes and the authorities upon it, if I were still what I once was as Saul of Tarsus, I would not be in this prison. That is an absolute fact. I would still be at liberty. There is no question at all about that. Well, why am I here then? I am here because of what happened to me that noonday on my way to Damascus. It is that event which has brought me to Rome and to this prison!

Once you begin to think in this manner you forget prison-bars and cells and discomforts and everything else. Paul was reminding himself of that amazing event in his life when he saw the face of Christ looking down upon him and heard the voice. The prison sends him back to think of his conversion and the amazing grace of God and the love of Christ. He reflects on the fact that, though he had been that blasphemous, injurious, persecuting person, Christ had nevertheless loved him and had died for him on the Cross to take his sins away, to reconcile him to God and to make him a child of God. All that came back to him. He is a prisoner of Jesus Christ. All that has happened to him as a Christian starts there.

And then he recalled the commission that Christ gave to him, as he is going to elaborate later – how by revelation Christ had made the truth plain to him. Christ had said to him; I am going to make you 'a minister and a witness, delivering you from the people and from the Gentiles unto whom now I send you', that you may testify unto them. The commission! It all came back to him. If those are the thoughts that occupy your mind in a prison, it becomes a palace. You are 'seated in heavenly places' though you may be suffering physically. That is the Apostle's method! He is Christ's prisoner.

But it does not stop at that! Paul also means that he is really suffering for Christ's sake, not for his own sake. He is not in prison because of any wrong he personally has committed. He is there because he is a preacher of Christ's gospel, because of his zeal for the name and the glory of Christ. He is literally suffering as a Christian, and for the sake of Christ. This to Paul was one of the most marvellous things of all. Writing to the Philippians he says, 'For unto you it is given in the behalf of Christ, not only to believe on him, but also to suffer for his sake' (Phil 1:29). Do not grumble and complain, he tells them, if you are suffering for Christ's sake. Rather regard it as the supreme honour of your lives. It was in this way that these early Christians always looked at their sufferings. They thanked God that at last they had been counted worthy to suffer for their Lord's sake. They did that even when they were dying in the arena, being mauled by lions. The supreme honour, the final crown of glory, was martyrdom. That is the way to look at it! This is where the glory and the triumphing come in.

But there is still something further. Paul's sufferings were to him an absolute proof of his calling and discipleship. This is argued out in what I have already quoted from his Second Epistle to Timothy: 'Yea, all that will live godly in Christ Jesus shall suffer persecution' (3:12). That is a searching statement. It means that if we are not, in some shape or form, suffering persecution for Christ's sake, we are not Christians. You believe the Scripture to be the Word of God? You believe that Paul is an inspired apostle? Then you must accept this categorical statement: 'Yea, and all that will live godly in Christ Jesus shall suffer persecution'. Therefore, if I am suffering persecution as a Christian in some shape or form, it is a proof of my discipleship. The Apostle James, in his Epistle, states that positively when he writes, 'My brethren, count it all joy when ye fall into divers trials' (1:2). Why? Because it is the proof, he says, of the calling and the discipleship of Christians. In the first chapter of his Epistle James reasons and argues it out. Paul is the prisoner of Jesus Christ in that sense also.

But the saying is true in yet another sense. One of the most amazing things the Apostle Paul ever said is found in his Epistle to the Colossians: 'Who now rejoice in my sufferings for you, and fill up that which is behind of the afflictions of Christ in my flesh for his body's sake, which is the church' (1:24). In other words, in respect of his own bodily sufferings, he has entered into the sufferings of Christ. In Philippians chapter 3 the same thought finds expression: 'That I may know him, and the fellowship of his sufferings' (v. 10). He needs the power of the resurrection to do that! 'That I may know him, and the power of his resurrection, and the fellowship of his sufferings'. In these sufferings, he says, I am filling up to the brim, as it were, what is left behind, what remains, of the sufferings of Christ, in my flesh, for His body's sake, which is the church. I am in prison, he says, but do not waste a tear on me, do not faint on my account. This is most glorious; I am having the greatest privilege of my life, I am making up what remains of my Lord's sufferings. He is having now the great and the high privilege of following in the very footsteps of Christ. Again, Peter brings out the same truth in his First Epistle: 'Follow his steps', he says, 'who did no sin, neither was guile found in his mouth; who when he suffered he threatened not' (2:21-23). That is the privilege: we are following in Christ's steps.

Finally, Paul suggests that it was his loyalty to the message that

Christ had given him that was the immediate cause of his imprison-ment. Note that he says 'I Paul, the prisoner of Jesus Christ for you Gentiles'. A better way of translating that would be, 'I Paul, the prisoner of Jesus Christ on behalf of you Gentiles' – 'for', 'on behalf of', 'you Gentiles'. What does he mean? The argument is roughly as follows: Why, precisely, is he in prison? 'For this cause' – the thing to which he has referred. What really put Paul into prison was that he went everywhere preaching that the gospel of Jesus Christ was as much for the Gentiles as for the Jews. It was this that above everything else infuriated the Jews. The accounts of Paul's arrest and imprisonment in the Book of the Acts of the Apostles, chapters 21 and 22, make it quite clear that that was the direct cause of his being arrested and kept in confine-ment and being sent to Rome. He persisted in preaching that Gentile believers were to be 'fellow heirs' with Jewish believers. If he had not emphasized this doctrine, the Jews might well have allowed him to continue preaching, but, to the Jew, Paul's teaching was absolutely intolerable, it was utterly impossible. So they opposed him, they nearly killed him, and he only escaped death by the intervention of the Roman authorities. 'For this cause'. So what the Apostle is really saying to these Ephesian Gentile Christians is that he is really suffering for their sakes, suffering because he persisted in saying that the Gentiles were to become the children of Abraham by faith in exactly the same way as the Jews. That you might enjoy the liberty of the gospel, I am in bonds, I am in prison, is what he told them. If I had withheld that aspect of the truth I would still be free; but I want you to know, he says, that I am suffering gladly for your sakes – I am rejoicing in it. I am in prison, but you are enjoying the glorious liberty of the children of God.

What a man! What a Christian! Some of us would be much more popular in the Church, as well as in the world, if we did not say certain things. If a preacher wants to be popular he must never offend. But Paul did not want to be popular. He was given the truth, and he preached the whole truth; he withheld nothing. If he had only withheld this particular aspect all would have been well. But no, he says, I was told to preach it, my Lord sent me to the Gentiles as well as to the Jews. So he is suffering gladly for their sakes.

But Paul goes even further. Notice his words in verse 13 – 'I desire that ye faint not at my tribulations for you, which is your glory'. There is a glory for them in his sufferings. How does it come about? We can seek an answer by asking what value the story of the martyrs has for us. We read the lives of the saints and the martyrs, but what is the precise value of the death of the martyrs to us? Why should we read Foxe's Book of Martyrs? Why should we read about the Scottish Covenanters? Why should we read of all the men and women who have laid down their lives for the Christian faith? The Apostle tells these Ephesians that his sufferings should reassure them with respect to the truth about themselves. Why is Paul in prison? The answer is, because he is so absolutely certain of the message that Christ has died for the Gentile as well as for the Jew. Though he knew it would mean prison and probably death, he nevertheless preached it because it was true. What a tremendous strengthening of the faith of the Ephesians would result from this! They would say to themselves, Paul must be absolutely certain of it; he would never undergo suffering in this way if there was any doubt about it at all! He is so sure about it, as he tells us, that rather than withhold it he will suffer anything for it. This then must be right, this is the truth about us, we are made one body with the Jews in Christ Jesus. We see, therefore, that Paul's suffering focuses attention on this most glorious aspect of the gospel from their standpoint; and this explains why he goes on to tell them in detail in the following verses how it was that Christ had revealed it to him personally, individually, in a special manner.

The Ephesian believers are being reminded that Christ has died for them and that his servant Paul is now, in his turn, suffering for them and is ready even to die for them, and that he regards it as a privilege. Many of them were but slaves and very ordinary and common people, but he tells them that the Son of God died for them, and that he as their Apostle considers it a great privilege to be in prison for them. When a man like Paul says a thing like that, you want to stand up and sing and shout. You feel unworthy, and yet you are aware of the privilege, the wonder and the glory of it all. And at the same time, in suffering in this way, what a wonderful example the Apostle gives Christians as to how these things should be faced. Is there anything that is more strengthening to faith than to read of the death of the martyrs? If ever you feel doubtful or hesitant about the Christian faith, if ever you feel the world attracting you, and wonder whether you should go on suffering persecution as a student, for example, or in your profession, or in your business, read the stories of the death of the martyrs. Mark the end of the perfect man, says the Psalmist (37:37). 'Remember them which have the rule over you', says the author of the Epistle to the Hebrews, 'considering the end of their conversation'. Look at the way in which they died. 'Jesus Christ is the same yesterday, today, and for ever' (13:7-8). There is nothing that so strengthens faith as that! These men faced the tyrants and 'the lions' gory mane' triumphantly because they knew Christ and the reality of the truth.

The Apostle is telling these Ephesians that if they but see the meaning of his imprisonment truly, if they but view these things in the right way, it will bring them into a knowledge of the glory of the Christian life such as they had never had before. What Paul is saying is that the Christian life to him is everything; Christ is his 'all and in all'. The Christian life is so glorious and so wonderful that it is much more precious to him than his personal liberty. It is much more precious than life itself. What he is really saying is what he said to the Philippians in the words, 'To me to live is Christ, and to die is gain' and 'that I might depart and be with Christ, which is far better' (1:21, 23).

There, then, is the beginning of the Apostle's argument; there are the elements, the fundamental principles. Are you rejoicing in tribulations? Are you discouraged by what has happened to you or by what is happening to the Church? If you are suffering as a Christian, face again the arguments as Paul presents them. Look at them, believe them, apply them, and end by standing up and thanking God, and glorying in the fact that unto you also 'it has been given in the behalf of Christ, not only to believe on him, but also to suffer for his sake' (Phil 1:29). 'I Paul, the prisoner of Christ Jesus for you Gentiles.' Have you understood it?

2

'The Mystery of Christ'

'If ye have heard of the dispensation of the grace of
God which is given me to you-ward: how that by
revelation he made known unto me the mystery; (as
I wrote afore in few words, whereby, when ye read,
ye may understand my knowledge in the mystery of
Christ) which in other ages was not made known
unto the sons of men, as it is now revealed unto his
holy apostles and prophets by the Spirit; that the
Gentiles should be fellow-heirs, and of the same
body, and partakers of his promise in Christ by the
gospel: whereof I was made a minister, according
to the gift of the grace of God given unto me by the
effectual working of his power.'

Ephesians 3:2–7

We turn now to the words found in verses 2–7 and we must look
at this as a whole because it is just one sentence with many sub-
divisions; and there is a sense in which, if we are to understand
any of its individual parts correctly, we must have some conception of the whole statement. It is the beginning of the long
digression which continues until the end of verse 13. We have seen
that its object was to help these Ephesians who were troubled
about the fact that he the Apostle was a prisoner. He wants them
to see things in such a way that not only – as he says in verse 13 –
will they not faint at it, but that they will even glory in it. He
himself is glorying in it, and he proceeds to show them why
they also should be glorying in it.

The Apostle begins to do so in verse 2: 'I Paul, the prisoner of
Jesus Christ for you Gentiles, If ye have heard of the dispensation
of the grace of God which is given me to you-ward'. That might
be translated, 'assuming you do know' or 'taking it for granted
that you are aware of the fact' that I am in this special position

with respect to you. Some commentators are in trouble over this expression, 'If ye have heard', as if the Apostle were doubtful about it. But it is not an expression of doubt, it is a way of saying 'assuming that, of course, you know', 'taking it for granted'. And yet, although the Apostle does assume that they know it, he nevertheless proceeds to tell them about it. Here again is one of the lessons we should never fail to learn as we read the Scriptures. You know all about this, says the Apostle, but I am going to remind you of it again. The very essence of good teaching is repetition. We all think and assume that we know certain things, but when we are examined about them we often discover that we do not know them. Not only so; though we may know things theoretically, somehow or another when we are in trouble, or in difficulty, we fail to apply the knowledge. It therefore becomes necessary that we should be reminded again of them. That is what the Apostle does here. They know all about this – he himself had told them, others had told them – yet because they are troubled about his imprisonment he must remind them of it again. He does this quite deliberately, for it is because they have not really understood it that they are misunderstanding his tribulations. At the same time, however, one cannot read this digression without feeling that the Apostle is very glad to go over the great story once more. It is such a magnificent and glorious story. There are some things which can never be said too often, they are so magnificent in and of themselves.

Paul's object is to bring the Ephesian Christians to see that it is only as they grasp what God has done for them through him as Christ's Apostle, that they will not only not be stumbled by the fact of his imprisonment but will indeed end by praising God as they see the perfection of His inscrutable ways. The same, of course, still applies to us. Beyond all doubt there is nothing which is quite so comforting, so reassuring to faith, nothing which is quite so exhilarating in the Christian life, as just to stand back and to contemplate, and to understand in some measure God's great plan and scheme and purpose of redemption. That is what the Apostle unfolds here to these Ephesians, and through them unfolds it to us. He is giving them a very hurried picture of how it was that the gospel ever came to them, pagans as they were. He remembers that they were living a godless life, worshipping a multiplicity of gods, and especially in Ephesus, worshipping the great goddess Diana, making images and idols, and, of course, living life on the very low moral level which always characterizes paganism and polytheism. Such they once were, but now they are saints in the church of God, and, together with the converted Jews, worshipping Him. That fact is quite astounding, it is almost incredible. But the great question is, How had it ever come to pass? The Apostle proceeds to tell them, and especially so in the long sentence beginning here at verse 2 and continuing to the end of verse 7.

As we look into this matter let us remind ourselves that it is not a mere matter of academic interest, or of interest in the history of the Apostle Paul. Some may wonder whether our enquiry is profitable in a world that is so full of troubles and problems, and ask what all this has to do with us. The answer is that the Apostle deals here with matters which are absolutely fundamental to the whole Christian position. At the same time he has things to say here which seem to me to be most important and relevant when considered in relation to present-day interest in ecumenicity and a possible great world church, even including Roman Catholicism, which could oppose Communism and the atheistic outlook in general. The Apostle introduces us here to certain cardinal principles the neglect of which will lead us into grievous error. In other words, as Paul relates here a part of his own personal history he is also instructing us in the New Testament teaching with regard to the Church, certain offices in the Church, and the whole nature of Christian truth.

The first thing he tells the Ephesian believers is that he is in prison at the moment because he is an apostle dedicated to their service: 'If ye have heard of the dispensation of the grace of God which is given me *to you-ward*; how that by revelation he made known unto me the mystery . . .' He goes on to say that this selfsame 'mystery' has been 'revealed to (the Lord's) holy apostles and prophets by the Spirit, whereof I was made a minister, according to the grace of God given unto me by the effectual working of his power' (vv. 2–7). Here, we begin to look at the extraordinary provision God has made for us and our salvation. Sad it is to realize how infrequently we stop to meditate upon all this! We are told so repeatedly in the Scriptures that God has planned and purposed our redemption 'before the foundation of the world', but how often do we contemplate that in detail? How often do we meditate on this great master plan of God, and realize how every part and portion has been planned and fore-ordained, and how when the fulness of the time had come God put it into operation? God had this great purpose of uniting Gentiles and Jews, and of sending this message of salvation throughout the whole world. In order to bring this to pass, as the Apostle will tell us in chapter 4, He has brought into being the Church. There is 'one Lord, one faith, one baptism, one God and Father of all' (vv. 5-6). He has also 'given gifts unto men', including a variety of offices: 'He gave some, apostles; and some, prophets; and some, evangelists; and some, pastors and teachers; for the perfecting of the saints, for the work of the ministry, for the edifying of the body of Christ' (vv. 11-12). What a perfect plan it is! All this has been ordained by God, the Apostle says, and as a part of it he was called by God to be an Apostle. Observe the beautiful language in which he expresses it: 'the dispensation of the grace of God which is given me to you-ward'. God, he says, has entrusted to me a stewardship of this marvellous grace of His. God has appointed me to be one of the custodians and guardians of this precious favour which He is showing to mankind in the Son of His love, our Lord and Saviour Jesus Christ.

We see now why it was that the Apostle does not apologize for repeating these things. He never got over the marvel and the wonder of it, that *he* who had been a blasphemer and a persecutor, a man who hated Christ and His cause and who thought he was doing God service by persecuting the Christian Church – that *he* had actually been given this dignity, this honour, this privilege of being called by God Himself to be an apostle of this message, a dispenser of this truth, one who was called to propagate the astounding good news that has come into the world through our Lord and Saviour Jesus Christ. In other words his claim is, as he tells us everywhere in his writings, that he is in the fullest sense of the term an apostle. He is as much an apostle as Peter and James and John and all the other apostles. He who had been so opposed to the gospel is one of the chief heralds of the gospel. 'This grace has been given unto me', he says. We must now look at what he includes in this definition, in this designation.

An apostle was one who had been very definitely and specifically called by God Himself, by the Lord Jesus Christ in particular. If you read the various epistles of Paul in the New Testament and pay close attention to his introductions, you will find that he almost invariably refers to himself as one who is 'called to be an apostle', which is better translated 'a called apostle'. No man could be an apostle unless he had been called in this unique and special manner. In other words, an apostle is someone who is not appointed by the church. No man can appoint or create an apostle. An essential part of the definition of an apostle is that in a unique and special and direct way he has been 'called of God'. Paul conveys that here in the expression, 'the grace of God which is given me to you-ward'; the gift has been given to me, the honour has been conferred upon me.

We have another instance of this emphasis in the letter to the Galatians: 'Paul, an apostle' – then, in brackets, 'not of men, neither by man, but by Jesus Christ, and God the Father, who raised him from the dead' (1:1). Note the way in which Paul puts it, and how important the negative is – 'not of men, neither by man'. You cannot be an apostle 'of' men or 'by' men. He emphasizes the statement for this good reason, that going round the churches in those early days were certain false apostles, men who said, 'I am an apostle', and who urged the people not to listen to the preaching of the Apostle Paul, who, they said, was not an apostle at all. They claimed that they were the true apostles, and they taught the people that they must be circumcised and submit to certain rites, and that the gospel of free salvation was not true. The Apostle always denounced them as false apostles. They were 'anti-Christs' as the Apostle John calls them; they were never called by God, they had been appointed either by themselves or by other men; they were 'of' men and 'by' men, and not by Jesus Christ and God the Father.

But Paul maintains that he is a true apostle: 'This grace', he says, 'has been given unto me'. What a term! The office itself is a grace; it is a dispensation of the grace; but it also includes the idea that when God called a man to be an apostle, by His grace He equipped him to be an apostle; He gave him certain gifts. Invariably there were certain 'signs' and 'marks' of an apostle. A true apostle was a man who was always given the grace and the power to work 'miracles and wonders and signs'. A man was not an apostle unless he was able to produce this authentication. There are many references to this in the New Testament Scriptures. One of the 'seals', the 'marks', the 'signs' of an apostle was that he had this supernatural, miraculous power. So when you read the Book of the Acts of the Apostles you find sentences such as, 'God wrought special miracles by the hands of Paul'. Special miracles! They were so profuse that people stood and marvelled and wondered at them. Indeed that had happened in this very city of Ephesus when Paul was there, and an uproar was caused, as can be read in chapter 19 of the Book of the Acts.

Above all this, and still more important for our immediate purpose, was the fact that an apostle was a man to whom God in a very special way gave the message of salvation. Paul says, 'A dispensation of the grace of God has been given to me'. The apostles were the 'stewards', the guardians, the custodians, of the mystery of the faith. There are several other places in the Epistles where the Apostle says the same thing. For instance, in the First Epistle to the Corinthians we read, 'Let a man so account of us, as of the ministers of Christ, and stewards of the mysteries of God' (4:1). All this is of tremendous importance for us. We have been told already by this Apostle, at the end of the second chapter, that the Church of God is established upon 'the foundation of the apostles and prophets' (v. 20). Here, the Apostle helps us to understand it. God takes these men, these certain men, and He makes them stewards, custodians, administrators of the message of His marvellous redeeming grace.

Here we see the working out of the plan of redemption. God the Father thought of it; He planned it. In 'the fulness of the time' He sent His only begotten Son into the world to do the work that was absolutely necessary. If the Son had not come and taught and died, bearing the sins of men and their punishment, and risen again, and gone back into heaven, salvation would never have been possible. The grace of God comes through the Lord Jesus Christ. Then God sent the Holy Spirit on the Day of Pentecost in order that this grace that had been prepared might be administered, that it might be dispensed to us. There would be no point in providing it unless the channel had been prepared by which it could come to us individually, that we might receive it and enjoy it. The Holy Spirit does this by giving this enabling and understanding, this power and ability to those men whom God has called and appointed to be the custodians and the guardians and the stewards of it.

At the beginning of the Book of the Acts of the Apostles this plan and purpose of God can be seen quite clearly. Our blessed Lord had risen from the dead and had manifested Himself for forty days to His disciples. They knew the facts about His life and death and resurrection, but still they were not in a condition to go and preach. They could not do that until they had received the fulness, the baptism of the Holy Spirit (Acts 1:8). But then they could, and they did. Full of the Spirit of God they went and preached this messege of the gospel.

That is what Paul means by saying that a dispensation, a stewardship of this amazing mystery of God's grace had been given even to him. God had filled him with His Spirit, had enabled him to understand. He had sent him out to preach and given him power to preach, and to attest the truth by the performance of miracles. In due course he had come to the Ephesians and preached to them, and those who believed were added to the Church. And now he tells them that he is in prison because of that.

What a tremendous thing this is! These Ephesian believers, most of whom were probably ordinary common slaves, had been included in this eternal plan and scheme of God. Do you realize the trouble to which God has gone in order that you and I might be redeemed and rescued and might become saints, and might eventually spend our eternity in His glorious presence? Now then, says Paul to the Ephesians, do not faint because of my tribulations, do not think so much of my chains in prison: think rather of this amazing thing that God has done – 'a dispensation of the grace of God has been given to me to you-ward'! He gave that dispensation to me on the road to Damascus when He told me that He had called me to be a 'minister and a witness'. I was appointed and commissioned to preach to the Jews and to the Gentiles. Think of that, says the Apostle; see this great purpose of God! Do not waste your sympathy upon me; I am glorying in the fact that I am suffering for His Name's sake and I want you to glory in it also.

Something, says the Apostle, has been committed to him. He has been made a steward. The picture is a familiar one. A great man owning a castle and great possessions cannot do everything himself; what he does is to appoint stewards. He puts one man in charge of this and another man in charge of that. They are responsible to him and on his behalf they administer his affairs according to the differing 'dispensations' entrusted to them. Paul, then, was made a steward. But of what was he a steward? He calls it a 'mystery' – 'how that by revelation he made known unto me the mystery' – and he repeats it – 'as I wrote afore in few words, whereby, when ye read, ye may understand my knowledge in the mystery of Christ'.

As we read these New Testament epistles we frequently meet this word 'mystery'; it is therefore essential that we should understand what the Apostle means by it. There are many who teach that this term 'mystery' means that the Christian message, the Christian faith, is something vague and indefinite and nebulous, something which really cannot be defined at all; in other words, they assert that Christianity is but some form of mysticism. At this point we see the practical relevance of this portion of Scripture to our position today. The whole tendency of 'modern thought' is to discount definition and doctrine and dogma and all theological formulation. It is asserted that definitions of faith divide Christians, and as the one thing that matters is that we should all be united we must not give heed to precise definitions. Indeed many go further and say that Christianity by its very nature is something that eludes definition. You must not try to define Christianity, they say, because it is a wonderful mystical experience, it is a mystery. You cannot say what it is, but you can be initiated into it; you cannot state it on paper, but you can feel it and experience it. The moment you try to say what it is and to define it – to say it *is* this and it *is not* that – you are destroying it, because it then ceases to be a mystery. So they interpret the word 'mystery' as meaning 'mysticism', or almost 'mistiness', a vague indefiniteness, something which cannot be expressed in propositions. But, surely, the Apostle himself here, and everywhere else, completely denies such an interpretation. What he says is that the mystery has been 'revealed', that he is a preacher of it because the mystery has been 'revealed' to him. It is not something vague and indefinite, but a message that has been made plain and clear to him.

'Mystery' in the New Testament sense is a technical term pertaining to a truth which, because of its character, can never be attained unto, or arrived at, by the unaided human intellect or by mere human ability. The thing itself is clear, but because man is what he is – finite and sinful – he cannot by his own unaided intellect arrive at it or understand it. The classic statement with respect to this is found in the First Epistle to the Corinthians where the Apostle has defined it once and for ever. 'Howbeit', he says, 'we speak wisdom among them that are perfect: yet not the wisdom of this world, nor of the princes of this world that come to nought: but we speak the wisdom of God in a mystery, even the hidden wisdom, which God ordained before the world unto our glory: which none of the princes of this world knew: for had they known it, they would not have crucified the Lord of glory. But as it is written, Eye hath not seen, nor ear heard, neither have entered into the heart of man, the things which God hath prepared for them that love him. But God hath revealed them unto us by his Spirit: for the Spirit searcheth all things, yea, the deep things of God' (2:6–10).

The wisdom that we speak, says Paul, is not 'the wisdom of this world', it is the 'hidden wisdom', the 'wisdom of God in a mystery'. The natural man, even though he may be a prince, does not understand it, he cannot arrive at it, his intellect is not adequate. 'But God hath revealed (it) unto us by his Spirit'. The 'mystery', we see, is not something vague and indefinite and nebulous; it is clear and definite, but man can never arrive at it unaided. He must 'receive' it from God; his mind must be enlightened and opened by the Holy Spirit to understand it and, as part of the preacher's calling, to expound it. So the Apostle is saying here that what God committed to him as a custodian, as a steward, as a trustee, was an insight into, and a knowledge of this amazing mystery. Hence he is able now to transmit it and to explain and expound it to others. That was his business and his privilege as an apostle.

He says also that this was something that was *revealed* to him: 'how that by *revelation* he made known unto me the mystery'. How constantly he impresses this upon us! He says repeatedly

[33]

that he had not arrived at this knowledge by his own ability or understanding. For instance, in addressing King Agrippa and the Roman governor Festus on a famous occasion, he says, 'I verily thought with myself that I ought to do many things contrary to the name of Jesus of Nazareth' (Acts 26:9). That was Paul's thinking as a natural man. And he would have continued until his death doing the same thing, denouncing the gospel of Christ, hating it, persecuting it, if he had continued to think with himself in terms of his own understanding. But something happened to him. I set out on the road to Damascus, he says, intending to exterminate the Christians of that city, 'breathing out threatenings and slaughter' against them, when suddenly about noonday I saw a light in the heavens above the brightness of the sun, and I heard a voice. It was the Lord Jesus Christ, the Lord of glory, appearing to me. And He said to me in effect, I have appeared unto you, Saul, in order to tell you certain things. He revealed the mystery to me concerning Himself and His great purpose, and He gave me this dispensation, He made me an apostle, and told me that He was about to send me to Jews and Gentiles.

We can never over-emphasize this aspect of truth. Go back again to the Epistle to the Galatians and note how the Apostle, having asserted it in that first verse of his letter repeats it in verses 11 and 12: 'I certify you, brethren, that the gospel which was preached of me is not after man; for I neither received it of man, neither was I taught it, but by the revelation of Jesus Christ'. They must not listen to any other teaching, and must not allow anyone or anything to upset their faith, because what he had preached to them he had received not from man, neither was he taught it; not even by the other apostles; he was taught it by the Lord Jesus Christ Himself when He appeared to him on the road to Damascus. He had received it by direct revelation. Christ had also appeared to him on another occasion when he was in the temple at Jerusalem, and on still another occasion when he was in Corinth. The 'mystery' had reached him 'by revelation'. It was not a message that he was originating; he was given it directly by the Lord. His authority is none other than the authority of the Lord of glory Himself. Hold on to this gospel, he says to the Ephesians. What makes me an apostle is that I have received it all by this direct revelation from the Lord Jesus Christ.

Observe that he says the same thing about all 'the holy apostles and prophets'. He reminds the Ephesians that the Church is 'built upon the foundation of the apostles and prophets' in the sense that it is to the apostles and prophets that God has revealed the mystery (2:20). The greatest men of the world could not understand it. They looked at Jesus of Nazareth and saw nothing but a man, a carpenter; they did not see that He was the Son of God. That has to be revealed as 'the mystery of Christ'. They could not see. It was not revealed to them. Christ Himself had said, 'I thank thee, O Father, Lord of heaven and earth, that thou hast hid these things from the wise and prudent and hast revealed them unto babes; even so, Father, for so it seemed good in thy sight' (Matt 11: 25–26). God has revealed this truth to the apostles and prophets once and for ever.

It is clear that the prophets were not apostles. The apostles were a select few, twelve men including Paul. The prophets were men who were given special understanding of the truth that had been revealed and could teach it to others. So what we have in the New Testament is the teaching of the apostles and prophets. The early Church, led by the Holy Spirit, would not admit any book into the New Testament canon unless it could be proved either that it had been written by an apostle or else under the influence of an apostle. Nothing is canonical unless it comes with apostolic authority. We have the apostolic message, the revelation of the mystery, here in the Word of God.

*　　　*　　　*

Let us learn certain vital lessons for ourselves from all this. The first is the glorious character of what God has done for us in the gospel of redemption. Has something of its glory come to us afresh as we have realized that the almighty, eternal God should have taken such trouble with those slaves in Ephesus, those pagans who came to know this truth and became the children of God? What a perfect plan! It is all of grace, it is all of God. It was not Saul of Tarsus who had decided to become a Christian and to go to preach in Ephesus. 'A dispensation' of this marvellous grace 'has been given to me', he said. The Lord had looked down upon him on the road to Damascus and had taken hold of him, because He had chosen him to be a steward of this mystery. The grace of God, the kindness, the mercy, the compassion of God! What an astounding truth! I fear that we modern Christians do not contemplate the plan of salvation as our fathers did. I mean the fathers of a century and two centuries and especially three centuries ago, and the great Protestant Fathers of the sixteenth century. They delighted in contemplating this great plan of redemption. As you and I do so we shall be made to glory in it and to triumph in it, even as Paul desired these Ephesians to do.

But further, let us learn a lesson about the nature and the character of an apostle. Have we realized that the office of an apostle is something entirely unique, that an apostle was one who was called directly by the Lord, that he had to be a witness to Christ's resurrection, that he was given a unique inspiration and authority, and that he was given power to attest his calling by miracles and signs and wonders? Do we see the unique character of an apostle, that an apostle belongs to the foundation of the Church and to the foundation only?

It is clear in Scripture that there can be no repetition of the apostleship, and that to talk of 'apostolic succession' is simply to deny the scriptural teaching. There can be no successor to the apostles; the truth has been revealed once and for ever. We do not need further revelation for the truth was revealed to the apostles and prophets. Because they transmitted it, and preached it, and their message was written, we have it. It is therefore implicit in the definition of an apostle that he is a man who received the revelation in a unique manner, and so he can obviously have no successor. In other words, our quarrel with the Roman Church and its followers is not political, it is scriptural; they are denying the Scriptures. A foundation is once and for ever: 'on the foundation of the apostles and prophets'.

Likewise I trust that we have seen again something of the nature of Christian truth. It is not ordinary knowledge. It is not something that the unaided human intellect can understand and receive. Without the enlightenment which the Holy Spirit alone can give, gospel truths remain as dark and as hidden to us as they did to 'the princes of this world' when the Lord of glory was actually amongst men. 'But God hath revealed them unto us by His Spirit'. 'We have received not the spirit of the world, but the Spirit that is of God, that we might know the things that are freely given to us of God' (1 Cor 2:12). This is not ordinary truth. Whatever the power of our intellect, whatever our brilliance, it will never be enough. We must all become 'as little children'. We need the inspiration and the anointing and the unction of the Holy Ghost before we can receive and understand divine truth.

Lastly, we are entirely dependent upon the Scriptures. We have no saving truth apart from what we find there. And obviously, in the light of all we have been saying, nothing can ever be added to Scripture. Once more we see where we separate from the church of Rome, which claims sometimes explicitly, sometimes implicitly, to have received further revelation. But surely there can be no further revelation, because revelation only comes through apostles and prophets, and there are no apostles now, and cannot be by definition. So we are entirely confined to the Scriptures, and we can add nothing to them. Neither must we take anything from them. We are in no position to pick and choose from them. We cannot say, I believe this and I reject that, I rather like the teaching of Jesus, but I do not believe in miracles; I admire the way in which He died, but I do not believe that He was born of a virgin or that He rose in the body from the grave. The moment you begin to do that you are denying revelation. You are saying that your unaided human intellect is capable of judging revelation, and sifting it and finding what is true and what is false. That is to deny the whole principle of revelation, of the apostolate, and of this unique work of the Holy Spirit.

How important, then, is this digression for us! We are shut in to the Bible and its teaching. I know nothing apart from that. I cannot add to it, I cannot subtract from it; I take it as given to us with the authority of the apostles. But if this standpoint is rejected and a person says, This is what I think, and this is what I believe, I reply: You are entitled to speak in that manner; but if you choose to do so, then according to this authoritative word of the apostles, the authoritative Word of God, you are in darkness, you are not enlightened; and you remain outside the life of God and without any experience of His grace, and His blessing in Jesus Christ our Lord.

Paul's message to these Ephesians is: I am a called apostle, a dispensation of the grace of God has been entrusted to me, and

I have delivered it to you. You have it, you are Christians, I am suffering for it. But forget that; think of the glory and the marvel and the wonder of what God has provided for you in His infinite love and kindness, and what you have become as the result of His amazing grace.

3
The Two Mysteries

'If ye have heard of the dispensation of the grace of
God which is given me to you-ward: how that by
revelation he made known unto me the mystery; (as
I wrote afore in few words, whereby, when ye read,
ye may understand my knowledge in the mystery of
Christ) which in other ages was not made known
unto the sons of men, as it is now revealed unto his
holy apostles and prophets by the Spirit; that the
Gentiles should be fellow-heirs, and of the same
body, and partakers of his promise in Christ by the
gospel: whereof I was made a minister, according
to the gift of the grace of God given unto me by the
effectual working of his power.'

Ephesians 3:2–7

As we continue our study of this sentence that runs from verse 2
to verse 7 we remind ourselves that we are interested in its
statements not simply because they are part of the exposition of
this great Epistle, but because they have a very important
practical relevance for us. We are living in a world in which many
Christian people are suffering acutely because they are Christians.
The faith of some of them may be shaken, and our faith may be
shaken because of what they are having to endure. Indeed a day
may come when we Christians may have to endure similar trials
in this land. The Apostle teaches us how to be prepared for such
an eventuality. But even apart from that, what can be more
profitable than that we should contemplate the greatness of this
plan of salvation? It is only as we grasp this that we shall praise
God as we ought, and worship Him as we were meant to
do.

The Apostle is reminding these Ephesian Christians of the
extraordinary way in which God had contrived to bring the

gospel to them. He reminds them that he, of all men, had been granted the great privilege of preaching the gospel to them in Ephesus; he, an apostle of equal rank and standing with the other apostles, though he was never with the Lord in the days of His flesh as they had been, and though he had not received his commission from the Lord while He was yet on earth as had the other apostles. But that special revelation had been made to him on the road to Damascus, and so he is an apostle of equal rank with the others, and he glories in it.

We now turn to the question as to the nature of this mystery that had been revealed to him. In this long sentence the Apostle uses the word 'mystery' twice, in verses 3 and 4, first, 'how that by revelation he made known unto me the mystery' – then in the Authorized Version there is a statement in brackets. Unfortunately the Revised Version and the Revised Standard Version and others do not use these brackets, and that confuses the issue. The Authorized Version very rightly starts with a parenthesis in brackets ('as I wrote afore in few words, whereby' – that is to say, 'when you look back at that' – 'when ye read, ye may understand my knowledge in the *mystery* of Christ'). Then, after the closing of the brackets, it continues: 'Which in other ages was not made known unto the sons of men'. It is clear that the statement within the brackets is very definitely a parenthesis. The main statement is: 'How that by revelation he made known unto me the mystery, which in other ages was not made known unto the sons of men, as it is now revealed unto his holy apostles and prophets by the Spirit; that the Gentiles should be fellow-heirs, and of the same body'. The words in the brackets are a subsidiary statement ('as I wrote afore in few words . . .'). Paul is referring there, not to some other supposed Epistle, but to what he has already said in chapters 1 and 2. Today we would express this by the words, 'As I said above, if you will read it again'. The Apostle reminds them that he has already indicated to them something of his 'knowledge in the mystery of Christ'.

It is quite clear that the Apostle is using the word *mystery* about two different things. We have already defined 'mystery' as meaning something that the human mind cannot attain unto by its own unaided effort, and which must be revealed by the Holy Spirit. It does not mean something which is misty or uncertain and about which you can never be clear in your minds; but something which without the enlightenment and revelation of the Holy Spirit we can never grasp. He uses this term in two senses. The mystery to which he refers in the parenthesis, in verse 4, is 'the mystery of Christ'. We may call that the *general* mystery. But what he is really concerned to elaborate is another mystery, the mystery he describes in verses 5 and 6. This is a mystery which 'in other ages was not made known unto the sons of men, as it is now revealed unto his holy apostles and prophets by the Spirit; that the Gentiles should be fellow-heirs'. That is the *particular* mystery.

This clarification is essential, for if we are not aware of the distinction we shall probably be muddled and confused about the entire statement. Once more it is interesting to observe, not only the working of the mind of this great Apostle, but also his spirit. It seems as if there are certain things which the Apostle cannot refrain from doing. Though it plays havoc with his literary style (as we have seen previously), he seems to be quite incapable of controlling himself. So while he is primarily concerned to expound the particular mystery he cannot refrain from saying just a word about the general mystery.

We start therefore with the general mystery, the mystery to which he refers in verse 4 and which he describes as the 'mystery of Christ'. Here he is referring to what he has already been expounding to these Ephesians. You need be in no uncertainty, he seems to say, as to my knowledge of this message that has been committed to me; I have said enough, I have written enough already for you to be sure of it. The 'mystery of Christ' is just another way of referring to the whole message of the gospel, or to the whole truth concerning the Lord Jesus Christ Himself; for He in reality is the gospel. It is all 'in Him'. In other words, the Apostle is referring to the message committed to him, the message he had already preached by word of mouth to these people. And that message is Christ, the mystery of Christ. No one can read Paul's writings without seeing that this is always his great theme and consuming passion. Read through the epistles of Paul and note down on paper every reference he makes to Christ, to the Lord Jesus Christ, to Christ Jesus my Lord, and so on. It is quite astounding and amazing. As someone once put it, he was a 'Christ-intoxicated' man. It is not surprising that he says, 'To me to live is Christ' – Christ the beginning, end, centre, soul, everything! His central message was that everything that God has for man is in Christ, and nowhere else. So we find him writing in his Epistle to the Colossians these words: 'In whom (Christ) are hid all the treasures of wisdom and knowledge' (2:3). It is all in Christ; and it is nowhere else. So Paul cannot pass on to deal with the particular mystery without saying a word about this great general mystery.

The same link is found in the Apostle's First Epistle to Timothy, which is very particularly a practical and pastoral Epistle in which he instructs Timothy about ordaining presbyters and deacons, and similar matters. The third chapter is one of the most practical passages in all his writings; but here again he is carried away by his controlling theme. He is concerned that Timothy should know how to behave himself in 'the house of God, which is the church of the living God, the pillar and ground of the truth'. Then suddenly, 'And without controversy great is the mystery of godliness: God was manifest in the flesh, justified in the Spirit, seen of angels, preached unto the Gentiles, believed on in the world, received up into glory' (3:16). 'Great is the mystery of godliness!'

Paul cannot refrain from making this statement because the coming of Christ into the world is the most thrilling, the most exciting, the greatest and most glorious thing that has ever happened in history. The mystery is the amazing way in which God has sent salvation to men; it is the way in which He has done it; it is all that has happened in and through the Lord Jesus Christ. What a mystery! Who would ever have had a glimpse of it, who would ever have known it, were it not for the illumination, the revelation that the Holy Ghost alone can give.

Let us look at it again. A Babe is born in Bethlehem and put in a manger. That must have happened frequently. A babe born! Thousands of babies are born daily. But the Babe of Bethlehem is the greatest mystery the world has ever known because that child, that babe is the eternal Son of God. The mystery is that of 'two natures in one person!' He is God, He is man. He is truly God, without any limitation. He is also truly man. Those two natures are in Him, and yet He is not two persons, He is one person. 'I do not understand that', says someone. Of course you don't, you are not meant to do so! If you think that your mind is big enough to grasp and to span such a concept you had better think again. This is 'the mystery of godliness'. This man, the Apostle Paul, who probably had a deeper insight into it than anyone who has ever lived, simply stands back and says, 'Great is the mystery of godliness'. It has been revealed to him, so he knows that there are the two natures in the one person. He knows now who that is; not by any mental process of his own, but, as he tells us, by the revelation which came through the Holy Spirit. Indeed the Son Himself had said to him, when on the road to Damascus he asked, 'Who art thou, Lord?', 'I am Jesus whom thou persecutest'. That is the mystery of Christ! This is God's way of salvation. God is the Almighty, the eternal and everlasting God, to whom 'the nations are but as the small dust of the balance', vanity, less than and lighter than vanity. It is He who made everything out of nothing and said 'Let there be light, and there was light'. So we would have thought that, when He desired to save man and to save the world, He would again have uttered some great word which would cause the whole universe to shake and quake. We would have expected some dramatic exhibition of power by which God would save men and would destroy evil. But God did not act in that manner. His way of salvation is found in this mystery of Christ, in a helpless babe. Nothing can be weaker or more helpless; nothing smaller, nothing more defenceless. That is God's way!

Then consider everything that happened to Him and in Him. Try to contemplate the whole process of the Incarnation. Consider how He divested Himself of the insignia of His eternal glory in order to be born a babe. Then go on to think of His humiliation and of all that He endured and suffered; then the death, the burial, the resurrection and ascension. That is God's way of salvation! That is God's way of dealing with the human predicament, the human problem! That is God's way of reconciling men unto Himself and of ultimately producing order and glory out of the chaos of things as they are now! That is the mystery to which Paul is referring! That is the mystery, the insight which he had been given into the mystery of Christ!

Let me now ask a question: Is the 'mystery of Christ' the most absorbing interest in your life? Is the 'mystery of Christ' to you

[43]

the most thrilling thing in the world? Is this at the centre of your life, the thing that is uppermost in your heart, the core of your meditation? In the Scriptures Christ is there always in that central position. The greatest of our hymns look at Him and contemplate Him and, with Paul, express amazement at the mystery. The mystery of Christ! It meant nothing to the Jews or the Gentiles. It is the last thing that Saul of Tarsus ever thought of, or ever even imagined. But it is fact, it is gospel. It is what Christ Himself had made known to Paul on the road to Damascus and had commissioned him to preach to the Jews and the Gentiles, telling them that in Him alone is remission of sins to be obtained, and eternal life, and the hope of everlasting glory.

I trust that we are now not quite as surprised as we may have been as to why Paul introduced the brackets and threw in his parenthesis, ignoring style. I have often felt that much of the explanation of the tragic state of the modern church lies in the fact that we no longer have parentheses! We are too perfect, our literary form is much too fine; the essay may be beautiful, but they are lifeless and achieve nothing. We are too much self-controlled; and it is because we have not seen 'the mystery of Christ'. Thank God for the brackets and the parentheses which remind us of 'the mystery of Christ'!

*　　　*　　　*

We must now turn to the *particular* mystery. The particular mystery to which the Apostle began to refer in verse 3 he now takes up again in verse 5: 'how that by revelation He made known unto me the mystery, which in other ages was not made known unto the sons of men, as it is now revealed unto his holy apostles and prophets by the Spirit; that the Gentiles should be fellow-heirs, and of the same body, and partakers of His promise in Christ by the gospel'. This refers to the particular matter of the relation of the Jew and the Gentile in the Christian Church. The Apostle tells us elsewhere that he glories in the fact that he is in particular 'the apostle to the Gentiles', and he glories in that office. He refers to it at this point because he is writing to Ephesian Christians who had been Gentiles and pagans, and his object, as I have said, is to enable them to realize the marvel and the wonder of their salvation.

But we have our own reason for paying careful attention to this particular statement. I say quite frankly that I would prefer not to have to deal with this subject, but the business of preaching is not only to exhort and to comfort, but also to instruct; and it is only as we grasp the doctrines with our minds that we can truly live the Christian life and enjoy it as we are meant to do. I am aware that there are those who use certain 'Bibles' in which are contained 'notes' which lay much stress on this particular statement, and out of it construct a whole outlook and scheme of teaching. I am referring to the teaching which is commonly known by the name of Dispensationalism, and I know that there is always a danger, when you find notes in a Bible, of believing unconsciously that the notes are as inspired as the text. We tend to swallow it all and to take it as authentic. We are driven therefore to glance at this statement from that particular standpoint.

The Dispensational teaching asserts that all the promises which you find in the Old Testament were made to the Jews and apply only to the Jews; that is to say, they do not apply to the Church; it is asserted that the Christian Church is something which has 'come in' – such is their term – as a kind of 'parenthesis'. Dispensationalists maintain that when the Lord Jesus Christ came into this world He came to offer the kingdom of heaven to the Jews, and it was only because the Jews refused it that the idea of the Church was introduced. If the Jews had accepted the kingdom, they say, there would never have been a Christian Church at all. But, the Jews having rejected the kingdom, the Church has come in as a new dispensation, as a kind of parenthesis. The Church will come to an end, and then once more there will be a restoration of the Jews as a nation and Christ will set up His kingdom among them. They draw a sharp line of division between the Church and the kingdom. They say that the Jews are still a separate and a special people, and that the Old Testament prophecies only apply to them.

The relevance of this to our position today is that those who believe the Dispensationalists' teaching are very busy preaching sermons and delivering addresses about Egypt and about what is happening in Palestine and in the Near East. Some even claim that they can foretell exactly what is going to happen, and when.

They find it all, they say, in the Scriptures. For this reason they make great use of the particular statement we are now examining. They emphasize that the Apostle says, 'how that by revelation he made known unto me the mystery, which in other ages was not made known unto the sons of men', and there they stop. Then they proceed to argue that these words make it perfectly clear that the 'mystery' pertaining to the Church was not known under the old dispensation; indeed, until it was revealed to the Apostle Paul. Some, indeed, even venture to say that the Old Testament nowhere teaches that Gentiles would be saved.

There is only one answer to give to such teaching. If its exponents would read the Old Testament without prejudice they would find many references to the matter in dispute between us. The promise was made to Abraham, as Paul reminds us in the third chapter of Galatians: 'In thee shall all nations be blessed' (3:8). In Isaiah there are references to 'the isles' and the 'Gentiles' and so on. That is the simple answer. But there are other answers and these are most important by way of reply to those who say that the Church as such was not known under the old dispensation. Here is a quotation from the Notes of a well-known 'Bible': 'The Church corporately is not in the vision of the Old Testament prophets', and then, in brackets to prove that contention, '(Ephesians 3:1-6)'. Ephesians 3:1-6, according to that statement, indicates that the Church corporately is not in the vision of the Old Testament prophet. That quotation is found in the introduction to the prophetic books of the Old Testament in those particular Notes. I perhaps might add, in order to make my statement complete, that there is a system of Ultra-Dispensationalism associated with the name of Dr Bullinger which goes so far as to say that it is only in the Epistles that we really have the New Testament Gospel which applies to us. Dr Bullinger taught that the gospels have nothing to do with us, that they were for the Jews only; it is here in Ephesians chapter 3 that we have the message for this age for Jews and Gentiles in the Church.

What is the answer to this teaching? Surely the doctrine concerning the Church was clearly taught by our Lord and Saviour Jesus Christ Himself. Consider what transpired at Caesarea Philippi when the Lord said to Peter, 'Upon this rock I will build my Church'. The famous Notes have to admit that He did so speak but they say that He did not elaborate it. But the fact is that He did say it: so this truth concerning the Church is not only revealed to Paul, it had been revealed before. Our Lord Himself taught it. Furthermore Peter preaching on the Day of Pentecost said, 'Repent, and be baptized in the name of the Lord Jesus Christ, and ye shall receive the Holy Ghost. For the promise is unto you, and to your children, and to as many as are afar off'. That clearly is a reference to the Gentiles. In the same way Peter and John obviously understood this principle when they recognized that the Samaritans, who were not Jews, had also received the benefits of salvation, and so laid their hands upon them that they might receive the Holy Ghost. Again Peter in the dramatic event that took place before he went to the house of Cornelius was brought to see the same truth. It took a vision from heaven to make Peter see it. As a Jew he could not understand this. In spite of the fact that he was a saved man and had passed through the experience of Pentecost the idea that the Gentiles should become joint-heirs with Jews was, in his view, impossible. But having seen the vision and witnessed the falling of the Holy Spirit on Cornelius and his household, he saw this truth once and for ever, and so admitted the Gentiles into the Church. He was attacked for doing so and defended himself as we are told in chapters 11 and 15 of the Book of the Acts of the Apostles. So it is clear that before Paul had become the apostle to the Gentiles this truth had already been preached.

But in fact this truth is found in the Old Testament. There are clear passages, such as Ezekiel 36 and elsewhere, which show this picture of the Church. And as Paul argues in the third chapter of Galatians, in the promise to Abraham it is clearly implicit. How important it is that we should realize the danger of starting with a theory and imposing it upon the Scriptures! What the Apostle actually says is, 'Which in other ages was not made known unto the sons of men' – then comes not a full stop but a comma – 'as it is now revealed unto his holy apostles and prophets by the Spirit'. The Apostle is not saying that it had never been revealed before. What he is saying is that it was not revealed before 'as', 'to the extent that', it is now revealed. It was there in embryo; it is now in full bloom and development. It was there in shadow as a suggestion; it is now fully revealed. The expression is, 'As it is *now* revealed . . .' How extraordinary are the subtleties of the human mind, even when it is Christian, and when it has received the Holy Spirit! It is not a matter of dishonesty. I am but indicating that our human minds are fallible, and that therefore we have to be careful as we study the Scripture lest we elaborate a whole system of teaching upon one text or the misunderstanding of a text.

The mystery that has *now* been made plain and clear is not simply the fact that the Gentiles are to be saved, but that Gentile and Jew are to be together in the Christian Church – in close relationship one to the other. Paul is not saying that the Gentiles are now to be allowed to become Jewish proselytes. That is what the Jews already believed; indeed they had practised proselytism. Many a Gentile had come to see the truth of God in the Old Testament Scriptures, and the Jews instructed him, and circumcised him, and so he became a Jewish proselyte. The Gentile was allowed to come in, but only as a proselyte; he was still not a complete Jew. But the mystery which had been made plain to Paul and the other apostles was that the Gentile had now come in, not as an addition, not as a proselyte, but into the new thing, the Church, in exactly the same way as the Jew had come in. He is asserting that the Church is now the Kingdom, that what the Jewish nation was in the Old Testament the Church is now; and that there is no longer that old distinction. In other words he is saying that our Lord's recorded prophecy in Matthew 21:43 has been fulfilled: 'Therefore say I unto you (the Jews), The kingdom of God shall be taken from you, and given to a nation bringing forth the fruits thereof'. The Apostle Peter repeats this in his own way by applying to the Church, consisting of Jew and Gentile, the very words that God used through Moses about the nation of Israel in Exodus 19, 'Ye are a royal priesthood, an holy nation, a peculiar people'. The Church is the present form of the Kingdom.

The Apostle's point is that the old distinction between the Jew and the Gentile is abolished once and for ever. He has already shown that in the second chapter, stating that 'the middle wall of partition' has gone, that Christ has demolished it, and has made 'one new man, so making peace'. The old distinction has gone. The particular manner in which the Apostle states it is most interesting. He expresses it by using the word 'fellow' three times (3–6). Unfortunately the Authorized Version misses this and says 'fellow-heirs, and of the same body, and partakers of his promise'. But Paul actually said, 'fellow-heirs, fellow-members of the body, fellow-partakers of the promise'.

The Gentiles, he says, are to be fellow-heirs with the Jews, which means that all the promises God had made to the Jewish people in the Old Testament are now open to the Gentiles. The Jew is an equal sharer with the Gentile, and the Gentile with the Jew. There is no difference. They are both fellow-heirs, they have the same place, as it were, in God's will; they are to receive the same benefits. This refers to the new covenant that God had promised. He had said that He was going to make a new covenant, not like the one that He had made when He brought them out of Egypt. It is, 'Your sins and your iniquities will I remember no more', 'I will be to you a God, and you shall be to me a people'. But this is no longer for the Jews only, but for Gentiles also; it is for you and for me. We are in God's will, we are heirs together with the Jews, the old nation, the ancient people of God, in this amazing promise of the benefits of the new covenant.

The second term is 'Fellow-members of the body'. We might have thought that 'fellow-heirs' tells us everything, and that nothing can go beyond it. This addition can be best explained perhaps by an illustration. Think of a man who has an only son, but also a family servant who has been with him perhaps for forty years and whom he has come to regard almost as a son. So when he makes his will he says that all his property is to be divided between his son and his faithful servant. A servant can be made a fellow-heir with a son, but he is still a servant. But it does not make him a member of the family; it does not mean he has the same blood in him; it does not mean that he has changed the essential relationship. So the Apostle adds to 'fellow-heirs' 'fellow-members of the body'. This is what demolishes all attempts to perpetuate a distinction between the Jew and the Gentile. It is not, says Paul, that the Gentiles are simply added on somewhat loosely; they are compacted together as joints in the same body, and no one joint is more 'in the body' than any other joint. We are jointed together, impacted as joints together in this one body. There is no distinction any longer; there is no superiority and no inferiority. The system of dispensationalism maintains that there is, that there is a 'heavenly people' and an 'earthly people', and that the Jews will be brought back and be given a very special place again at some future time. Such teaching is a denial of what we are told here, that all that is finished for ever, that there is one body, and that Jew and Gentile are equally joints impacted together in the one body.

The Apostle goes even a step further, and says that we are 'fellow-partakers together of the promise'. In the light of other Scriptures this means two things. In Galatians 3:14 we read: 'That the blessing of Abraham might come on the Gentiles through Jesus Christ; that we might receive the promise of the Spirit through faith'. This is also called 'the promise of the Father', and that runs as a golden thread through the Old Testament. It is what happened on the Day of Pentecost which Peter explained thus: 'This is that which was spoken by the prophet Joel'. The promise of the Father is the shedding forth of the Spirit, and all the results that flow from it. You are fellow-partakers of the promise, says Paul to the Ephesians, you have received the fulness of the Spirit exactly as the Jew has done. But I believe that the words have a further meaning. Another great promise was the promise of the resurrection and of the glorious kingdom of the Son of God. Paul states this very clearly in Acts 26, verses 6–8, while making his defence before King Agrippa and Festus. 'And now', he says, 'I stand and am judged for the hope of the promise made of God unto our fathers: unto which promise our twelve tribes, instantly serving God day and night, hope to come. For which hope's sake, king Agrippa, I am accused of the Jews. Why should it be thought a thing incredible with you, that God should raise the dead?' The promise is that a Messiah would come who would even conquer death and the grave and bring life and immortality to light. It is the promise of resurrection, the final resurrection, and the coming of the glorious Kingdom, 'the new heavens and the new earth wherein dwelleth righteousness'. That was something which the Jew prized above everything else. He had to suffer much in his life in this world, but he looked beyond it all, as we are told in Hebrews 11 – he looked for the fulfilment of that great promise, the resurrection and the life of glory. That promise was at first confined to the Jew; the Gentile was without hope, without God in the world, as Paul has already said in chapter 2, verse 12; but now he says that Gentiles are fellow-partakers of God's promise in Christ by the gospel'.

To us it means that we can look forward to the resurrection of the body, to a glorified body. We can look forward to dwelling on a new earth under new heavens, wherein dwelleth righteousness; fellow-partakers of the promise, 'Christ in you, the hope of glory'.

Those are the two mysteries which the Apostle tells us he has been given to preach; the general mystery, the mystery of Christ, and the particular mystery that God's purpose is now manifest and in operation in the Church; and that the Church is the final form of this purpose until it is completed. Jew and Gentile are in Christ together, are sharing God's blessings now, and shall share the benefits of the everlasting and eternal glory. They shall wonder and be amazed to all eternity at the grace of God that ever made it possible, that ever brought us in, and that made us and the Jews together fellow-heirs, fellow-members of the body, and fellow-partakers of such a blessed hope.

4
'Unsearchable Riches'

'Whereof I was made a minister, according to the
gift of the grace of God given unto me by the effectual
working of his power.
'Unto me, who am less than the least of all saints, is
this grace given, that I should preach among the
Gentiles the unsearchable riches of Christ;'

Ephesians 3:7–8

Having described the nature of the message which the Lord God
revealed to him, and commissioned him to preach, the Apostle
Paul goes on to deal with this in a yet more profound manner and
in a most moving statement. He begins by saying that he has been
made 'a minister' of the gospel. A minister is one who serves in
the interests and for the benefit of others; so what Paul is saying
is that the 'mystery' had been revealed to him by God in order
that he might teach the Gentiles, that he might bring to them this
great benefit. They were as 'aliens from the commonwealth of
Israel, and strangers from the covenants of promise, without
hope and without God in the world'; they were in the darkness
of paganism, and he had been given this dispensation of the
grace of God in order that he might bring to them great blessing.
So he went and he preached to them. He was called to do so, and
was enabled to do so.

The Apostle is particularly concerned that the Ephesian
Christians should realize that all the benefits which they were now
enjoying as fellow-heirs with the Jews had come to them through
the gospel which he had preached, and of which he was a
minister. And here he gives a wonderful picture of the Christian
ministry as a divine calling. Conceivably this is perhaps the first
thing the Christian Church needs to recapture at this present
time. That the Church counts for so little in the modern world is
largely the result of her failure to realize the origin and character

of the ministerial calling. The whole idea of the ministry has become debased. It has often been regarded as a profession. The eldest son in a family goes perhaps into the Navy, another son into the Army, another into Parliament; and then the remaining son 'goes into' the Christian ministry. Others think of a minister as a man who organizes games and pleasant entertainments for young people; one who visits and has a pleasant cup of tea with older people. Such conceptions of the Christian ministry have become far too current. But they are a travesty. The minister is a herald of the glad tidings, he is a preacher of the gospel. It is largely because the true conception of the work of a minister has become debased that the ministry has lost its authority and counts for so little at the present time. Pray God that at a time such as this men may be brought back to this old, this New Testament conception of the ministry. The world needs a Savonarola today. Men and women need to be shaken out of their lethargy, their sinfulness, their indulgence and their slackness. Ministers are called primarily to teach men and women God's great revelation concerning Himself, concerning man, concerning the only way of reconciliation, concerning the kind of life mankind is meant to live.

The Apostle then goes on to express his amazement that this call to the ministry should ever have come to him. Note the way in which he does so. 'Unto me, who am less than the least of all saints, is this grace given'. This is not 'mock modesty' or affectation or hypocrisy. At the same time it is in no sense a contradiction of what he says elsewhere about himself when he claims that he is 'not a whit behind the very chiefest apostles' (2 Cor 11:5). How do we reconcile such statements? The answer is that he never ceased to be amazed at the fact that the blaspheming and injurious Saul of Tarsus had ever been called, not only into the Christian life, but also to be an apostle, and given the unique privilege of being in a very special manner 'the Apostle to the Gentiles'. It is a bad day in the life of any Christian when he forgets his origin, when he forgets 'the hole of the pit out of which he has been digged'. This does not mean that we should look perpetually backwards and become morbid, and for ever be reminding ourselves of our sins. The essence of the Christian position is that we should always realize that it is by grace we are saved, that we are what we are solely and entirely by the grace of God. If we fail to do so we shall lose the element of thanksgiving and praise in our Christian witness. The Apostle never lapsed into that condition. He never forgot that he was what he was 'by the grace of God'. Oh, the privilege of it all!

But there was another element also in this situation. Paul was a man who lived so near to his Lord that he was conscious of his deficiencies and shortcomings. Labouring as he did indefatigably, he was nevertheless conscious of how little he had done, and of how much more he might have done. He expresses this in many places, thereby demonstrating true humility, true Christian meekness. If a man is not always conscious of the honour and dignity of being a Christian at all, and especially of having the privilege of preaching the gospel and of his own inadequacy and insufficiency, he is in a very false position. The more we realize these things, the more we shall be amazed, with the Apostle, at the grace and goodness and kindness of God.

Furthermore the Apostle explains to the Ephesians, and to us, how all this had happened to him; and once more his explanation is that it is all 'of the grace of God'. Note how he keeps on repeating this word 'given': 'Whereof', he says in verse 7, 'I was made a minister, according to the *gift* of the grace of God *given* unto me by the effectual working of his power. Unto me, who am less than the least of all saints, is this grace *given*'. This is the word that introduces the gospel and salvation – 'given'. It is all of grace, it is all 'given'. The Apostle did not feel worthy of any- thing; everything had been given to him freely in God's love and mercy and compassion. I say again that if we do not realize this it is because our whole understanding of salvation is defective.

But Paul goes on to tell us that the gift was *given* in a particular manner: it was 'by the effectual working of his power'. Un- fortunately the Revised Standard Version which is so popular today, is very weak at this point. It simply has 'by the working of his power'. But the word is much stronger; and the Authorized Version rightly translates, 'by the effectual working of his power'. We might also translate it as 'by the energetic working of his power'. The word used conveys that idea; and the Apostle used it in order to explain what it was that turned that persecuting, blaspheming hater of Christ into one of His foremost preachers and apostles. Nothing else can produce such a change.

One of the most fundamental questions confronting us as we preach the gospel is, What can turn any man from being a hater of God into one who loves God? What is it that can turn the natural man, to whom the things of God are 'foolishness', into a man who delights in them, and enjoys them, and lives for them, and whose highest ambition is to know them more and more? According to the Apostle there is only one answer; it is the 'effectual working' of the power of God – nothing else!

The Apostle Paul himself was very conscious of this power. Had he been left to himself he would still have been the persecuting, blaspheming Pharisee. He had heard about the preaching of Christ, he had heard the preaching of Stephen; he knew all that Christians claimed. But he hated the 'good news': he saw nothing in it except blasphemy. What happened to this man? There is only one answer; he had been made a new man. He had been regenerated, born again, 'a new creation', nothing less than that! And this was the result of the 'effectual working' of the power of God.

It is the effectual working of the power of God that makes anyone a Christian. It means a rebirth, a regeneration. It is not the result of our decision, it is not something that you and I decide to do; it is what is done to us! 'The effectual working of his power!' Paul would never have been a Christian at all were it not for this power. But even after becoming a Christian he would have been ineffective apart from this same power. It is this working, it is this power of God, that not only transformed his whole outlook, but it called him into the ministry and gave him the gifts that are requisite to the ministry, the understanding of the truth, the power to speak, the power to write, the power to teach. It was all of God. The Apostle deals with this in detail in the next chapter and says that when Christ rose from the dead and ascended up on high He 'gave gifts unto men', to some, apostles, to some, prophets, to some, evangelists; and to some, pastors and teachers.

All is given by God. Ministers are given to the Church by God, and every gift and help in the Church is given by God. We are helpless in and of ourselves. No man can truly preach the gospel in his own strength and power. He can talk perhaps and talk eloquently; but talk is not preaching, and it will lead to nothing. Whenever there is an effectual ministry it is because of this 'working', this 'energetic working' of the power of God through the Holy Spirit. As the Apostle tells us in 1 Corinthians chapter 2, his preaching was 'not with enticing words of man's wisdom'. He did not depend upon any human gifts or methods or contrivances. It was 'in demonstration of the Spirit and of power'. So here, again, he emphasizes that he has received his ministry, and has been put into his position by the 'energetic working' of divine power.

Do we know anything about this? Have you felt the hand of God upon you? Do you know God's working in your own life and in your own soul? Do you know what it is to be dealt with and to be moulded and to be fashioned? This is involved in true Christianity. It is all the result of 'the energetic working of his power'. The Apostle sums this up perfectly in a great phrase in the first chapter of the Epistle to the Colossians (v. 29). He has been saying that he preaches, 'warning every man, teaching every man, that he may present every man perfect in Christ Jesus', and then adds, 'Whereunto I also labour, striving according to his working, which worketh in me mightily'. I am labouring, says Paul, I am working, as it were agonizing in my labours. Yes, but this is the result of what He is doing to me and working in me! I am working out what He is working in. I am labouring, yes, but according to this tremendous working of God which worketh in me mightily. So we have this perfect blending of the divine and the human, the power of God energizing a man and enabling him to carry on his work in the ministry.

*　　*　　*

The Apostle says that in this way he has been prepared and equipped and called in order that he might preach among the Gentiles 'the unsearchable riches of Christ'. What a phrase! what a profound, what a sublime statement! But it is also a statement that tests us and examines us. I do not hesitate to assert that the test of all preaching is its conformity to this definition of the message, and to this standard. The business of any man who claims to have been called to be a minister of the gospel is to preach 'the unsearchable riches of Christ'.

Let us look at this task and calling of the minister, first of all negatively. He is not simply to preach about current events. There are those who would criticize the spending of our time Sunday by Sunday in this examination of Ephesians 3, because of the world situation and the many pressing international, political, industrial and economic problems. They feel that preaching, to be relevant, should deal directly with such matters. But is that the business of the Christian minister? Is it his business to express his view as to what the Government should have done last week or what it should not have done? Is it the business of the Church to be sending perpetual resolutions to governments and statesmen, and proffering their detailed advice on many specific issues? My answer is that I do not claim that I know any more about the international situation than any other church member. I do not have all the facts before me; so for me to express an opinion would be an impertinence. I have my views, as we all have, but I am in no position to stand and address a company of Christian people as to whether I think the Government has acted rightly or wrongly. That, I repeat, is not the primary business of the Christian minister. And I have a feeling that it is because the Church has so often done that kind of thing that not only is the Church as she is, but the world is as it is today. There is very powerful evidence to suggest that it was the action of the 'Church', and certain people in the Church in particular in the 1930s, that directly led to the war of 1939–1945. An impression was given to Hitler and others in Germany that his country had gone completely pacifist and would on no account engage in another war. It is dangerous for ministers, whether their position in the Church be exalted or otherwise, to express their opinions on these matters. The Christian minister is called to preach 'the unsearchable riches of Christ'.

But again, it is not the business of the Christian Church to preach patriotism. It has often done so. The Church has often been nothing but a recruiting agency, a recruiting station in times of war. That is a travesty of the Christian ministry. The world was in great trouble when Paul wrote these things; the world has always been in trouble; but the peculiar business and task of the Church and its ministers is to do what the Apostle tells us here. Far too often Christian ministers have been nothing but some kind of Court Chaplain, mouthing vague generalities.

Neither is it the business of preaching simply to preach and to inculcate a general public morality or some general ethic. There has been much of this during the last hundred years, and the ministry has become less and less prophetic. Christianity has become more and more diluted and consequently ineffective. The business of Christianity is not to produce 'perfect little gentlemen'. The world can preach morality and ethics, and it has done so in various ways. The philosophers can do so and have done so. The Jews of the first century A.D. were teaching morality; and the pagan philosophers had been preaching morality before Paul was ever called into the ministry. But Paul was called to preach 'the unsearchable riches of Christ'.

Yet further, the business of the preacher of the gospel is not merely to preach religion. Not even religion! Not even godliness in general! Judaism had been preaching the importance of religion and the vital importance of godliness. Let me go further. It is not the primary business of the preacher of the gospel even to tell people to pray and to conform to certain standards and to discipline themselves. Mohammedanism does that, and does so very effectively indeed. It preaches a very stern discipline. It preaches a worship of God. But that is not Christianity. In a sense you can have godliness without Christianity. It is a false godliness, I know, but it is a kind of godliness. Likewise you can have religion, and be very zealous in it. But that is not what Paul had been called to preach. He had been doing all that as a Pharisee.

I go one step further; it is not the primary business of Christian ministers to teach and to preach even the teaching of Christ with regard to certain specific matters. There are men who seem to reduce 'the unsearchable riches of Christ' to nothing more than pacifism. They preach it every Sunday: war is the absolute sin, and if we only behaved in a nice way to other people, and refused to fight about anything we would be much happier. To them that is the sum total of Christianity. All these things fall hopelessly short of this great wondrous definition of the gospel which is given here by the Apostle. Think of all the pompous pronouncements upon the international situation which are made by ministers Sunday by Sunday. Where do 'the unsearchable riches of Christ' come in? Think of all the ethical moral appeals, and appeals in the name of the country so regularly repeated. Where does Christ and His unsearchable riches come into it all? It is a travesty of the gospel; it is a waste of time. It is an abnegation of the duty and the task given to us.

What then does Paul preach? What are we to preach? Primarily and essentially, the Lord Jesus Christ Himself. The riches are 'the unsearchable riches of Christ'! The essence of the gospel is Christ and what He gives to us. Not what we do, not what He asks us to do. That comes later. The obvious beginning and essence of the gospel is what He gives us, what we receive from Him. Paul is thrilled at the very thought of this. He says in effect: I was given this great privilege of coming to you, and I have given you the good news, the marvellous and thrilling good news concerning the riches of Christ, what Christ has given to you, and what He can, and what He will give to you, 'the unsearchable riches of Christ'. The first message, then, is about the gift of God, before there is any call to us to do anything.

*   *   *

Next we must try to analyse this gospel – 'try' because the very attempt is almost ridiculous. Ultimately we cannot analyse it but because there is such a tendency in us merely to repeat these resounding phrases without considering what they mean, we must at least venture upon the work. Fortunately the Apostle himself goes on to analyse the 'good news' in the remainder of the chapter.

The first thing we must emphasize is that the gospel is Christ Himself. 'The unsearchable riches of Christ'. Not first of all the unsearchable riches that He has to give us, but Christ Himself as the unsearchable riches. This includes, of course, what we have already considered under the term *mystery* – 'the mystery of Christ'. The 'riches' are in Him because of the mystery of His incarnation and His taking unto Himself human nature and becoming truly man. The message of Christianity is Christ Himself. As has often been pointed out, 'Christianity is Christ'. Everything is in Him, and there is nothing apart from Him. God has treasured up all His riches in His Son; and everything that you and I ever derive in the Christian life is derived from Him directly. Without contact with Him we have nothing. 'Apart from me', He said, 'ye can do nothing'. John in the first chapter of his Gospel says: 'Of his fulness have all we received, and grace upon grace' (v. 16) – 'of his fulness'! We are united to Him and we draw from Him; He is the fountain head. So, then, the message of the gospel is Christ Himself; what He gives, though of vast importance, takes second place.

But look at Paul's second word, the word *unsearchable*. If we could but see what is in Christ! But it is unsearchable, untraceable. This reminds us of our definition of the word *mystery*. It is a mystery, but it has been revealed. Thank God that this is so, otherwise we would know nothing at all about it. It follows that no man can ever find and lay hold on those riches in and of himself. Many a man has tried to do so. Many a man has approached Christianity philosophically, and he has tried to understand it from the outside. He might as well have given up at the beginning for it can never be done. The riches are untraceable, they are unsearchable; of himself man is incapable of getting at them.

But, further, the riches that are in Christ are unsearchable in this respect, that no man, not even a Christian, can ever fully comprehend them. As Paul continued in the Christian life he was more and more amazed at these riches. He may have thought at times that he had been to every room in this great treasury, but then he found another. There is always some further inner room, and yet another and another. We shall spend our eternity in discovering fresh aspects and facets of the unsearchable riches of Christ. Unsearchable, untraceable!

Another meaning of this term is that the riches can never be fully described. Hence Paul has to pile superlative on superlative – language fails him. The 'unsearchable riches', the 'exceeding riches' of His grace, he says. Now and again he talks about superabundance, and says that 'God is able to do exceeding abundantly above all that we ask or think' (3:20). These are his terms, and they mean that the riches cannot be described because they are glorious and endless in the extreme. The next thing the term means is that the riches of Christ are inexhaustible; they can never fail. Though men and women for centuries have been drawing from them, there is still as much remaining as there was at the beginning. They can never be diminished. They are 'a never-ebbing sea', as one of our hymns reminds us. The unsearchable riches of Christ! How much do we know about them? Are we thrilled by the very term? Does it mean something concrete and real to you?

What are these unsearchable riches of Christ? Although they cannot be described we must try to mention some of them. What is there in Christ for any one of us at this moment? Let us look at it in the following manner. I am poor, I am empty-handed, I am a pauper; what do I need? Christ has everything that I need. What are the things I need most of all? The answer is found in a sentence of Paul's in the First Epistle to the Corinthians, where he says, '. . . who of God is made unto us wisdom, and righteousness, and sanctification, and redemption' (1:30). These are the riches, the 'unsearchable riches'.

The first thing we need is 'wisdom', that is, knowledge and understanding. Here we are in this great world, perplexing in its problems and possibilities. The first questions to be answered are, What is it all about? Why is man as he is? Is there a God? Why is not God doing something about it all? How can I know God? As I see the world collapsing around and about me is there no place of steadiness and steadfastness? That is our fundamental and primary need. And that is why I am not preaching directly about the international situation. I could not help you if I did so. But this is the Christian way of helping you. If you and I know God, well then, what we read in Psalm 112 is true of us. 'He shall not be afraid of evil tidings: his heart is fixed, trusting in the Lord' (v. 7). How then can we arrive at this knowledge and this wisdom? Note the Apostle's answer: it is in Christ. '(He) of God is made unto us *wisdom*'.

The Lord Jesus Christ teaches me about God, but that makes me conscious of my sinfulness. I feel that I dare not approach such a God. I am in agony, I am in a crisis; because I may die at any moment and have to stand before God. How can a sinful man stand before God? 'How should man be just with God?' (Job 9:2). Christ is made unto us 'righteousness'. Though you have lived a life of sin till this moment, if you believe on the Lord Jesus Christ your sins will be forgiven, and you will be clothed with the righteousness of Jesus Christ at this very moment, and you can stand in the presence of God! *Righteousness* is part of 'the unsearchable riches of Christ'.

But it does not end there; I want to go on. How can I continue with God? Though I know I am forgiven, and given the right-eousness of Christ, I know that sin is still within me, and I know that the devil is still my enemy. How can I stand up in the fight against evil and sin? Paul answers: Christ is made unto us not only wisdom and righteousness, but also *sanctification*. Whenever we come to die we can be sure of this, that in Christ we shall stand before God 'faultless and blameless'. He is our sanctification, and He helps us to work it out in our daily lives by putting His Holy Spirit within us.

And Christ is also *redemption*, which means that He will raise my body and glorify it and change it. The redemption is complete and entire, there will be nothing lacking in body, mind or spirit. In your poverty, in your need, you are confronted by 'the unsearchable riches of Christ'. He is everything you need.

> *Ransomed, healed, restored, forgiven,*
> *Who like thee His praise should sing?*

Or look at it thus: What do we really need, what is our greatest need? Our greatest need is life. Most people today are but existing; they have no life. When their pleasures are shut off, when because of war the cinemas and theatres and public houses and dance halls have to be closed they have nothing. They have not got life; they are but existing, and dependent upon things outside themselves; they need life. But where can life be found? It is Christ again who has said, 'I am come that they might have life, and that they might have it more abundantly' (John 10:10). Life means spiritual life; life means a relationship to God and an enjoyment of His fellowship; and Christ our Lord has it in all its fulness. He says, 'He that cometh unto me shall never hunger, and he that believeth on me shall never thirst' (John 6:35). 'The water that I shall give you', He says to the woman of Samaria, 'shall be in you a well of water springing up into ever-lasting life'. Though the world may take everything from you, though you may be naked and bereft of all things, this life from Christ will still go on springing up eternally within you.

The Apostle works this out still further at the end of this third chapter, but I must emphasize again that Christ Himself is the riches, and it is as I know Him and possess Him that I am a participator in the riches. The Apostle had a personal knowledge of the Lord Jesus Christ, and that is the greatest treasure in the world. We often say, and it is true, that the greatest blessing that we can have in this world is to have a good husband or wife or friend. We say that that is a priceless possession. But in the gospel we are offered this knowledge of, and this companionship with, Christ. The Apostle in writing to the Philippians says, 'To me to live is Christ' (Phil 1:21). It is life to him – to know Christ. Then he proceeds to say that his greatest ambition is 'that I may know him'. He does not mean simply to know about Him, he means to know Him, so that he can go and talk to Him and listen to Him. That is how the Apostle Paul lived. He was in this state of communion with Christ. Christ was nearer to him and dearer to him, and more real to him, than anything in the world. He is enjoying this already, and he wants more and more of it.

He prays for others 'that Christ may dwell in (their) hearts by faith'. Our Lord comes into the heart and He dwells there. He Himself says, 'Behold, I stand at the door, and knock: if any man hear my voice, and open the door, I will come in to him, and will sup with him, and he with me' (Rev 3:20). All the riches and treasures of God are in Christ, and He comes into the life and into the heart, and He dwells there, 'Christ in you the hope of glory' (Col 1:27). The Apostle goes on to pray for these Ephesians that they might be 'strengthened with might by his Spirit in the inner man, that Christ may dwell in your hearts by faith'. And the object of this is that they may know 'the breadth and length and depth and height; and to know the love of Christ which passeth knowledge'. Nothing in the whole world is comparable to that, to be loved by Christ, to feel it and to know it. What are the riches of the whole universe in comparison with this! To be loved by the Son of God! 'The unsearchable riches of Christ.'

But apart from the gift of Himself Christ also gives us His own Holy Spirit. 'I indeed baptize you with water', says John the Baptist; 'He shall baptize you with the Holy Ghost and with fire' (Matt 3:11). We receive the gift of the indwelling of the Holy Spirit resident within us; and, further, His power activating us and enabling us to 'work out our own salvation' and to be witnesses of all this to others.

But there are also certain particular riches which result from this. The first that Christ gives us is rest: 'Come unto me, all ye that labour and are heavy laden, and I will give you rest' (Matt 11:28). Do you know this? He is able to give it superabundantly. Then there is peace. This is what He says: 'Peace I leave with you, my peace I give unto you; not as the world giveth, give I unto you. Let not your heart be troubled, neither let it be afraid' (John 14:27). I cannot help any needy troubled soul by preaching about the international situation, but here is His message to you: 'Peace I give unto you', no matter what may be happening to you. Young men may be called to fight, I do not know; calamities may come, I do not know, but I do know that what we always need is peace within. Whatever may happen in the world outside He gives us His peace. 'In nothing be anxious, therefore', says Paul; that is, 'In nothing be crushed with anxious care'; whatever may happen to your husband or to your children, do not be anxious, 'But in all things by prayer and supplication with thanksgiving let your requests be made known unto God'. And then, 'the peace of God that passeth all understanding shall keep your heart and mind through Christ Jesus' (Phil 4:6–7). All this is included in the riches.

Then think of the joy. 'Hitherto', the Lord says, 'ye have asked nothing in my name; ask, and ye shall receive, that your joy may be full'. That was said in the context, 'In the world ye shall have tribulation, but be of good cheer; I have overcome the world' (John 16:24, 33). Or do you need wisdom? 'If any of you lack wisdom, let him ask of God who giveth to all men liberally and upbraideth not', says James in his Epistle (1:5). The Lord offers us guidance, understanding, wisdom and discretion. This leads to one of the most wonderful things of all, namely, the ability to be content with our lot whatever may take place. Paul tells the Philippians, 'I have learned in whatsoever state I am, therewith to be content. I know both how to be abased and I know how to abound. . . . I can do all things through Christ which strengtheneth me' (4:11–13). What a way to face the future, dark and trouble-some though it may be! Whatever may happen we can face it quietly and steadily. 'I can do *all things* through Christ which strengtheneth me'.

The Lord is able also even to transfigure death. 'To me to live is Christ, and to die is gain', says Paul to the Philippians (1:21). Oh, 'the riches of His grace'! The blessed hope He holds out before us because we are children of God, and 'if children then heirs, heirs of God and joint-heirs with Christ', enables us to smile even in the face of death. Though atomic and hydrogen bombs may be used, and our world blasted to nothing, there remains for us 'an inheritance which is incorruptible and undefiled and that fadeth not away' (1 Peter 1:3-5).

I have but started telling you about the riches, but these are some of the things that are found in the treasure-house of God's grace. Are you enjoying these riches, 'the unsearchable riches of Christ'? Are you unhappy? Are you miserable? Are you troubled and perplexed? Do you feel that you are bereft of everything? May God have mercy upon you! With all these treasures that are freely given we have no right to be in need; and we are a disgrace to Christ if we are in that condition. Are you enjoying Christ Himself? He stands at the door and knocks. That is not a text for the unconverted, but for the converted. It is a message to the Church of Laodicea (Rev 3:20). He is standing at your door and knocking; He wants to come in and fill you with peace and joy and all you need. Let Him in! Do we contemplate these riches? Do we dwell upon them? Are we thrilled as we think of them? Are we receiving them more and more? Is your desire for them becoming greater and greater and greater? Do you live for these things? How are you going to spend the rest of this day? Is it in terms of 'the unsearchable riches of Christ', or are you going to fall back on the newspapers or on some novel or on the Radio or Television? It is in Christ that riches abound. God forbid that we should be like the Laodiceans, who thought that they had everything and were very rich! The message of the Son of God to such is, 'Because thou sayest, I am rich and increased with goods . . .' If you tend to say, I am converted, I am not like those unbelievers; I am a fundamentalist and not a modernist; I am 'all right' and I can sit down and relax; if you think so and believe that you have need of nothing, the truth about you is, 'Thou knowest not that thou art wretched and miserable and poor and blind and naked'. Or are you doubtful about yourself and what you have? If so, this is the Lord's word to you: 'I counsel thee to buy of me gold tried in the fire, that you mayest be rich; and white raiment that thou mayest be clothed, and that the shame of thy nakedness do not appear; and anoint thine eyes with eyesalve that thou mayest see' (Rev 3:18). Thus He offers to all who believe in Him His 'unsearchable riches'.

God forbid that any of us should live like paupers! God forbid that any of us should be in penury and need and want and trouble and alarm and unsteadiness! The world today is presenting us with a unique opportunity of telling men and women about 'the unsearchable riches of Christ'. We are being watched, we are being observed; and many in their spiritual bankruptcy are wondering whether, after all, the answer is in Christ. The world judges Him by what it sees in us. If we give the impression that, after all, to be a Christian does not help very much when there is a crisis, they will not listen to our message or look to Him. But if they find that we are entirely different from them, and able to maintain a calm and balance and peace and poise, and even joy in the midst of the hurricane of life, under God that may be the means of opening their eyes, and leading them to repentance, and bringing them to the Lord Jesus Christ and His 'unsearchable riches'.

5
'The Manifold Wisdom of God'

'And to make all men see what is the fellowship of
the mystery, which from the beginning of the world
hath been hid in God, who created all things by
Jesus Christ: to the intent that now unto the
principalities and powers in heavenly places might
be known by the church the manifold wisdom of
God, according to the eternal purpose which he
purposed in Christ Jesus our Lord.'

Ephesians 3:9–11

In these words the Apostle, as the word *And* indicates, continues
with the theme of the task of the Christian ministry to make
known the message of the gospel. So far he has been dealing with
the personal, particular, individual benefits we can all derive if
we believe in the Lord Jesus Christ and His gospel. But the
message does not stop at that point. He continues: 'And to make
all men see what is the fellowship of the mystery, which from the
beginning of the world hath been hid in God, who created all
things'. In other words, the Christian message and the Christian
salvation are not only personal. The gospel is personal, and it
always starts with the personal; but it goes on beyond the personal
and the individual to something greater and larger. This larger
purpose is achieved, as we shall see, through the personal; but it
is important for us to realize that the Gospel of Jesus Christ,
over and above what it gives us by way of personal salvation, has
also a larger ambit, a wider scope. To this the Apostle directs the
attention of the Ephesians in these three verses.

The gospel has always to be preached in a world of troubles and
trials, of war and of bloodshed, a world in which people are
perplexed and are asking questions. The commonest question
they put to the Church is: What has Christianity to say about the
world situation? What has Christianity to say about all the
problems confronting mankind in such an acute manner at this

present time? Does Christianity hold out any hope? Has it any light to give us on the situation, the grievous situation, in which we find ourselves? These are perfectly fair and legitimate questions; indeed we should encourage people to ask them more and more, for in these three verses we have the Apostle's inspired answer to these very questions. Nothing is more relevant to the situation of this present time than the statement before us. Indeed there is no question that can ever occur to any man but will be answered completely and finally somewhere in Holy Writ. So what has Christianity to say about the world? Is there any hope of a lasting peace? Can this message in one way or another bring to pass the concord and the amity between nations and amongst men which men throughout the world claim to long for and desire. In reply we have but to unfold and to expound what the Apostle says in these three verses. As we do so, let us remember that this is not a personal opinion of the Apostle Paul, but that this was 'given' to him, 'revealed' to him. It is not his personal philosophy, but is what the Lord Jesus Christ had communicated to him. In other words we are going to consider God's answer to the questions and problems of mankind at this present time.

*　　*　　*

The first thing the Apostle says is that there is much darkness with respect to this whole matter. He says, 'And to make all men see what is the fellowship of the mystery'. The word *see*, I must point out, does not adequately translate the word the Apostle used, which means 'to illuminate', 'to impart light', 'to shed light upon'. A part of his calling he says, is to illuminate the minds of men with regard to this problem; the implication being, as I have said, that there is very great darkness in the minds of men as to all this. Were men and women honest they would be ready to confess their ignorance. Are *you* clear as to what is happening in the world? Does the present situation fit into your philosophy, and into your ideas with regard to life and history and man? As I read the papers and the books and the journals it seems to me that there is a gross darkness and terrible confusion. There are many theories, of course, being put forward still, as they have always been put forward, which attempt to explain the course of history and what is happening in the world. There are some who say – and perhaps it is the most popular theory at the moment because it has behind it the name of Professor Arnold Toynbee – that the whole process of history is, in a sense, just a matter of cycles. A great power rises up, but the very fact that it rises means that it stimulates those whom it tends to keep down and to oppress, to rise up against it. Not only so, but because it has arrived at a position of supremacy it tends to slacken its efforts, so that there is a kind of seed of decay in its greatness and its glory. So, as it tends to go down, other powers, stimulated by its decline, tend to arise; and the time comes when the great power is overcome by these other powers. It falls, they rise; but they, in turn, by rising finally provoke others to rise against themselves, and so the whole process is repeated again. That, says Toynbee, is the explanation of history – rise and fall; no real advance, men are just going round and round in circles. As you look at history superficially there seems to be much to be said for that idea. Many a great empire, nation and kingdom has risen, has waxed mighty, and has then waned, and yet the whole world seems to be very much as it was before.

Another great historian, the late Mr H. A. L. Fisher, quite honestly and frankly said that after spending a lifetime in studying history he had come to the solemn and the simple conclusion that no purpose whatsoever was to be found in history. In it, he says, there seems to be no end or purpose, no objective whatsoever. Many agree whole-heartedly with his profound pessimism with regard to life and to history. Things just happen and no one knows why or for what reason.

Another group, which is not as vocal as it once was, consists of the so-called humanists and optimists. These were the people who talked so loudly and vociferously at the end of the Victorian age, and in the Edwardian period. One of the surest signs of a Christian understanding is that we see through the utter folly of Victorianism and Edwardianism, with their utterly false optimism. They believed that the world was advancing and developing and progressing quite inevitably. With Tennyson they sang about the coming of 'the Parliament of man' and 'the Federation of the world'. The twentieth century was expected to be marvellous, all as the result of secular knowledge, especially scientific, and education and culture. As regards the Bible they would hold on to the ethical, moral teaching of our Lord in the Sermon on the Mount. But, of course, they were too clever, they were too scientific, to believe in miracles or the supernatural. As long as we taught everyone the 'ethics of Jesus' all men would embrace and love one another and there would never be another war. We do not hear so much about that now, and of course it is not surprising. After having experienced the horrors of two World Wars, and in the light of what is happening in the world at this present time, there is little evidence to suggest that we have arrived at the golden era in which men, having achieved sanity as the result of education, turn their swords into ploughshares. The evidence points to an almost opposite conclusion. The foolish, vapid optimism of the Victorian and Edwardian periods, which lingered on to 1914, and which some tried to revive even after 1918, presents rather a pathetic aspect today.

The fact is, I say, that mankind is really in the dark about the whole world situation. In spite of all the thinking of the greatest thinkers, and every attempt to work out a plan or a scheme for history, and to hold out some hope for the future, there is nothing but darkness. Indeed, intellectually speaking, the present position is precisely that which was expressed time and again by the writer of the Book of Ecclesiastes: 'Vanity of vanities; all is vanity'. Or, as Paul describes the position of the Gentiles in chapter 2 of Ephesians: 'Without hope'. Such is the position of the world at this present time. Gross darkness!

The great good news of the gospel, says Paul, is that, in spite of the darkness, light is available, but only in the gospel. He has been called not only to preach 'the unsearchable riches of Christ' in a personal sense, but to make all men see; his work is to illuminate, to enlighten, to throw light upon, the world situation. There is light! This is the claim of the whole of the Bible and of the gospel in particular. The Apostle tells us that he had been given this great and high privilege of holding this light before the Gentiles, before all men, to give them an understanding and an insight into what was happening in their world and what was going to happen. This was the claim of the Lord Jesus Christ Himself. He said, 'I am the light of the world', and He spoke the words in such a way as to mean, 'I, and I alone, am the light of the world'. You will never obtain this light from your statesmen or from your philosophers, or from your sociologists, your humanists, your hedonists. There is no light anywhere, except here in the Lord Jesus Christ. That is why the Christian Church stands at this hour in such an important and unique position. She is the only body which has a message that can give people any light at all; she is called to enlighten.

The light which the Apostle had received to give to all men was this; that God has a plan and a purpose for this world. He states it in these words: 'To make all men see what is the fellowship of the mystery'. 'Fellowship' is an unfortunate translation; it really means the 'plan' of the mystery, or the 'administration' of the mystery, or the 'stewardship' of the mystery, or the 'carrying out' of the mystery. This is God's plan for the ages. He states it again in verse 11, 'According to the eternal purpose' – the purpose of the ages – 'which He purposed' – and has already started to bring to pass – 'in Christ Jesus our Lord'.

As a part of the Christian faith this is absolutely fundamental. God has a plan, a purpose, a great scheme, for the whole of life in this world and for man. The Bible is the great revelation of that plan and purpose. Foolish and ignorant people say that the Bible is remote, and that they want something practical. So they run to their newspaper or some other medium. They turn to the historians and philosophers. But do they find what they seek? If they want something practical they should go to the Bible. The whole theme of this Book, its one great message, is to give men an understanding of life in this world – what it is all about, and what is going to happen to it. This therefore becomes a very good test as to whether we are truly Christian. Do we know God's plan for this world? That is a part of Christian knowledge. Christian people should have a unique understanding of the world situation at this moment; and if we have not got it we are very poor, and very ignorant Christians. For too long we have been stopping at the personal blessings, and spending our time in feeling our own spiritual pulse and coddling ourselves spiritually. But we must go beyond that if we are to help others. We must have an understanding of God's plan for the whole cosmos if we are to remove this gross darkness from the minds of people at the present time.

*   *   *

The second thing the Apostle says is that this plan was in God's mind before the beginning of time. He writes, 'And to make all men see what is the fellowship of the mystery, which from the beginning of the world' – or better, 'from the beginning of the ages' – 'has been hid in God'. God has hidden it from the ages until the point of time when Christ came and began to reveal it; but until then, throughout the ages and the centuries, it was hid in the mind of God. But it was there! This is the grand truth we must grasp. Thank God for it! History has not got out of God's hands. The first thing we have to realize is that God does not belong to the flux of time. He is not subject to all the changes in the policies of nations, to all the lying and dishonesty. He is entirely above it all. He dwells in eternity. He looks down upon time and upon the world, but He is not in it or subject to it. It is surely the most consoling fact one can ever discover at a time such as this, that God's plan was made perfect and complete before the world was made, before the time process began. It is there irrespective of all that is happening; and it is certain. There is nothing contingent about God's plan. God never had to improvise, or to modify His policy because of what someone else has done. It was a plan before the beginning of the ages, before time itself was created. It is an eternal purpose. If, in the light of that truth you do not feel that you are standing on the 'Rock of Ages' I doubt whether you are a Christian at all. It is the most glorious news one can ever receive in a world such as this.

> *When all around my soul gives way*
> *He then is all my hope and stay;*
> *On Christ, the solid Rock, I stand,*
> *All other ground is sinking sand.*

The Apostle then says that this truth has been hidden. He has been calling it a mystery, and we have seen that a mystery is something which does exist, but which has not yet been fully revealed, and which the mind of man can never arrive at by its own efforts. But God has revealed it, says Paul. There is a difference between what was the case in the past and what is true now. It had been hidden throughout the ages but '. . . now', he says, 'unto the principalities and powers in heavenly places shall be demonstrated by the church the manifold wisdom of God'.

This is so wonderful, he says, that it had not only been hidden from man, but even from the angels, the 'principalities and powers in heavenly places'. There is a suggestion that those bright angelic spirits were caused to wonder; they knew that God was about to do something, but they did not know what it was. They are to be enlightened, says Paul, by the Church, by what happens to you and to me. But even though God's plan and purpose was not yet clearly revealed, it was there, and it was being worked out slowly and surely by God. It is seen in the whole story of the Old Testament, through which it runs as a golden thread if you but have eyes to see it. Things often seem to be going wrong, but God's purpose goes steadily on; though hidden it is still in being. Through the ages there is one eternal purpose of God, sure and certain.

That brings us to the crucial question: What is this plan which God purposed before the foundation of the world, which He kept hidden from men and from angels, which is nevertheless in being and in process of being carried out? The answer is given in the phrase at the end of verse 9: 'And to make all men see what is the fellowship of the mystery, which from the beginning of the world hath been hid in God, who created all things'. Why does the Apostle, when he uses the name of God, add 'who created all things'? There I find the key to the answer to this question. The Apostle is reminding us of the fact that, after all, this is God's world. It is not man's world; it is the world of Him 'who created all things'. If ever there was a time when man needed to be told the truth about creation, it is now. We have become so clever, we can split the atom. How marvellous, how wonderful we are! We believe we have made everything and are responsible for all things. What blind dogs we are in our ignorance! It is God's world – 'He created all things'. If you desire to try to understand what is happening in the world today, that is the point at which you must start. This world has not been brought into being by man, but by God. He made it, and He made it perfect. It was never meant to be as it is now; we but see a travesty of it. This is not the world as God made it. Fundamentally it is so, but it is sin and evil that have brought the world into its present condition. Sin has brought in warfare and bloodshed and spite and malice and envy and hatred, and all other vile and abominable things. What is

[73]

described so perfectly in the early chapters of Genesis is the cause of our trouble. God made the world, and He looked upon it and saw 'that it was very good' (Gen 1:31). It was perfect, it was a Paradise.

Part of the message of the gospel is to get men to hold this truth clearly in their mind. It is God's world, it belongs to Him. Man has made it what it is because in his folly he listened to the temptation of Satan. But – and here is the glory of the message – God's plan is to redeem it again and restore it to perfection. The Apostle has said all this previously in the tenth verse of the first chapter of this epistle; 'That in the dispensation of the fulness of times he might gather together in one all things in Christ, both which are in heaven, and which are on earth; even in him'. Everything is to be re-united in Christ. That is the message of the Christian gospel to this war-ridden, torn, warring, distracted world of ours. And God's plan to re-unite everything again, Paul tells us, is to be worked out in and through the Lord Jesus Christ: 'according to the eternal purpose which he purposed in Christ Jesus our Lord'.

Let me assert it very dogmatically; there is no hope whatsoever for this world apart from our Lord Jesus Christ. Have you found any? I say again, search your newspapers, your books on history, philosophy, poetry, science; go the complete round; where is there any vestige of hope? There is none. But God has purposed to restore all things in Christ Jesus our Lord. He is the only way.

As we now proceed to consider how God is going to accomplish His purposes in Christ Jesus it is essential to start with certain negatives because of the popularity of false views. We start by saying that the work is not going to be done simply by the preaching of the ethical teaching of Jesus Christ. Of all the fatuous and foolish teachings of today, there is none that is more erroneous than that which says that all we need to do is to take the Christian teaching and apply it to the modern position. Some say that we simply have to teach people the ethic of Christ and then they will apply it. They say that men can have peace at the present time in this world if only they accept the teaching of Christ and follow His example. Very deliberately and solemnly I assert that such a claim involves one of the completest denials of the Christian message imaginable. As a solution of the world's problem it is utterly impossible. It is because it is impossible that Christ came and died on the Cross. The Lord Jesus Christ came into this world because all men and all their scheming had utterly failed.

If all that is necessary is that men should be told and encouraged to follow Christ's teaching and example, then the law which God gave to the children of Israel through Moses would have solved the problem and put everything right. If men had practised the Ten Commandments and the moral law, all problems would have been solved. There would never have been another war, never another difficulty. But the children of Israel, the people of God, completely failed to keep them. Not a single individual has fully kept that law. The Apostle himself emphasizes this in writing to the Romans: 'What the law could not do, in that it was weak through the flesh . . .' The law is perfect; so where is the trouble? It is in man. The law is perfect, but man has to carry out the law; and therein lies the difficulty. Man does not desire to carry out the law, and man has not the power to carry out the law. Therefore I argue that if man cannot keep the Ten Commandments, how can he possibly keep the Sermon on the Mount? If man cannot even come up to his own standards, how can he conceivably follow the pattern of the Lord Jesus Christ? To assert otherwise is sheer nonsense; it is a denial of the gospel. Anyone who preaches the Christian faith as merely that kind of behaviour is denying Christ. There could be no greater denial of the gospel. It is sheer heresy.

*　　　*　　　*

How then does God accomplish His purpose in Christ Jesus our Lord? The answer has already been given in the second chapter of this Epistle. It is not that Christ merely tells us what we have to do. God's great purpose is brought to pass through what Christ Himself has done for us. Salvation is the activity of God, not your activity and mine. 'We are his workmanship, created in Christ Jesus'. It is what God has done and is doing in Christ that will yet bring this great divine purpose to pass.

The first thing we all need is to be reconciled to God. We cannot be blessed by God while we are His enemies. God will not bless us unless we are in the right relationship to Him, unless we are reconciled to Him. How can man be reconciled to God? There is only one answer; it is through Jesus Christ and Him crucified. 'God was in Christ, reconciling the world unto himself, not imputing their trespasses unto them'. 'He hath made him to be sin for us, who knew no sin, that we might be made the righteousness of God in him' (2 Cor 5:19-21). That is the first step. The enmity has to be taken out of us; we have to be reconciled to God, and God does this in Christ. He has put our sins upon Christ, He has punished them in Him, and therefore He looks at us and forgives us. He makes us His children, He adopts us into His family.

That leads us to the astounding statement made by the Apostle here in this very verse: 'To the intent that now unto the principalities and powers in heavenly places might be known by the church the manifold wisdom of God'. This means that God will ultimately restore peace and unity and concord in the world through Christ, and by the medium of the Church. God who created the world at the beginning and made it perfect, and who in His own inscrutable will allowed and permitted sin and evil to enter in through the devil, has purposed, because it is His world, to restore the entire universe again to perfection. He has planned to do so by means of a new creation. Part of that new creation is the Church. This is a vital part of the biblical message. The situation of man in sin is such that nothing less than a new creation can deal with it. Mankind by various external applications can never be brought again to perfection. There must be a new beginning, a new creation. And what God is doing in Christ is to bring into being this new creation, this new humanity, this new body, this 'one new man' in Christ containing the Jew and the Gentile; in other words, the Church. All divisions are abolished, a new thing is brought into being. It is not that Jew and Gentile are loosely stuck together, but both are created anew, and are thereby fashioned into one body, of which they all become members.

This is a chief part of the great message of Christianity. Ever since the Lord Jesus Christ was in this world this new humanity is being formed. Wars and periods of peace have alternated; there have been times of bloodshed and times of concord. Nothing apart from this is to be found in the secular history books. But we see more than the mere outward show – we see God in every generation drawing out a people unto Himself from the world, creating them anew in Christ Jesus, adding them to the Church. We see a new body, a new humanity, gathered in, spreading, increasing, progressing and developing – something absolutely new! We see a new race of people, Christ the firstborn, and all of us His brethren, born out of Him. We see God gathering them together, preparing them and us for the day of manifestation. It is an on-going process. Do you see it even now? It is going on at this moment. It is God's grand purpose, and it will be carried on until God's plan is completed. And when it is completed He will send the Lord Jesus Christ back again into this world, riding on the clouds of heaven, as 'King of kings and Lord of lords'. He will come back in judgment and He will destroy all His enemies, Satan and all his forces, and all who have followed him and rejected Christ; indeed, all evil and iniquity and sin in every shape and form, will be cast into a lake of fire and perdition. The universe will be cleansed and purified.

A day is coming, described by the Lord Himself as a time of 'regeneration, when the Son of man shall sit in the throne of his glory' (Matt 19:28). There is to be a regeneration of the whole cosmos; the very physical world itself will be perfect. There will be 'new heavens and a new earth, wherein dwelleth righteousness' (2 Peter 3:13). 'The wolf shall lie down with the lamb . . . and the lion shall eat straw like the ox', and 'a little child shall lead them' (Isa 11:6–7). Absolute perfection! It is coming! It is the ultimate end of God's purpose. There is a new world awaiting us.

> One God, one law, one element,
> And one far-off divine event
> To which the whole creation moves.

This is what had been revealed to Paul; this is what he is longing for all men to see; this is the light which is shining in the darkness today.

Because this is God's plan it is absolutely certain of fulfilment, for He is still the Creator, and this is still His world. He is still the God who said, 'Let there be light' and 'there was light'. Let man do as he pleases, let him do his utmost to frustrate this plan, nothing can thwart it. God is He who created all things by the word of His power, and in spite of hell He will go on with His purpose. In the Old Testament we see how, in spite of all that happened to the contrary, God went on with His plan. Christ came; king Herod tried to kill Him, His enemies tried to molest and hinder Him; still it went on. They crucified Him; but He rose again. Let the world do what it can, let hell be let loose, God's purpose, because He is the Creator, can never be frustrated.

But let me add this: This revelation of God's plan gives us but few details of particular incidents and happenings. Many of those whom the world has regarded as great and of vital importance are not even mentioned – the Kaisers, Hitlers, Stalins, and many others. It does not give us such details. It is man's self-importance that makes him look for such things. All we are told bears upon the great eternal purpose. The Bible does not deal with trivialities, with mere incidents of time. Nations may rise and fall, but God's plan goes steadily on.

Furthermore, the plan will not be modified to suit the whims and fancies, the likes and the dislikes of any individual or of any nation. Indeed we must be prepared for some strange surprises with regard to this plan. We may think at times that everything is going wrong. The churches may be empty and people will ask, Where is your God's plan? The answer is that the churches have been empty many times before; but in the fulness of His time God sends a revival, and if it is His will He will send one again.

But above all, I emphasize and repeat that God's plan is always in terms of the Lord Jesus Christ. He is both centre and circumference, He is everything, all is fulfilled in Him. It is also fulfilled through the Church. There are no benefits to anyone except those who are in the Church. If you are not a Christian you have no right to look to God for benefits and blessings. All His blessings come through Christ, and through the Church, to those who belong to the body. All else is incidental. This message holds out no hope whatsoever of peace on earth and amongst the nations until Christ comes back to His final victory. That is an essential part of the gospel. There is not held out a vestige of hope in the Bible for peace among men and nations in this world until Christ comes back again and finally destroys sin and evil. While there is sin and lust and passion in the human heart there will be fighting and war. There is no promise to the contrary. But He will return again in spite of all; He will rout His enemies, He will purge the universe of sin. Then, and only then, will war be no more, and sorrow and sighing flee away. Then peace shall reign universally and for ever and for ever. ,

*　　　*　　　*

Are you tempted to say that you are disappointed with this message, that you find it very depressing, that you thought you might hear some immediate hope for the world, and that you are no longer interested in Christianity? If that is so I have two things to say to you. The first is that quite patently you are not a Christian, for no Christian speaks in that manner. A Christian is not merely interested in personal comfort and solace. The Christian is one who is concerned about the glory of God and the greatness of His holy name. Such comfort as you seek is given by the cults and by the various travesties of the Christian message. In the second place, I say to any who feel that such preaching is irrelevant and does not help men in the present situations, that this is the only message that tells them the truth about the present situation. This alone explains why the world is as it is. Do you feel that this is irrelevant to you? If you do, and if you continue in that belief and that opinion until your grave, a day will come when you will suddenly discover that there was nothing else that was more relevant. You are involved in God's purpose and plan. God will 'judge the world in righteousness', and as a citizen of this world you will be judged in righteousness. This is the eternal purpose which God purposed before the foundation of the world. It is certainly being carried out, and will be carried out. All who belong to the devil and his forces, all who reject this gospel because it does not give some little temporary comfort or solace, all who reject the Lord will find themselves rejected on that great day, and will not be among the company who shall bask in the brightness of God's glory, and reign with Christ as 'kings and priests to God' throughout eternity. Thank God for the light of the gospel in this dark hour, the light which shews that in spite of all we see in the world, God is still on the throne. His purpose is certainly and surely being carried out; and carried out even in and through us who are truly members of the Church, truly members of the body of Christ.

6

God's Strange Design

'To the intent that now unto the principalities and powers in heavenly places might be known by the church the manifold wisdom of God.'

Ephesians 3:10

These words come as a part of the statement which begins in verse 9 and ends at verse 11. It is a part of the Apostle's explanation of the whole purpose of his calling and his ministry. We have seen what it means in terms of God's world plan, God's purpose for the world which He is surely bringing to pass. But here, in connection with that second statement, the Apostle interjects this remark concerning principalities and powers. Through the gospel message, he says, and as the result of his preaching, namely, the ingathering of the Church of which the Ephesian Christians are a part, the staggering and astounding truth is that even the principalities and powers in the heavenly places are being instructed. Something is happening through all who are members of the Church which is even enlarging the understanding of these august and mighty beings. This is the matter which we must now examine.

We must realize that when the Apostle writes of the principalities and powers in the heavenly places, or in the heavenlies, he is referring to the angels, including the brightest and the most glorious of them. Some have thought that the reference is rather to fallen angels that is, to devils. But it seems to me that if we accept that interpretation we miss the real object which the Apostle has in mind here, and we certainly miss the thrill and the glory of what he is saying. Doubtless the fallen angels, the devils, are made to understand, and are given to see their utter folly partly through the Church; but what we have here is something still more staggering. If you take this expression as you find it in

Scripture, you will discover that invariably it refers to the angels that are ever, always, in the presence of God; and the Apostle is asserting that what is happening in the Church is so stupendous, so glorious, that even the bright angelic beings who have spent their entire existence in the presence of God, even they are staggered and amazed at what they see in and through the Church. These angels, created by God, have always been immediately in the presence of God; but according to the Apostle, what takes place in the Church is something that even they had never thought of or imagined. It surpasses even their knowledge, their comprehension, and even their imagination. What concerns us is that this information concerning God's eternal purpose should have come to them; and the statement is that it is 'through the Church', through us. In other words, we are given here a portrayal of the Church in her dignity and greatness and glory which, in a sense, really seems to surpass anything the Apostle has ever said about her. Nothing, surely, can be higher than this, so let us look at it in the form of a number of principles which will bring out this glory.

*   *   *

The first proposition is that Christianity, and salvation in and through Christ is the supreme, the highest, the greatest manifestation of the wisdom of God. We can define the wisdom of God by saying that it is that attribute by which He arranges His purposes and His plans, and arranges the means which bring forth the results that He purposes. That is also wisdom on the human level. Wisdom is that rare faculty and quality which enables a man so to view a situation that he can decide what to do and how to bring about the most desirable result. There is a vast difference between knowledge and wisdom. Many men have knowledge but they do not have wisdom. Wisdom in one of its aspects is the capacity and the power to make use of knowledge. A man may be very learned, but if he lacks wisdom he is of little value in society. This applies in every profession and indeed in every walk of life. Over and above a knowledge of the facts, that which differentiates the supreme artist, the great scientist, the great man in any profession, is that he has this further quality of being able to use and to harness all that he knows in order to lead to the desired result. So the Bible tells us that wisdom is one of the attributes in the character and being of God. And what the Apostle says here is that in and through the Church this attribute of God is being revealed to the principalities and the powers in the heavenly places in a greater manner than ever before.

The principalities and the powers in the heavenly places obviously already knew much about the wisdom of God. Dwelling ever in the presence of God they are in that wonderful position of being able to observe what God does and arranges. Thus they were always aware of the wisdom of God. They had seen it, for instance, in nature and in creation. For anyone who has an eye to see, the wisdom of God can be seen in a marvellous manner in things that are made. Take any flower and dissect it, and you will find that it has been built up and constructed on a very definite plan and design. In many ways the greatest characteristic of all God's handiwork in nature is the essential simplicity of the pattern on which He always works. Some flowers appear to be highly complex, but if you dissect them you will always find a very simple pattern, and that what appears to be complex is but a collection of a number of very simple patterns. This principle runs throughout the whole of nature. God's essential wisdom is displayed in this simple pattern. This is indeed the outstanding characteristic of all genius, of supreme competence in any department. The great artist always gives the impression that what he is doing is quite simple. A man who at his work is fussy and who gives the impression that what he is doing is really difficult, reveals that he is not competent.

This is true in any profession, in any calling. The real expert, the genius, always reduces complexity to simplicity. Think of the difference between a great teacher and a pupil, or a great professional and an amateur in any sport, or in music. This is seen supremely, of course, in the preaching of our blessed Lord and Saviour. Though He handled such profundities His essential pattern was always a very simple one. How often has this been forgotten in life and in the Christian church herself! Many people seem to have the foolish idea that the really great and profound is the complex and involved, that which they cannot understand. But the truth is the exact opposite to this. If the mind is not clear and able to express itself clearly it is a sign of confusion and of a lack of ability, as is seen to perfection in the whole realm of nature. The angels had been observing this; they had been viewing the work of God's hand in accordance with His planning of creation, and the orderly sequence every year of spring, summer, autumn, and winter. The same every year! how simple it all is! See how the flower starts as a simple bud; it grows and develops, then begins to blossom and to bloom and to reach its maturity; then it fades, withers and dies. Always the same process! There we see something of the glorious wisdom of God.

The angels had seen this wisdom also in history. They had been watching over human affairs through all the history that is recorded in the Old Testament, and they had seen how God had been handling the nations. They watched as He patiently allowed some great tyrant to rise up and 'stride the world as a colossus' and cause all the nations to quake and to be terrified and alarmed. They had perhaps even begun to wonder what was happening; and then they found that at a given moment God would arise and scatter His enemies and cause them to disappear as if they had never been. In such ways as these they had often seen the wisdom of God in history. So at a time such as this it is profitable for us to read it, of course, with a Christian eye. If you do not read history with a Christian and a biblical eye you will come to Hegel's conclusion, which was that 'History teaches us that history teaches us nothing'. But if you look at history with a biblical mind, with a Christian eye you will find that it is full of instruction because, at the back of all, you will see the wisdom of God allowing, permitting this and that, but always in control. The Lord God reigns; and He is always present as the 'I am', and in His own time He does various things.

The angels had been watching all this, and admiring it, and worshipping God as they did so. And very particularly they had been watching and observing the whole history of the Jews. One day they saw God looking at a man whose name was Abram. He lived in a pagan country among a pagan people, and they could not understand God's interest in this one man. But they watched, and they saw Him calling Abram out of his own country and taking him to a strange land. Abram did not know where he was going but he went; and the angels began to see that God was forming a nation for Himself, creating a people for Himself. They watched the calling of Abraham, his coming to Canaan, Ishmael and Isaac being born. To their amazement they saw God's purpose being furthered through Isaac, not Ishmael, and then through Jacob and not Esau; and in every such event they saw the wisdom of God. They may well have thought at first that Esau was to be the chosen man, but no, it was Jacob. Esau was a much nicer man, a hunter and generous, a hale and hearty fellow, quite unlike the cringing Jacob who spent his time in the house, always at his mother's apron-strings, a scheming type of man. But Jacob is the one whom God chooses. They could not understand it; but they began to see God's purpose unfolding, and that God was giving an illustration of the fact that His ways are to call, not the righteous, but sinners to repentance, to take hold of the worst and turn it into the best. Thus they had seen God revealing His great wisdom.

Then, too, the angels had seen the children of Israel going down into Egypt and eventually becoming helpless slaves there. Then suddenly they saw how God smote Pharaoh and his hosts in the Red Sea and brought the children of Israel back into Canaan, and they had observed the entire subsequent history including the captivity in Babylon. In it all they had seen a tremendous manifestation of the wisdom of God.

But, says the Apostle, it was not through all that that they have really seen the wisdom of God. It is rather through the results of the message entrusted to Paul, the message of the Gospel of Christ, and especially the message about the Church, that these principalities and powers in the heavenly places have been able to see the manifold wisdom of God. It is here that the many-sidedness, the variegated character, the great varieties of colours in God's wisdom, appear. They already knew the essence of it; but here is the full bloom in its glory. In other words, the Apostle's argument is, that the angels, these principalities and powers, have been brought to see, through the Church, that God's wisdom is greater than they had ever imagined; that it is more varied, more variegated; that there are tints and colours in it of which they had never been aware. There were hidden glories in it of which even they knew nothing, even though they had always lived in the presence of God. By employing the word *manifold* the Apostle conveys to us the idea that the light, the whiteness of the light of God's wisdom, has suddenly, as it were, been broken up into these various colours of the spectrum, and exhibited it in its component parts. The angels had seen but the whiteness; they are now seeing all the shades, all the varieties of colour – the variegated wisdom of God.

*   *   *

The second principle is that the Church is the medium through which this wisdom becomes manifest. The Church is a kind of prism that is placed in the path of the light to break up the whiteness into the colours of the spectrum. What a conception of the Christian Church! Without this the angels could see the light, could see the wisdom in general, but not the amazing variety. It is through the Church as a medium, that the angels have received this new conception of the transcendent glory of the wisdom of God. What we have to grasp and realize therefore is that the Christian Church to which you and I belong is the most astonishing phenomenon the world has ever seen. The Christian Church is more wonderful than anything seen in nature. We are all interested in the wonders of nature; we will travel miles in order to see them. We go to Switzerland to look at the great mountains; we travel to America to look at the Grand Canyon. Marvellous! Wonderful! Thrilling! we say. The Apostle's assertion is that all these things pale into insignificance when put side by side with the Christian Church, when put side by side with those of us who are Christians, who are gathered together in congregations. As members of the body of Christ we are the most wonderful phenomenon in the universe, the most amazing thing that God has ever done.

You cannot explain the great mountains or the great phenomena without God. You cannot explain the meanest flower without Him. I remember hearing the story of a man who lived here in London who went on a holiday into the country in early September. He happened to look at a great field of wheat, ripe unto harvest. There it was in all its golden splendour, with a gentle breeze playing upon it. As he looked at it he said the only thing that anyone should say when he looks at such a sight, was 'Well done, God'. He saw the wisdom and the marvel of God's handiwork. But it is the Church, this body to which we belong, this body of which we are parts, that is the supreme and highest manifestation of God's handiwork.

We must draw two very important conclusions at this point. How terribly wrong it is for those who call themselves Dispensationalists to say that the Christian Church was a mere afterthought in the mind of God, that He had never really intended it in eternity, that the Lord Jesus Christ came to earth to preach the gospel of the Kingdom to the Jews, and that it was because they did not receive it that God introduced the Church as an afterthought. The greatest thing in the universe, the greatest manifestation of God's own wisdom, an afterthought! Thus we deny Scripture by our theories. The Church, far from being an afterthought, is the brightest shining of the wisdom of God. It is equally wrong to say that the Church is only temporary, and that a time will come when she will be removed and the gospel of the kingdom will again be preached to the Jews! There is nothing beyond the Church. She is the highest and the most supreme manifestation of the wisdom of God; and to look forward to something beyond the Church is to deny not only this verse but many another verse in the Scripture. The Church is the final expression of the wisdom of God, the thing above all others that enables even the angels to comprehend the wisdom of God.

*　　*　　*

To explain the third principle, I must show how God shows and manifests His variegated wisdom in and through the Church and in salvation. Let us try to meditate upon this for this will be the theme of our praises to all eternity. The Apostle Peter says concerning this in the first chapter of his First Epistle: 'Which things the angels desire to look into' (v. 12). He is referring to the Christian salvation and the Christian Church. A better translation says that the angels of God are 'stooping down in order to look into it'. That is the actual meaning of the word Peter used. The angels in glory are looking down from heaven, are stooping down to look at you and me, to look at the Christian Church, this manifestation of the many-coloured wisdom of God. They have never seen anything like it, though they have spent their eternity in the presence of God. Should *we* not be looking at it *now* with the whole of our being, for hereafter we shall be looking at it to all eternity, and will never cease to be surprised and amazed at it.

What do we see? Think for a moment of the amazing way in which God has solved the problem by sin. It is here we see the wisdom of God. What the Apostle is saying here in a sense concerns – and I say it with reverence – the greatest problem that has ever confronted God. That is why salvation is the greatest manifestation of the wisdom of God. It was not difficult for God to create the light and the sun; all He said was, 'Let there be light' and 'there was light'. Look at the great mountains; they are nothing to God! The nations are like 'a drop of a bucket' and 'the small dust of the balance'. To send a pestilence, to cause an earthquake, is nothing to God. Such things to Him are no problem. Here is the problem – man in sin! I say with reverence, here was the greatest problem God ever had faced or ever will face; there is nothing beyond this! So the greatest wisdom is needed to solve this problem. Anyone who thinks that the salvation of man was a simple matter for God is simply proclaiming that he does not know either the Old Testament or the New Testament. If you imagine that forgiveness is a simple matter for God, and that because God is love He simply has to say, 'Very well, I will forgive you' you might as well burn your Bible. The forgiveness of sins, I dare to say, taxed even the wisdom of God. At any rate I am certain when I say that the angels could see no way through this problem. That is why they are surprised when they see what God has done about it. They knew that some of their fellows had sinned and had been cast down and reserved in chains in hell by God, as Peter tells us in the second chapter of his second Epistle. Then also they saw the fall of Adam and Eve. But they could not imagine what God could do about this. They saw no way through the problem. The problem of the salvation of man, the salvation of a single soul, the forgiveness of sins, is the most profound problem that has ever arisen or can ever arise in the whole of the universe, and even for God Himself.

The essence of the problem lies in the fact that God is not only love, but also just, and righteous and holy. 'God is the Father of lights, with whom is no variableness, neither shadow of turning', and He cannot deny Himself. Eternally He is ever the same; in His perfection there is never any shadow of contradiction. Hence

[87]

the problem raised by sin. If God is to forgive sin He must do so in a manner that not only manifests His love, but equally manifests His justice, His righteousness, His holiness, His truth, His eternal glory, and His unchangeableness. Is this possible? Must not the love of God inevitably come into conflict with His justice? Can His mercy be made compatible with His righteousness? Such is the problem; and the central glory of the gospel is that it is the revelation of how the eternal wisdom of God solved this problem.

In the third chapter of the Epistle to the Romans we find all this stated perfectly and in most glorious fashion by this same Apostle. The problem is: How can 'God be just, and the justifier of him that believeth in Jesus'? How can God justify the covering over of the sins of the children of Israel under the Old Testament? God gave the law; in exercising forgiveness is He not putting the law on one side? No, says Paul, He is establishing the law! In the way of salvation that He has devised He is not making the law void, He is establishing it. How can God at one and the same time carry out the law and forgive the sinner? God has found the way; He has reconciled His own love and justice and mercy and compassion. They are all one, and are to be seen shining gloriously together. The Psalmist who wrote the 85th Psalm (v. 10) had had a preview of this. He did not understand it, but he said, 'Mercy and truth are met together; righteousness and peace have kissed each other'.

> O, *loving wisdom of our God!*
> *When all was sin and shame,*
> *A second Adam to the fight*
> *And to the rescue came.*

Do you see that nothing but the eternal wisdom of God could have enabled him to do this and yet to remain God, unchanged and shining in every direction with the same glory and the same perfection? I know of nothing more thrilling than to contemplate that mystery. We rob God of His glory if we imagine that forgiveness and salvation are simple and easy. They constituted a problem in the mind of the eternal. They baffled angels. It was God alone who could solve the problem.

That was the problem seen as a whole, but now let us look at it in detail. In order to solve the problem God sent His own Son into the world. How can fallen humanity be redeemed? God said: 'I will send my Son down into the world of sin and shame. He will take humanity unto Himself, and He will raise it up. Who could have thought of such a thing? Who could have imagined such a thing? The angels never imagined that the Second Person in the blessed Holy Trinity, who was substance of the eternal substance, the only begotten Son in the bosom of the Father, would humble Himself and be born as a babe in Bethlehem and live as a man. And when they saw it they were amazed at it. Here they saw the wisdom of God manifesting itself in facets and angles that had never entered into their minds. Then they watched the Son living as a man amongst men, 'made under the law', and giving perfect obedience to it. Can we imagine their thoughts and their feelings as they saw Him who was the brightness and effulgence of the Father's glory working as a carpenter in His father's workshop in Nazareth.

Again, look at another aspect of this amazing wisdom. The Father did not send His Son to be born in a king's palace, but in a stable. Oh! the wisdom of God! Who could ever have expected such a thing? But we can see the purpose shining through it all. If He had not so come into poverty and need and in lowliness, He could not have raised the lowest. We, in our wisdom, would have acted in a very spectacular manner, would we not? But God acts in this essentially simple manner through a helpless Babe and all that followed from it.

And yet again, when the angels saw Him on the Cross they must have been perplexed as to what was happening. This seemed to be the hour of triumph of hell and of the devil and the world at its worst. But it was not so. What was happening there, says Paul in his Epistle to the Colossians, chapter 2, is that on the Cross, and by dying there, our Lord was putting all the forces that were against Him 'to an open shame, triumphing over them in it'. God was using them and their cleverness to bring His own great and glorious purposes to pass; for at the Cross God was making His own Son to be our Sin-bearer. He was putting our sins upon Him and dealing with them. He was punishing them; so God remains just and righteous because the sin is punished and the law is fulfilled. Our Lord had kept the law perfectly, and on the tree He was bearing its penalty for us. The law was honoured in

[89]

every particular, and Christ was establishing it. But at the same time God was opening a way of forgiveness for our sins. That is God's wisdom.

Thus we can go on working it out in every detail, and in doing so we shall understand increasingly what the Apostle had in his mind when in writing his First Epistle to Timothy he says: 'Without controversy, great is the mystery of godliness: God was manifest in the flesh, justified in the Spirit, seen of angels, preached unto the Gentiles, believed on in the world, received up into glory' (3:16). We have been expounding the meaning of the phrase 'seen of angels'. They were watching all this, and they were amazed and astonished as they did so. But they realized that this is the wisdom of God which they thought they knew.

*　　*　　*

The result of all this is that we are entitled to say that the saved Church is the final and the supreme manifestation of God's wisdom. We have seen how He has reconciled His own attributes; but at the same time and in a very striking way He has brought about what is particularly in the mind of the Apostle at this point, namely, He has brought Jew and Gentile together. This is amazing! Jew and Gentile seemed hopelessly irreconcilable. They were entirely different, and traditional enemies, with all their traditions at variance. The angels had seen the world divided into Jew and Gentile and had contemplated the apparently hopeless problem. They watched the futile attempts of the greatest philosophers to deal with it as they wrote about their utopias, and as they still do. There appeared to be no solution. But now they see it happening in the Church. Jew and Gentile are brought together in the Church, not in a temporary truce, not by putting some kind of force between them to prevent them getting at one another and killing one another; not by some police action. No, they are made one, made fellow-members in one body.

But we see the wisdom of God yet more clearly in the way in which He has done this. He has not just taken the two as they are and somehow brought them together. He first of all took the Jew and abased him to the ground. He then took the Gentile and did the same thing to him. He makes them both see that they are sinners, that there is 'none righteous, no, not one'. The Jew, having seen himself as he is in the sight of God, has nothing to be proud of; neither has the Gentile. We see both parties licking the dust and seeing their unutterable hopelessness and helplessness, and at the same time seeing that they are identical, and that there is no difference. Then, having brought them down, God raises them up, but not simply as they were: He makes new men of each of them. The Jew is no longer a Jew as such, and the Gentile is no longer a Gentile; each is a new man in Christ Jesus. According to the flesh they are still Jew and Gentile, but that is forgotten in Christ. As new men, new creations, they are identical, they are both members of the same body, interlocked together as joints in a body. That is the wisdom of God!

Again think of the variety of ways in which God does all this, the ways in which He treats us all individually. A Saul of Tarsus has to be struck to the ground on the road to Damascus, and the risen Lord appears to him. Lydia's heart is opened quietly. An earthquake is used to save the Philippian jailer. There is no end to the variation in personal experiences, and each one gives a further glimpse of this many-sided wisdom of God. He knows us each one individually and the precise treatment we need.

Then consider the timing, the way in which God times all this. Look at the Old Testament. There we see God's people crying out and asking, 'How long, O Lord? why do you not come, why do you not send the Messiah?' But God sent Him when 'the fulness of the time was come'. That was after He had given the children of Israel sufficient time to see that the law, the mere possession of the law, could not save them. They believed that it could; so He gave them sufficient time to be completely convinced that it could not. At the same time God gave the philosophical Greeks enough time to see that their philosophy also could not save the world. If God had sent Christ before these two things had happened, people might have gone on thinking that if philosophy had only had a longer opportunity it would have succeeded. So God allowed Socrates, Plato and Aristotle, and all the rest, to come and to teach and set up their schools, and to gain their followings, all to lead to nothing. Then, having proved beyond doubt that nothing could solve the problem of man in sin, He did it in His own way. Thus His glorious wisdom shines forth.

And as we follow the subsequent history of the Church we

find evidences of the same eternal wisdom. How many times have men thought that the Christian Church had failed and come to the end! How many times have they laughed at her and ridiculed her and almost buried her; but as they were about to put her in the grave and to deliver their funeral orations, suddenly there is a resurrection, a revival! And so God confounds His enemies and displays His wisdom. So we can say with the Psalmist that 'Surely the wrath of man shall praise Thee' (Psa 76:10). Do you realize that, out of the present manifestation of the wrath of man in the twentieth century, God is manifesting His wisdom? The end of all this modern confusion, as of all similar happenings in the past, is going to be that 'the wrath of man shall praise God'. 'His purposes will ripen fast'. Man can never stop them nor frustrate them. What God has purposed He will most surely perform.

The question that comes to us is this: Are we manifesting this wisdom of God? It is through the Church God shows it. Is it being seen in us? Are we reflectors in our little way of this bright shining of the eternal wisdom? Are you somewhere in the spectrum? Is the light being reflected through you? God forgive us if we are failing. The way to shine is to meditate upon these things, to look at them, to realize the truth about yourself as a part of the Church. Then keep on meditating upon it, and dedicate yourself to Him daily. And then, through you, the light will shine in one of its variegated colours, and the angels will be filled with amazement at what they see in you. It was our blessed Lord Himself who said that 'There is rejoicing in the presence of the angels of God over one sinner that repenteth' (Luke 15:10).

> 'Tis mystery all! The Immortal dies!
> Who can explore His strange design?
> In vain the first-born seraph tries
> To sound the depths of love divine!
> 'Tis mercy all! let earth adore,
> Let angel minds inquire no more.

(Charles Wesley)

7
Boldness, Access, Confidence

'In whom we have boldness and access with
confidence by the faith of him.'

Ephesians 3:12

This is obviously a statement which connects with the previous
statement. 'In whom' is a reference to the One of whom he
speaks in verse 11, where he says, 'According to the eternal
purpose which he purposed in Christ Jesus our Lord'. As we
look at this verse we must remind ourselves that the grand
objective which the Apostle has in his mind as he writes the
whole of what we have found in this chapter is that these
Ephesian Christians might be kept from fainting at the tribulations
and the trials which the Apostle himself was being called upon
to endure. One of the first things we always tend to ask in a time
of trouble is, Why is this? In view of the fact that we are what we
are, why should this happen to us? Why should this be allowed?
It is a temptation that the devil is ever ready to insinuate into the
minds of God's people, and the Apostle deals with it here in the
case of these Ephesians.

In this particular statement Paul brings this part of his message
to a kind of grand climax and conclusion. In a sense we can say
that everything the Apostle has been saying would have been of
no value to the Ephesians unless it brings them inevitably to this
particular conclusion. In other words the ultimate purpose of all
Christian doctrine, Christian teaching, indeed the end of the
Christian salvation itself, is to bring us to what we are told in this
verse. We need to be reminded of it, because we are living in days
when many think of the Christian salvation and its benefits in
other terms, such as some particular blessing we desire, or some
particular need which we want to be satisfied. Thank God all

these things are true, and we can never thank God too much for them. But, over and above them all, and indeed before them all, the grand objective towards which all is designed, is to bring us into the presence of God, and to enable us to worship and to pray.

The Apostle is telling the Ephesians that they need not faint or be troubled and unhappy on his account. He says that he is not fainting, and he needs no sympathy. He is perfectly happy because he is in contact with the eternal God, and is enjoying access into His presence. And his desire is that his Ephesian friends may realize that the same experience is open to them and possible for them. Hence if they are attacked, and made to feel sad and perplexed, they need not spend any time in looking at these happenings, but must go straight into the presence of God. As they do so all their problems will take on a new aspect; they will see a purpose even in trials and troubles and testings, and they will end by praising God and glorifying His holy name. For the same reasons we also must consider this particular verse.

There is a principle here which we ignore or forget at our peril. All Christian doctrine is meant to lead, and is designed to lead, to a practical result and outcome. This cannot be over-emphasized. Truth is not merely something for the mind or the intellect. It is, of course, primarily for the mind and the intellect, and it is taken in with the mind and the intellect. But it is fatal to think that truth or doctrine or theology – call it what you will – is to be regarded as an end in itself, something that you are aware of and that you can appropriate with your mind, that you can discuss and argue about, and nothing more. If doctrine stops at that point I do not hesitate to assert that it can even be a curse. Doctrine is meant and designed to bring us to God. It is meant to be practical.

We have a perfect illustration of this truth in the very section we are examining. Here the Apostle, as we have seen, introduces us to some of the profoundest doctrines, yet he makes it clear that it is to lead us into an experience which enables us to say, 'In whom we have boldness and access with confidence by the faith of him'. Nothing is more remarkable about the Apostle Paul, nothing more moving, than this, that though he can soar into the heavens his feet are always fixed firmly on earth. Like

Wordsworth's Skylark he always remains 'true to the kindred points of heaven and home'. He is never a mere theoretical theologian; he is not an intellectual who enjoys bandying terms about. He was the supreme theologian, but his object, his intent, his purpose is always this practical end and result. In other words, if your knowledge of doctrine does not make you a great man or woman of prayer, you had better examine yourself again. The more you know, the more it should show itself in your prayer life, in your holy living, in every other respect. That is why you never find doctrine or theology in isolation in the Scriptures. You generally find it at the beginning of every epistle. But the Apostles do not stop there. 'Therefore', they say – they always apply it, they lead us on to see how all doctrine must be reflected in our life. So let us realize that the first eleven verses of the third chapter of the Epistle to the Ephesians are intended to bring us to verse 12 with its all-important statement.

We must, of course, put equal emphasis on the other side in order that we may be balanced. Doctrine, I repeat, is meant to be practical and is meant to lead to a great richness in the Christian life. But it is equally important to say that your Christian life will never be rich unless you know and apprehend doctrine. These things must not be separated; they are one and indivisible. One of the main causes of trouble in the Church is that we tend to divide ourselves up into sections. Some are only interested in the doctrines and are consumed with that interest. We rarely hear them praying, and we are not struck by the holiness and the sanctity of their lives. But their minds are full of doctrine. To a second group doctrine is of no value at all. Those other people they say, only talk and discuss theology; we are the practical people, we know nothing about doctrine. But to speak thus is to be as wrong as those whom you are criticizing. These two things must always go together; doctrine must not be separated from the practical element, nor the practical from the doctrine. We must ever learn and strive to preserve the balance of Scripture, 'rightly dividing the word of truth' (2 Tim 2:15). We must take it all as we find it in Scripture. You have no right to say, 'I am a practical man, therefore I do not read chapters 1, 2, 3 and part of 4 in the Epistle to the Ephesians; I start reading halfway through chapter 4'. If so you are doing violence to the

Word of God. But if, on the other hand, you stop at the middle of chapter 4 and do not go on to the end of the Epistle you are equally guilty.

So the real purpose of all that the Apostle has been reminding these Ephesians – that they who had been Gentiles and aliens and strangers from the covenants of promise, without hope and without God in the world, have now by this glorious gospel that he had preached unto them been made fellow-heirs with the saints, and fellow-members of the body with the Jews, and fellow-partakers of the great promises – the real purpose, I say, is that they should rejoice in it because it is by means of it that they 'have boldness and access with confidence' into the presence of God. The thing Paul is anxious for them to rejoice in, is that now they who were once estranged from God have been brought nigh, and can enter into the presence of God, and can pray as the Jews always prayed.

This is something of which we also need to remind ourselves, for it is in many ways the highest pinnacle of salvation. Of all the blessings of Christian salvation none is greater than this, that we have access to God in prayer. Before we come to the details, let us note the word 'we' – 'in whom *we* have boldness and access'. In other words, says Paul, what I am going to say does not apply only to apostles, or to certain people who have given themselves entirely to the cultivation of the Christian life. It applies to all Christians. That is the glory of it all. Let us banish from our thinking once and for ever that artificial and unscriptural, and indeed sinful, dichotomy which is found in all forms of Catholic teaching, the teaching which divides people into two groups, the 'religious' and the 'laity'. There is no such distinction in Scripture. 'We', says Paul – I the apostle, you who were formerly Gentiles – 'We' all together have this boldness and access with confidence.

*   *   *

Looking at this in a practical manner, therefore, let us consider the manner of our approach to God in prayer. We can well introduce it by asking a question: How do you pray? What is the character of your prayer life? How do you feel when you get on your knees in prayer to God? What happens? Do you enjoy it? Is it free? Is it certain? Is it assured? What kind of praying is your praying? According to the Apostle our approach should be one which is characterized by 'boldness'. 'Access with confidence' is true Christian prayer. The terms are worthy of separate consideration.

Boldness means fearlessness, a freedom from all apprehension, and from all doubt that we may be rejected. It means freedom from all sense of evil which tends to make true prayer impossible. Boldness obviously means an absence of restraint or fear in any shape or form. When we think of a bold man, we think of one who steps straight forward, who is afraid of nothing. Though facing a mighty enemy the bold man walks with chest high and with confidence and with assurance. He is not conscious of inhibitions, he is not hesitant or doubtful or uncertain. Boldness is the exact opposite of all that indicates weakness.

The second term is *access*. This can be translated as 'entrée'. A man says that he has gained an entrée into some exclusive club; many people are not allowed in, but he has found a way of getting in, a means of entry. It connotes the privilege of entrance, of admission. Paul's use of the term means, then, that there is a relationship existing between us and God whereby we know that we are acceptable to Him and have an assurance that He is favourably disposed towards us. That is the essence of this term 'access'. We know that God is ready to look upon us favourably and that He is waiting to receive us. So we do not hesitate as it were on the doorstep, we have a right of entry, an access, an entrée. This is a very strong term which the Apostle has already used in verse 18 of the second chapter.

Then the Apostle adds another word – *confidence*. The Apostle is so much concerned about establishing this point that he says the same thing as it were in three different ways. Some pedants would call it verbosity or tautology; the Apostle does it for emphasis. And he does so, of course, because he knows how slow we are to learn these things. He knows our failure in prayer, so he keeps on emphasizing it and repeating it again and again. Confidence is always the end of a process. When you have confidence it means that you have been practising something so diligently that you are now confident with respect to it.

Think, for instance, of learning to ride a bicycle. The first moment when the hand of the one teaching you was taken away you were hesitant and uncertain and frightened. But you soon reached a point, when, having ridden alone a number of times, you attained confidence, and you are ready to go alone on the street and round corners and up and down hills. You have developed confidence. It is always the result of a process. A speaker may be nervous when he starts speaking, but after he has spoken a few sentences he loses his nervousness and gains confidence. Such is the term the Apostle uses, and it means that we go into the presence of God with confidence because of a process through which we have gone; it is the result of something that has taken place.

Throughout the New Testament we are taught that confidence is an essential element in true prayer: boldness, access, confidence! An eminent instance of this teaching is found in chapter 10 of the Epistle to the Hebrews: 'Having, therefore, brethren, boldness to enter into the holiest . . . let us draw near with a true heart in full assurance of faith. . . .' (vv. 19–22).

*   *   *

We must now turn to the second principle and consider what it is that makes this way of entry into God's presence possible. How can I have this boldness and this access with confidence? Only one answer can be given, and, because of its importance, the Apostle says it twice in this one verse: 'In *whom* we have boldness and access with confidence by the faith of *Him*'. Whom! Him! The faith of Him means the faith of which He is the object. It could be stated thus: 'In whom we have boldness and access with confidence by means of our faith in him (the Lord Jesus Christ)'. This is obviously a basic fundamental truth. And yet how obvious it is that people who talk about prayer often leave it out altogether! A central message of the New Testament is that there is no possibility of prayer, or of entry into the presence of God, except in and through and by our Lord and Saviour Jesus Christ. He Himself said, 'I am the way, the truth, and the life: no man cometh unto the Father, but by me' (John 14:6). Paul in writing to Timothy says: 'There is one God, and one mediator between God and man, the man Christ Jesus' (1 Tim 2:5). Christ is the only way, and there is none other. Do we always go to God in

Him, and by the faith of Him, and through Him? There is always much interest in prayer when the world is in trouble. When people are driven to their wits' end they turn to prayer and to God. But according to the Scriptures – and I have no other knowledge apart from this – there is no entrance into the presence of God except in and through the Lord Jesus Christ. If there were other ways of entering He need never have come into this world. He came and did all that needed to be done 'to bring us to God'.

Let us state this in a practical manner. If we realize who and what God is, how can we possibly think of coming to Him in any other way? Think of the descriptions He has given of Himself as, for example, to the children of Israel of old, descriptions of His holiness, of His eternity, of His majesty, of His power. The Son of God Himself, when in this world, addressed Him in prayer as 'Holy Father' (John 17:11). 'God is light, and in him is no darkness at all', says the Apostle John (1 John 1:5). 'Our God is a consuming fire', says the Epistle to the Hebrews (12:29). I fear that we often do not stop to think about God before we pray to Him. Indeed we are encouraged at times by certain types of teaching to think that an easy familiarity with God is the hallmark of spirituality. But that is never found in the Scriptures.

Look at all the instructions God gave to the children of Israel in the Old Testament as to how He should be worshipped. Why did they have to build a tabernacle and later a temple? Why were these structures divided into various compartments and sections? Why was the innermost compartment called 'The Holiest of all', into which no one was allowed to enter except the high priest, and he only once a year? Why did God institute all the ceremonial, including numerous sacrifices – burnt offerings, sin offerings, trespass offerings, and others? What is the meaning of it all? It was God who gave the instructions, not men. They were not conjured up out of the minds of men. God called Moses to ascend a mountain and taught him how He was to be worshipped, saying, 'See that thou make all things according to the pattern shewed to thee in the mount' (Heb 8:5). There is but one explanation of all this: God was teaching His people about His holiness and His eternity and His majesty, and He taught them that that was the only way in which they could come into His presence. They could only come as they brought the sacrifices and the offerings; and yet there are those who teach that we can rush into the presence of God easily, and the Name of Christ is never mentioned. It is all quite simple, they say; there is no need to be concerned about theology, they tell us; praying is very simple, it is as simple as breathing.

Such teaching is a denial of the whole of the Old Testament. And it is a denial of the New Testament with its teaching about the absolute necessity of the Lord Jesus Christ and His atoning work. Surely such teaching is nothing but psychology, a form of self-hypnotism which persuades people that they are talking to God. The fact that it makes them feel better or satisfied is no answer. Psychology can often make one feel better. You can persuade yourself of many things. The cults thrive on that fact. The only authority we have in this matter is the Scripture itself. How can I approach God? 'Who among us shall dwell with the devouring fire?', is a question asked by one of the Old Testament prophets (Isa 33:14). Every time any one of them was given some dim vision of God you find him falling on his face in dread, because of the holiness and the majesty of God.

Then again, what do I say to my conscience? When I go into the presence of God I am reminded by my conscience of my sins, of my unworthiness, of the evil I have done and have thought. How can I go to God with a clear conscience and with an assurance that God will forgive me? Then, over and above that consideration, how can I possibly hold communion and fellowship with God? I know what it is to be nervous in the presence of great men and women; I know what it is to feel that I am a worm, and less than a worm, when I am in the presence of a saint. How can I therefore hold converse with God? I feel I am vile and filthy and unworthy; how can I do this? These are the questions: How can I be assured that God is well disposed towards me? How can I go in with boldness? How can I be sure that I have an entrée, an access, that I am accepted? How can I have confidence? There is only one answer, it is 'by the faith of him'.

The only way of going with assurance into the presence of God is to know that the Son of God has borne my sins and their guilt and their punishment in His own body on the tree. It is only when I know that God has taken my sin and guilt away, that He Himself has clothed me with the righteousness of His own Son, and that as I stand before Him He does not see my filthy rags but the perfect robe of righteousness wrought for me by Jesus Christ, that I can go with boldness to God. It is God's Son who has prepared that robe, it is He who has given it to me; so I know that I am accepted. There is no other way. As the 10th chapter of Hebrews says: 'It is not possible that the blood of bulls and of goats should take away sins' (v. 4). They covered over sin for the time being but they could not really cleanse the conscience. And yet there are those who teach that you do not need any offering at all – neither the blood of bulls nor of goats, nor the ashes of an heifer, nor the Son of God and His shed blood – you simply go to God as you are!

Without Christ we cannot truly pray. As the author of the Epistle to the Hebrews says again: 'Seeing that we have a great high priest, that is passed into the heavens, Jesus the Son of God, let us hold fast our profession. For we have not an high priest which cannot be touched with the feeling of our infirmities; but was in all points tempted like as we are, yet without sin. Let us therefore come boldly unto the throne of grace, that we may obtain mercy, and find grace to help in time of need' (4:14–16). We know what would happen to the kind of person who thinks that he can walk into Buckingham Palace and appear before the Queen at any time he likes; he would very soon be dealt with and thrown out, and perhaps cast into prison, as he would deserve to be. And yet people imagine that just as they are, without any meditation or mediation, they can go into the presence of God. There is only One who can introduce you, there is only One who can countersign your visiting card. It is the Son of God, and He has written His Name with His own blood. Thank God, it matters not who you are or what you are, nor the depths of sin to which you may have sunk, nor in what gutters you may have spent your life, walking and grovelling in sin. If you have that card with that blood-written signature upon it, the gates of heaven are open to you, and you can enter with 'boldness', you have 'access with confidence' by the faith of Him!

*   *   *

To be yet more practical, let us consider another question. If this is the only way in which I can have this boldness and access with confidence, what have I to do in order to make it real to myself and in my own experience? The teaching we have been considering must be applied; it does not apply itself. It is possible for Christians to believe all I have been saying and yet never really to know what it is to pray with 'boldness' and to 'have access with confidence'. This is because they have never applied what they know. They have never really taken hold by faith of the vital truth and used it in the right way; for there are certain things that we must do if we would have this boldness and access with confidence.

The first is that we must realize that we must not rely upon our feelings or moods or states. This is quite basic. When you kneel to pray, have you not often found that you suddenly become hard, and that your mind seems to wander far away. You do not feel like praying, you are full of doubts and of uncertainties, your sins are brought back to you, and you feel that prayer is almost impossible? If you listen to such moods and thoughts you will never pray. The first thing we have to do is to deal with all these moods and feelings and states and inward conditions. We have to realize that they arise not only from the body but also from the devil, whose supreme object is to keep us from this communion with God. We must regard them all as sent by him. They are the 'fiery darts' which the devil throws at you, and especially when you are on your knees in prayer. Recognize their source and origin, recognize that they are 'of the devil', and taking yourself firmly in hand, reject them. You have to do it. Prayer is hard work, it is a task. You must not 'relax' as the cults teach, but rather energize yourself and discipline yourself. You must learn to agonize in prayer.

Then, having thus dealt with your feelings and moods and states, you must begin to preach to yourself. I am more than ever convinced that the trouble with many Christian people is that they do not preach to themselves. We should spend time every day preaching to ourselves, and never more so than when we get on our knees in prayer. By preaching to yourself I mean that, when you are on your knees, and all these thoughts and doubts and uncertainties come crowding in upon you, and your sins rise up against you, and you feel you have no right to pray at all, and that you are almost a cad in doing so – I say, you must first realize where they come from and then begin to remind yourself of the central truths of the Christian faith. You must remind yourself of the great doctrine which we have been considering together. You say: 'Of course I am a sinner; when the devil told me I was a sinner, he was quite right. He said it to discourage me; but I am going to use it to help myself. Of course I am a sinner! God is holy and I am vile, and I do not realize even yet how vile I am. Well then, how can I pray? How can I go into the presence of God? The answer is, that God Himself has opened the way for me; He has provided it. He has sent His only Son into this world to bear my sins, to die for me. Christ has kept the law for me and has 'put His own perfect robe of righteousness upon me. With this on me I can go into the presence of God'. Having convinced yourself of that, you gain confidence and begin to pray.

Thus you have solemnly and specifically to remind yourself of what you are, and of what you are doing, also that the God whom you are addressing is the God who has revealed Himself. You have to see the absolute necessity of Christ, and to know that He really covers you in every respect. So with Christ's righteousness upon you, and Christ with you, you go into the presence of God. John in his First Epistle states it thus: 'If we confess our sins, he is faithful and just to forgive us our sins and to cleanse us from all unrighteousness'. He says that in the context of 'the blood of Jesus Christ which cleanseth us from all sin' (1:7-9). He goes on to say, 'If any man sin, we have an advocate with the Father, Jesus Christ the righteous, and he is the propitiation for our sins' (2:1-2). That is what you say to yourself. You do not wait until a better mood comes; and you do not simply go on talking in spite of your mood or state. You have to say to yourself 'Although I am a sinner, and though I feel nothing, I believe in the Lord Jesus Christ. I know that I can never fit myself to go into the presence of God; but I believe this record in the Scriptures. I therefore believe, whatever I may feel or not feel, that Christ the Son of God has died for me and my sins; and that therefore I have as much right to go into the presence of God as the greatest saint'.

And then you immediately thank God for it all – 'By prayer and supplication with thanksgiving', says this apostle in teaching the Philippians how to pray (Phil 4:6). Forget for the moment all your needs and desires, even that particular thing which led you to pray. Before you ever come even to that, just thank God for His love, thank Him for His mercy and compassion, thank Him for sending His Son into a world such as this; thank Him for going to the Cross and dying for you, thank Him for rising again, thank Him for sending the Holy Spirit. Pour out your heart in praise and thanksgiving. Soon you will find freedom; your heart will be moved, and you will know for the first time in your life 'boldness and access with confidence'. Then pray that God will shed His Holy Spirit abroad in your heart so that you may experience the authentication of all these things. We need to go into the presence of God using the words that Count Zinzendorf wrote, and that John Wesley translated in the following way:

> Jesus, Thy blood and righteousness
> My beauty are, my glorious dress;
> 'Midst flaming worlds in these arrayed
> With joy shall I lift up my head.

> Bold shall I stand in Thy great day;
> For who aught to my charge shall lay?
> Fully absolved through these I am,
> From sin and fear, from guilt and shame.

If we do what I have been trying to say, and then go with boldness into the presence of God, do you know what will happen? (It is not surprising that the Apostle brought these Ephesians to this practical point.) This is what will happen. I use the words of the Apostle James in the fourth chapter of his Epistle, 'Draw nigh to God, and he will draw nigh to you' (v. 8). That is the greatest thing one can ever hear in this life. Go into the presence of God with boldness and access with confidence in the faith of Jesus Christ, and you will meet God. You will realize His presence; you will be supported not only by a sense of His glory and His comfort, His strength and His might, but also by a sense of His love and kindness and compassion. You will know that you are His child and that He is your Father. You will know, and you will be able to say, that 'all things work together for good to them that love God'. You will be persuaded that 'neither death nor life, nor angels, nor principalities, nor powers, nor things present, nor things to come, nor height, nor depth, nor any other creature, shall be able to separate you from the love of God which is in Christ Jesus our Lord'. You will be able to say, as another hymn expresses it,

> *In heavenly love abiding*
> > *No change my heart shall fear;*
> *And safe is such confiding,*
> > *For nothing changes here:*
> *The storm may roar without me,*
> > *My heart may low be laid;*
> *But God is round about me,*
> > *And can I be dismayed?*

'Draw nigh to God, and he will draw nigh to you'.

8
Praying to the Father

'For this cause I bow my knees unto the Father of our
Lord Jesus Christ, of whom the whole family in
heaven and earth is named.'

Ephesians 3:14–15

The Revised Version leaves out the words 'of our Lord Jesus
Christ' and translates thus, 'For this cause I bow my knees unto
the Father, from whom every family in heaven and on earth is
named'. With a slight variation the Revised Standard Version
follows suit. With these words the Apostle takes up the matter
which he had obviously intended to take up at the beginning
of the chapter, as we saw when we were looking at verse 1.
Observe that verse 1 starts with the words 'For this cause', as
does also verse 14. He was about to say what he now goes on to
say beyond verse 15. His great concern, as he says in verse 13, is,
'Wherefore I desire that ye faint not at my tribulations for you,
which is your glory'. He has worked his way through the great
digression, and now he comes back to that which he had
originally intended to say.

The expression 'For this cause' in verse 14 as in verse 1 refers
to what the Apostle had been saying at the end of chapter 2. We
must be careful therefore in our exposition of the statement that
we are going to examine to make sure that it does connect with
what had been said at the end of chapter 2. His essential point
was to show these Ephesians that they had been brought into a
state of complete unity in the Christian Church with the Jews
who had also believed the gospel. You are, he assured them, 'no
more strangers and foreigners, but fellow-citizens with the saints,
and of the household of God; and are built upon the foundation
of the apostles and prophets, Jesus Christ himself being the chief
corner stone; in whom all the building fitly framed together

groweth unto an holy temple in the Lord: in whom ye also are builded together for an habitation of God through the Spirit'. That was the exalted conception and description which he gives there of the Christian Church.

*   *   *

The connection is clearly important for us to bear in mind, for it is only as we remember what Paul has been saying that we can possibly understand what he is now about to say. This further truth, this prayer that he is now going to offer for these Ephesians, arises because of their position as fellow-citizens with the saints and as members of the household of God. They belonged to God's family, and constituted a part of the holy temple in the Lord in which God takes up His habitation through the Spirit. Bearing all that in our minds we can follow the Apostle when he tells these Ephesian believers that he is praying for them. 'I bow my knees unto the Father'.

For the moment I propose only to make a number of comments upon the way in which the Apostle introduces the great prayer which he offers for the Ephesians. The first thing to be emphasized is that he does pray for them. And, taking it in its setting, this is something which is of great value to us. When the Apostle was writing this letter he was a prisoner; it is one of the 'prison epistles'. He was probably a prisoner in Rome but that is immaterial. The important thing for us to realize is that what he is saying in effect is, that though he is a prisoner, though a malignant enemy has arrested him, and has put him into bonds, and has made it impossible for him to visit them at Ephesus and to preach to them, or to go anywhere else to preach, there is one thing that the enemy cannot do, and that is, he cannot prevent him from praying. He can still pray. The enemy can confine him to a cell, he can bolt and bar doors, he can chain him to soldiers, he can put bars in the windows, he can hem him in and confine him physically, but he can never obstruct the way from the heart of the humblest believer to the heart of the Eternal God. In many ways in this uncertain modern world of ours this is one of the most comforting and consoling truths we can ever learn. Think of what this means to hundreds, not to say thousands, of Christian people in various parts of the world at this moment. Some are in prison, and some in labour camps. They are subject to untold suffering and indignities but thank God they can still assert that 'stone walls do not a prison make, nor iron bars a cage'. The spirit of prayer is still free in spite of all the malignity of cruel tyrants. Men may forbid us to speak with our lips, but even were they to stitch our lips together we can still pray in our spirits, still keep on praying to God.

This is always applicable to us whatever our circumstances and conditions may happen to be. There are times when as Christians we seem to be in some kind of prison. We may be hemmed in and tied down, perhaps by illness or some physical weakness or by circumstances, or circumstances may prevent us from coming to the House of God or of having fellowship with others. Christian people often find themselves in some such circumstance or condition. So let us remember that whatever circumstances or evil men may do to us, there is always open to us this particular ministry and activity. Nothing need ever hinder it. In other words if you find yourself ill and confined to a sick bed, that does not mean that you are useless for the time being, it does not mean that you can do nothing. You can still go on praying. You can pray for yourself; you can pray for others; you can be taking part in a great ministry of intercession.

I fear at times that we tend to forget this. We have become a generation of Christians that tend to live on meetings. That may sound strange at a time when church attendance is very low. Nevertheless I think it is true that those who still gather together tend to depend overmuch on their attendances and to feel that, when they are laid aside on their beds in sickness, there is nothing that they can do, except wait until they get well again. That is an utter fallacy. Paul was very active and busy in prison. He spent his time, we gather, in praying for various churches. We find in the prison epistles that he says he is praying constantly, daily, for them. He was occasionally able to send them a letter though but few of them survive; but he was constantly surrounding all the churches with his prayers, and praying for individuals in them. He was exercising a great ministry in prison. It was not his usual ministry, for he was a preacher, an evangelist, an incomparable teacher. He does not tell his friends that he can now do nothing as he is languishing in prison and can but hope that somehow or other he will soon be set free. Not at all! This tremendous prayer activity is continuing. Let us bear this fact in mind.

And how much there is to pray for at the present time with the world as it is, and so many Christian people suffering as they are! May I ask a simple and obvious question: How much of our time are we giving day by day to praying for Christians in other countries? We have the time and the leisure; we are not even in prison. We have the time to do many things that are not at all essential or even profitable. How much time are we giving to intercession and to prayer for other people? We are called to bear one another's burdens, to share in one another's woes. Here is a man who did so in prison with everything against him. Let us, I say, heed this call to prayer. As Paul knew that he could help the Ephesians by praying for them, we can also help people – people we may never have met perhaps, but whom we know to be suffering at this very hour, and who are in trouble in various respects. Let us spend time at the throne of grace on their behalf.

*   *   *

In the next place, we are reminded here by the Apostle, that prayer is always as necessary as is instruction. It would be a very great fallacy if we got the impression that the Apostle was praying for these Ephesians only because he could not preach to them. I have emphasized that he was praying for them, in one sense, because he could not preach to them; but I want to make it equally clear that that is not his only reason for praying for them. Were he at liberty he would still be praying for them. Here, once more, is a principle which seems to be somewhat neglected by us. It is as essential that we should pray for ourselves as it is that we should instruct ourselves. We believe we need instruction; we read our Bibles, we meditate upon them; we read books about the Bible, we read commentaries, we read books on Church History, we read books on doctrine. It is right that we should do so, it is essential; we can never know too much. We need instruction, we need enlightenment – that is why these epistles were written. The Apostle believes that doctrine is essential; instruction must have priority. But to impart knowledge is not enough. It is equally essential that we should pray – pray for ourselves, that we may be made receptive to the knowledge and instruction; pray that we may be able to harness it and apply it; pray that it may not stop merely in our minds but that it may grip our hearts and bend our wills and affect the whole man. Knowledge and instruction and prayer must always go together; they must never be separated.

Prayer is also equally necessary in our dealings with others. That is what is most prominent here, of course. Paul was writing this rich, profound doctrine, and he knows that the Ephesians were going to read and discuss and study it together. But he knows that that is not enough, so he is praying that his teaching of them may be made real to them. And he knows that it never can be made real to them except under the direct blessing of God. The best teaching in the world is useless unless the Holy Spirit takes hold of it and applies it and opens our understanding to it, and gives it a deep lodging place in our whole being. We have already seen in the first chapter how the Apostle had been praying for the Ephesian Christians that 'the eyes of their understanding might be enlightened'. For if the Holy Spirit did not open 'the eyes of their understanding' Paul's teaching would be quite useless and void.

Let us learn a very practical lesson from this. We all have friends who are not Christians, about whom we are concerned. We are anxious to help them, and we talk to them about these things. We quote Scriptures to them and explain them. We try to show them the Christian attitude and position with respect to present conditions and the whole of life. But I must emphasize that if we leave it at that, it may come to nothing. You cannot reason anyone into the Christian life. You can give the reasons for believing but you cannot reason them into belief. You can put the case before them, but you cannot prove it as if it were a matter of a theorem in geometry. We must realize that while we are instructing them, we must also be praying for them. It is only as the Holy Spirit deals with them and prepares them and opens their understanding that they can receive the truth.

The Apostle is perfectly consistent with his own doctrine. He knew that it was as essential that he should pray for these Ephesians as that he should instruct them by his Epistle. We, likewise, must never forget that instruction and prayer go together.

If you are interested in a particular person, and desire his salvation, you must not stop at befriending him, helping him, spending time with him, and putting the truth before him; equally you must pray for him. Indeed I would go so far as to say that unless you are giving more weight to your prayer than to your instruction your work is likely to be a failure. Note the place that is given to intercessory prayer in the New Testament. It is extraordinary and quite amazing, and is exemplified particularly in the Apostle Paul. Notice, too, how very dependent Paul was upon the prayers of other Christians. In most of his letters he pleads with them to pray for him. He urges them to pray that he may have a door of opportunity, that he may have liberty, and so on. He fully realized his dependence upon the prayers of others. In some respects this is a great mystery; and some are tempted to say, God is all powerful, there is nothing He cannot do, why therefore is there any need of prayer? The answer to that query is that God has chosen in His own eternal wisdom to work in this way. He divides up the work, and somehow or other He uses our prayers, and brings His great purposes to pass through the means and the instrumentality of the intercession of the saints.

*   *   *

Another important matter we must note is the way in which the Apostle prays; in other words we must pay attention to the method, the mode, or the manner of his prayer. Here is something very striking and significant. 'For this cause I bow my knees unto the Father.' There is no need to assert that, at the very moment he was writing, the Apostle literally went down on his knees. He may have done so; I do not know. But what he is clearly saying is that he was praying for them, and what interests us is the way in which he chooses to describe prayer. He did not pray haphazardly, accidentally, but does so very deliberately. A man under divine inspiration does not speak casually, does not say things accidentally. Very deliberately, when he comes to talk about himself praying, he says, 'I bow my knees'.

This expression brings us face to face with the whole question of our posture in prayer. This is a matter which has troubled people in two diametrically opposed ways; they tend to go to one extreme or the other. But the Scripture is quite clear on the matter. It teaches that sometimes men bow their knees or they kneel in prayer; but it is equally clear in its teaching that others stand in prayer. Both methods are mentioned in the Scripture, and even others, such as lying prostrate on the ground.

This question must detain us for a moment because it can so easily be handled in a wrong, and even foolish, manner. There are two extremes to be noted. The one extreme is formalism, and the other is thoughtlessness or casualness. Formalism virtually teaches that unless we actually kneel we are not praying at all. There are people who honestly believe that nonconformists never truly pray in a church simply because they do not kneel. To such people the kneeling is vital and essential to prayer. They forget all about the references to standing in the Bible. We can put into this selfsame category all who think that forms of liturgy are absolutely essential. On the other side are those who assert the principle of liberty. But the principle of liberty can also be pressed too far, with the result that it becomes licence, looseness, laxity, and thoughtlessness and can lead to a manner of prayer that is totally unworthy of God.

Surely the vital principle involved is that it is not the posture or the attitude in and of itself that matters; but what it represents and what it indicates. Bowing the knees is an indication of reverence, of what the author of the Epistle to the Hebrews means when he writes in Chapter 12 of 'reverence and godly fear'. It is indicative of an attitude of worship and of adoration and of praise. It is obvious that you can drop on your knees mechanically when certain words are uttered, but your heart may be far away. There are people whose reverence is entirely determined by the type of building in which they are found. If they are in certain cathedral-like types of building they walk softly and they speak in whispers; but the moment they go outside they may be blaspheming and cursing. So what they are doing in the building is not displaying reverence, it is simply the case that the building has affected them psychologically. Scripture is not interested in that type of behaviour. There are men who may be most devout in their postures, in their crossing of themselves, and in striking other attitudes; but that is valueless unless it is truly an expression of the state of their hearts. But – and this must be emphasized – the state of the heart does express itself, inevitably.

And it is here that the expression used by the Apostle is so important and so interesting.

This matter is directly connected with what we have been considering in the Apostle's magnificent and encouraging statement, 'In whom we have boldness and access with confidence by the faith of him'. How vital it is that that should always be coupled with 'I bow my knees', in order to remind us that boldness does not mean brazenness, that confidence does not mean an easy familiarity. Boldness at the throne of grace is not presumption. Confidence is not cheek. I emphasize this because there are those who seem to think that it is the hallmark of spirituality, and of assurance of salvation, that one should pray to God with an easy, glib familiarity, which is an utter denial of what is taught here and throughout Scripture.

There is a type of person who thinks that if you want to prove how spiritual you are, you should be very businesslike in your prayers. You must utter brief petitions, almost telegraphic petitions. They teach that you should be so assured of your position before God that you are a complete stranger to 'fear and trembling', indeed to any preliminary worship and adoration before you present your requests. I have often noticed this, alas, in conferences among evangelical people. The prayer-meeting is often conducted in the following manner. A list of things that should be prayed for, so-called prayer-requests, is read out, and the chairman then says, 'Well now, let us get busy, let us get to prayer'. And so the people present get up one after another and just offer very brief petitions concerning these various problems. I have been in such prayer-meetings where, I do not hesitate to assert, there has been no worship whatsoever. God has not been worshipped, has not been praised, has not been adored. He has not even been thanked for His great mercies. There has been no mention of His majesty and His glory. There has been no 'bowing of the knees'. Some were perhaps literally on their knees, but their spirits were not bowed. All was taken for granted.

Such is the attitude which the Apostle's statement corrects so drastically. It is an attitude which, far from being a sign of spirituality, indeed becomes the very reverse. It is based on ignorance of Scripture, and on ignorance of God. If ever a man knew God, and if ever a man knew the way into God's presence, it was this mighty Apostle; and yet he 'bows his knees'. He knew whom he was approaching. He is not on terms of glib familiarity with God. 'Boldness and access with confidence', yes! but accompanied by 'reverence and godly fear' for 'our God is a consuming fire'. Let us recall the true interpretation of that previous verse 12, which is, that we are to be free from a craven fear because we know the grounds of our standing, and also know that we have access and entry into God's presence. But that does not mean that we can walk boldly with chest forward, as it were, into the presence of Almighty God. We are to be always humbly aware of our great privilege. We know that we have access, but we remember that it is access into the presence of the living God in all His glory and His power. 'I bow my knees.' Worship, adoration, praise! We must never proceed to particular petitions until we have first worshipped and praised and thanked God, and submitted ourselves utterly and entirely to Him.

The little word *unto* – 'I bow my knees unto' – is a very expressive word, which means 'facing', or 'face to face'. He bows his knees in order to come face to face with God. The moment we realize that prayer means coming face to face with God, we cannot but bend our knees. When Isaiah had his vision of God he said, 'Woe is me, for I am a man of unclean lips' (6:5). When John had his vision on Patmos he fell to the ground as one dead (Rev 1:17). There would be no need for this exhortation if we had some real conception of the glory of God. If we had but a glimpse of God, we would tremble at being face to face with Him. Let us thank God again for this. Wherever we may be, whatever our circumstances, in and through the Lord Jesus Christ we can always come face to face with God. 'We all, with open face beholding as in a glass the glory of the Lord . . .' says the same Apostle to the Corinthians (2 Cor 3:18).

*   *   *

Lastly we come to the Apostle's description here of God, the One to whom he comes thus humbled in spirit and bowing in his heart. He says that he comes to 'the Father, of whom the whole family in heaven and earth is named'. The Authorized Version has 'the Father of our Lord Jesus Christ', whereas certain other Versions simply have 'the Father'. This is purely a question of textual criticism which does not affect the meaning to the slightest extent. The Apostle has already made it abundantly clear that God is only our Father in and through the Lord Jesus Christ. Some of the old manuscripts have the addition; some have not.

In verse 15 we have a most interesting statement. The 'of whom' really means 'after whom', or indeed 'from whom'. As to the remainder of the statement, the Authorized Version has 'Of whom the whole family in heaven and earth is named'. Certain other translations have 'Of whom (or from whom) every family in heaven and earth is named'. In the final analysis the difference is not a serious one; but the particular interpretation varies according to which of these two translations or renderings is adopted. The translation, 'Of whom (or from whom) every family in heaven and earth is named' places the emphasis upon the word 'family', as meaning 'belonging to a common stock'. Such is the meaning of the word 'family' in and of itself. It may also mean a tribe or a class or a nation. Furthermore, every family has a family name. The family name derives from some original father; the tribes of Israel all took their names from a particular man. 'Our Lord came from the family and lineage of David'; He was 'of the seed of David according to the flesh'. All groups are given their names from some such origin. And so, according to this interpretation, what the Apostle is saying here is that all these distinctions and divisions into families and tribes and groups and nations, which all acknowledge some earthly leader or father, are but pale reflections of the fact that God is the Father of all; He is the Father of all families, the Father of every family. He is the One from whom every subsidiary parenthood or fatherhood is derived. Ultimately, therefore, He is the Father of all.

We note that the Apostle says, not only 'on earth' but also 'in heaven' – 'every family in heaven and on earth' – and the line of interpretation to which I have just referred gives the following explanation. In verse 10 Paul says: 'To the intent that now unto the principalities and powers in the heavenly places'; and at the end of the 1st chapter he has written in still greater detail, saying that Christ is 'above all principality and power and might and dominion, and every name that is named'. There are different groups in heaven; angelic beings are divided into angels and archangels, and various other sub-divisions. They are, as it were, divided into groups, families, and tribes. So here, it is asserted, the Apostle is saying that not only does every earthly fatherhood and nation and tribe and division untimately derive from the Fatherhood of God, but the very groupings in heaven are all under this universal Fatherhood. Indeed they say that the Old Testament refers to the angels as 'the sons of God', so that in a sense they are children of God, and God is their Father.

This line of exposition is true; but it is true only in the sense that God is the Creator of all. The Apostle Paul took this line when, preaching in Athens, He said, 'We are also his (God's) offspring' (Acts 17:29). The whole world is in that sense the offspring of God. He is the Father in the sense that He is the Creator of all. If this is borne in mind, then the interpretation to which I have been referring is legitimate and is true. And yet, for myself, I do not accept it here, and for the reason that it does not seem to fit the context; it seems to drag in something which at this particular point is irrelevant.

The expression, 'For this cause', as we have seen, refers back to chapter 2, and there, surely, we have the key to the explanation of what Paul means here. For in verse 18 of chapter 2 we read: 'For through Him (Christ) we both have access by one Spirit unto the Father'. Take note of this reference to the Father. Again, 'Now therefore ye are no more strangers and foreigners, but fellow-citizens with the saints, and of the household of God' – 'the family of God'! Here we have the two terms, the 'Father' and the 'family'. Surely what the Apostle is saying here in verse 15 of chapter 3 is that God is the Father of the whole family. What family? The family of the redeemed! Of this 'family' of the redeemed some are in heaven already, and some are still on earth; but they all belong to the same family, the whole family. In other words I suggest that the Apostle is saying here precisely what the author of the Epistle to the Hebrew says in chapter 12 of his Epistle. His word runs: 'Ye are not come to the mount that might be touched' . . . 'Ye are come unto mount Zion, and unto the city of the living God, the heavenly Jerusalem, and to an innumerable company of angels, to the general assembly and church of the firstborn, which are written in heaven, and to God the Judge of all, and to the spirits of just men made perfect, and to Jesus'. So the Apostle is saying that he is praying on behalf of the Ephesians, to the One who is the Father of all. He is their Father now, since they have come into the Church, as well as the Father of the Apostle. He is the Father of all who believe. Now there is neither Gentile nor Jew . . . Barbarian, Scythian, bond nor free (Col 3:11). No longer afar off, Christians have been made nigh.

I believe the Apostle used this form of expression in order to teach these Ephesian Christians not to think of themselves any longer as Gentiles. They were to think of themselves now as the children of God, as belonging to God's great family. This was the wonderful result of what had happened to them, they had been made 'members of the household of God', 'fellow-heirs' with the Jews, members of the same body, partakers of the same promises; they had been brought into the great family of God.

Nothing we can ever learn is more precious for us than to realize this glorious truth. You may be unknown by the world, you may be insignificant, or you may feel that you are forgotten, that no one knows anything about you; and that may be true. But if you are 'in Christ', if you are a Christian, you belong to God, you are in His family, and your Father has His eye upon you. Nothing can happen to you apart from Him and without His permission; 'the hairs of your head are all numbered'. You are as much His child as the greatest saint, the mightiest apostle, that has ever lived. There is only one family, the 'whole family', and He is the Father of the whole family, the Church 'militant' as well as the Church 'triumphant'. We all have this access into His presence. And here this great brother, the Apostle Paul, this mighty brother who was so advanced in knowledge, is telling his humble brethren, his young brothers there in Ephesus, that he is going to 'our Father' on their behalf, and is about to ask Him to do certain things for them.

We belong to this family, this 'whole family'. Let us never forget it; and especially as we pray and approach God in worship. But let us never forget it also in our conduct and behaviour. We know what it is to be proud of our families and of 'the family name'. We know what it is to be proud of country, of a class, or group, or school – proud of the name! So as Christians let us always remember that the Name that is on us is the Name of God, 'from whom the whole family in heaven and on earth is named'.

What matters is no longer the family of David, no longer this tribe or that tribe, no longer this country or that country, this class or that class, this group or that group. No! The family name which I claim is the Name of God, and I am to live in this world as one who represents that family, as one who represents that Father. His Name is on me; so may it never be besmirched! May men never think meanly of Him and His Name because of what they see in me!

May God open our eyes to the privileges that are ours through the Name that is on us, and also to the high, and in many ways the dread responsibility of having upon us the Name of God!

9
'The Inner Man'

'That he would grant you, according to the riches of
his glory, to be strengthened with might by his
Spirit in the inner man.'

Ephesians 3:16

These words are part of the larger statement which, beginning
at verse 14, goes on to verse 21: 'For this cause I bow my knees
unto the Father of our Lord Jesus Christ, of whom the whole
family in heaven and earth is named, that he would grant you,
according to the riches of his glory, to be strengthened with
might by his Spirit in the inner man; that Christ may dwell in
your hearts by faith; that ye, being rooted and grounded in love,
may be able to comprehend with all saints what is the breadth,
and length, and depth, and height; and to know the love of
Christ, which passeth knowledge, that ye might be filled with all
the fulness of God. Now unto him that is able to do exceeding
abundantly above all that we ask or think, according to the power
that worketh in us, unto him be glory in the church by Christ
Jesus throughout all ages, world without end. Amen'.

However long you may live in this world, whatever orator may
arise, you will never hear anything equal to that for eloquence,
for elevation of thought, for profundity of language and for
conception. It is undoubtedly one of the great mountain peaks
in the Scripture. Indeed, there are many who would say that this
is the highest peak of all in the entire glorious range of Scripture
truth and divine revelation. We are looking, let us remember,
at the actual prayer which the Apostle offers for the Christian
people in Ephesus. We have studied the way in which he
approaches God, and noted how careful he is to remind us of
its essentials and of our need to be conformed to it. He 'bows his
knees' before the Father, the One whom we, through our blessed

Lord and Saviour, are also entitled to call 'our Father'. Having thus entered into the presence of God, what is it that the Apostle prays for these Ephesian Christians who are so much upon his heart?

In the New Testament we have several recorded prayers of Paul, and they all are worthy of our most careful and serious consideration, but there is surely no prayer of his which rises higher than this one. Here, he lifts us right into the heavens and prays for things which are almost incredible, rising to the climax 'that ye might be filled with all the fulness of God'. Remember that he is praying thus for converted pagans, many of whom had been slaves, and were perhaps slaves still, people who were unknown. Because they were Christians the Apostle offers this prayer for them, and takes us, as he does so, to the very highest reaches, the topmost level of Christian experience and of what is possible for men and women in this present world. This is the real key to true Christian living; therefore we cannot examine it too closely.

*   *   *

Coming then to the actual content of his prayer, let us note first of all what he does not pray for. In Scripture the negative is always significant. At times, it is almost as important as the positive. And, here, what Paul does not pray for is noteworthy. Imagine yourself in the position of the Apostle. How would you have prayed for these Ephesians? What do we pray for one another? When we know that others are in trouble and in difficulties, what do we petition for them, what is the character of our intercession? Paul does not pray for any change in circumstances, either for himself or for them. His prayer is not that he may be brought out of prison in order that he may return to preach to them in Ephesus. That would have been very desirable; and no doubt he did pray in that way; but that is not the big thing, it is not what he puts in the centre, it is not the thing he wants to impress upon them. Neither does he merely offer some kind of general prayer for them that God may bless them and that God may be good to them. I emphasize this particularly because it seems to me that far too often our prayers are of this character. We pray God's blessing upon people. We pray that

God may be gracious unto them, and may look upon them; and we leave it as some kind of general prayer.

Positively, the Apostle's first petition is, 'That he would grant you, according to the riches of his glory, to be strengthened with might by his Spirit in the inner man'. Here we have what is always characteristic of Paul's prayers, and at the same time characteristic of all the biblical prayers, Old Testament and New. At the same time we are introduced to the characteristic Christian way of viewing the problems which are incidental to our lives in this world, many of which arise directly because of our profession of the Christian faith.

The first characteristic is that his prayer is exclusively spiritual. He is concerned, not about the material but the spiritual. He focuses his attention and his concern on the spiritual state of the Ephesians. His entire attitude to life is a spiritual one, and he always starts with the spiritual. This is a principle which we ignore at our peril. In this matter he is following our Lord Himself who taught, 'Seek ye first the kingdom of God and his righteousness; and all these (other) things shall be added unto you' (Matt 6:33). Our Lord was there dealing with people who were always worrying about food and drink and clothing and material things. The trouble with you, He says in effect, is that you are starting at the wrong end, you are starting with the material and with the seen; start with the unseen, 'Seek ye first the kingdom of God and his righteousness'. That is precisely what the Apostle does here. It is the spiritual condition and welfare of these people that is uppermost in his mind, and in his heart.

The second characteristic of Paul's prayer is that it is a very specific one. As I say, it is not a mere general prayer; he singles out certain matters, he isolates certain particulars and brings them forward one by one in his prayer to God on behalf of the Ephesians. True Christian praying – praying in the Spirit, praying in Christ – is not only spiritual in character, but it is always specific also. We betray much of the truth concerning ourselves in our prayers and in our praying. Ultimately there is no better index of one's spiritual state and condition than one's prayers. If a man's prayers are formal it means that his whole position is formal. If he is more concerned about beauty of language and of diction you can be sure that his main concern again is with the externals. Is there freedom, is there spirituality in the prayer? Is there displayed an understanding of the essential character and nature of the Christian life? Let us face this individually for ourselves. When you pray to God what is your greatest concern about yourself? Are you concerned chiefly about circumstances and ambitions – your body, your affairs – or are you primarily concerned about your spiritual state and condition? Which is it that receives chief attention and most time in your personal prayers and devotions? Are you primarily concerned about the whole question of your spiritual growth and development, your knowledge of God, your relationship to Him, and your enjoyment of Him? Is that the big thing? Or do you give priority to the things that belong to the externals of life? The Apostle's prayers are not only essentially spiritual, but also specific. There are certain aspects of the spiritual prosperity of the Ephesians that he is concerned about in particular, and so he mentions them one by one.

*   *   *

Take note that Paul does not make light of the problems involved. The New Testament, the truly Christian approach to the problems of life, never makes light of them. It is characteristic of psychology, however, that it generally does so. Being primarily concerned merely to make us happy, it is not over-particular as to how it does so. So it comes to us and gives us a general assurance that all will be well, and that the worst may never happen. Or it may look into one's situation and say that, after all, it is not quite as bad as it might have been. That is not the Apostle's method at all, neither is it found anywhere in the New Testament. Scripture never tries to minimize a problem or a difficulty: it does the exact opposite. The worldly way of trying to help us when we are in trouble is to pat us on the back and to say, 'It's all right!' But it is very wrong to say that all is right if it is not so. An essential honesty always characterizes the scriptural and Christian approach.

Neither does the Christian method lightly promise that the problem or the difficulty, or whatever it is, will soon be removed. Nothing is so characteristic of the Scripture as its realism. I emphasize this because it is the key to the understanding of this prayer. The New Testament tells us very frankly and plainly, 'In the world ye shall have tribulation' (John 16:33). It does not promise us an easy time. It is not a cheery kind of optimism. It does not say that once you come to Christ the whole world will be changed; that you will walk with a light step and never again have any problems. On the contrary these are its statements: 'We must through much tribulation enter into the kingdom of God' (Acts 14:22). 'Unto you it is given in the behalf of Christ, not only to believe on him, but also to suffer for his sake' (Phil 1:29). 'Yea, and all that will live godly in Christ Jesus shall suffer persecution' (2 Tim 3:12). The Book of Revelation likewise is full of prophecies of trials and troubles and tribulations. Nothing in the New Testament leads us to think that all our difficulties are suddenly going to be removed and that we shall walk into some kind of magic circle. Quite the reverse! If the New Testament did not speak to us in this realistic way it would not help us to meet the situations in which we find ourselves, and to overcome them, and to be more than conquerors.

It is of the essence of the Bible's method to show us that because this is a sinful world there must of necessity be trials and troubles and problems and tribulations in it. A Christian should not be surprised at the state of the world, for sin has sad consequences. It is the philosophers, and pyschologists, and false optimists who should be surprised, for they believe that it is within man's power to put everything in order in this world. But the Christian starts with this principle, that while there is sin left in this world there will be trouble. 'The way of transgressors is hard' (Prov 13:15). 'There is no peace, saith my God, to the wicked' (Isa 57:21). There is not, and there will not be, and there cannot be. Sin, the lust that is in the human breast and heart, is the cause of war and discord and of all our troubles, and while it continues thus there will be troubles. If you suggest that this is a very pessimistic view, I reply that it is realistic. It is not pessimistic to face the facts. Pessimism arises after you have faced the facts, and especially as the result of how you face them. It is not true optimism to refuse to look at the facts honestly, because true optimism is always thoroughly realistic. It starts by looking at everything as it is, at its very worst, and then overcomes it. And here the Apostle does not promise anything easy or simple. There are no short cuts in the spiritual life.

[123]

Notice further that Paul does not pray that some method may be evolved for fighting these problems and difficulties and situations directly. Christianity is never concerned primarily with the destruction of our enemies, or the solving of our difficulties and problems. The Apostle's method is rather to pray that, face to face with all these things, in the face of imprisonment and all else God might permit, we might 'according to the riches of his glory' 'be strengthened with might by his Spirit in the inner man'. In other words, the Christian way of dealing with all life's problems is not, in the first place, to do anything about them, but to deal with our own spiritual state. The Christian method is to build up our resistance in our inner man, by the Spirit.

An illustration will throw light on my meaning. The biblical teaching concerning our response to attacks is analogous to that which happens in nature in the case of the physical body and disease. It is a convenient way of looking at this whole problem. Sin and evil and Satan and all the forces that would get us down, and depress us, and destroy us, are like diseases resulting from the attacks of germs and microbes and viruses which are very powerful and potent, and even capable of destroying life. We are all constantly being attacked in this way, whether we are aware of it or not. They are inside us; our bodies are full of many billions of germs any of which at any moment can become lethal and destroy us. How does the body deal with these things? There is a mechanism in the body which is designed to resist such attacks. It is a question of infection and resistance. Resistance is sometimes referred to as man's natural constitution; some term it his physique. Some men are born with better, stronger constitutions than others, so when two men are exposed to the same infection, while one may be struck down the other is unaffected. This is because the latter has a better resistance. You have heard say of a certain child who has been vaccinated that it did not 'take'. The doctor may think that there has been some mistake, so he repeats the vaccination. But still it does not 'take'. The doctor then comes to the conclusion that the child has a 'natural immunity'. It is a part of that child's nature, his constitution.

There is a mechanism for resistance in the body. The resistance is not always very strong, indeed may be very poor. So what is needed to meet infection is to build up the resistance. There are

many ways of doing this. One is to take exercise, to get out into
the open and fill your lungs with fresh air and oxygen. Another
is to take the right kind of food. However, there is another line
of approach, namely, to take drugs of various kinds and to try to
attack the enemy directly. This approach is not concerned with
building up the resistance, it deals in a direct manner with the
invading germs. Another possible method is to operate and
remove some infected organ.

Now the method that is being employed by the Apostle is that
of building up the resistance of the Ephesian Christians. There are
the circumstances, there is the attack, so the Apostle prays that
God 'according to the riches of his glory, may strengthen them
with might in the inner man'. Whatever the attack may be, the
resistance can be so strengthened that they will be made more
than conqueror. This is the essential biblical teaching as to how
to live in a world such as this, and how to keep going in it, and
how to be 'more than conqueror' in spite of everything that
happens in it.

Our blessed Lord teaches this in verse 1 of chapter 18 of the
Gospel according to St Luke, where He says 'that men ought
always to pray and not to faint'. He says, if you want to avoid
fainting, pray. What prayer does, as it were, is to fill the lungs of
the soul with the oxygen of the Holy Spirit and His power. If
you want to stand on your feet and not to falter, fill yourself
with the life of God. 'Pray, and not faint.' In other words we are
not to spend our time in considering the things that are tending
to defeat us; we are to build up ourselves 'on our most holy faith',
as Jude exhorts us.

This is the only way whereby we can ever come to know what
it is to rejoice in tribulation. This is the only way of being what
the Apostle calls 'more than conquerors' in spite of everything
that attacks us. Or, as he states it in chapter 4 of his Second Epistle
to the Corinthians, if you desire to be able to say 'Our light
affliction which is but for a moment worketh for us a far more
exceeding and eternal weight of glory', you must also be able to
say, 'While we look not at the things which are seen, but at the
things which are not seen' (vv. 17–18). The same principle
operates everywhere in the spiritual realm. Build up the inner
man. Strengthen the resistance.

The principle should be obvious to all. And yet we so tend to ignore it or to fail to see it, that it needs to be repeated and re-emphasized constantly. Another way of stating it is to say: Put the centre right and the rest will look after itself. Put the source right and you need not worry much about the strains and stresses. The trouble is generally in the source, so we have to go back to the beginning. There is a proverb which says, 'As a man thinketh in his heart, so is he' (Prov. 23:7), and it is perfectly true to life. So to put the man right, put his thinking right. Do not deal with him in a piecemeal manner, dealing with this problem and then with that, and simply patching up; go back to the centre. It is the man's thinking that is wrong, so put his thinking right. Or take the way in which the wise man who wrote the Book of Proverbs expresses it in chapter 4, verse 23: 'Keep thy heart with all diligence; for out of it are the issues of life'. The heart really does control everything; and the 'heart' here means the centre of the personality, not merely the seat of the emotions. Put that right and everything else will be right.

Our Lord stated the matter negatively when He said that it is not that which goes into a man which pollutes the man but rather that which comes out of him. It is 'out of the heart that come evil thoughts, adulteries, fornications, murders', and all such things (Mark 7:20–23). In other words, in the last analysis it is not the temptations that meet us on the streets that determine our conduct; it is the heart of the man who faces them. Two men may face the same conditions; one falls, the other stands. The difference is not in the temptation but in the heart of the man. 'Out of the heart . . .'! So we must pay attention to the heart.

Ezra expresses this in a more lyrical manner. He understood this principle when he said, 'The joy of the Lord is your strength' (Neh 8:10). How true that is! When you want strength to do your work and to face some task that is waiting for you, the tendency is to pay attention to your muscles alone. That is right within limits. But it matters not how physically fit you may be if you have something preying on your mind. If you have some worry or anxiety you will not be able to do your work. You may be a hundred per cent physically fit, but if there is something gnawing at your heart, and upsetting you, and worrying you, you will feel physically weak. On the other hand, though you may be fairly weak in your physique, when suddenly something comes which fills you with joy and gladness, you feel like a giant refreshed and find that you have unusual power. 'The joy of the Lord is your strength'. The heart really governs everything.

*   *   *

The Apostle enunciates this great principle in this interesting form, 'That he would grant you according to the riches of his glory, to be strengthened with might by his Spirit in the inner man'.

Let us consider further what is meant by the 'inner man'. We have the answer in 2 Corinthians 4, verse 16 where the Apostle says, 'But though our outward man perish, yet the inward man is renewed day by day'. Again the Apostle says in Romans 7, verse 22, 'I delight in the law of God after the inward man'. There are two men in him. There is a law in his members dragging him down, but he says 'I delight in the law of God after the inward man'. Obviously this inner man is the opposite of the outward man. Yet most people in the world never know or realize that there is a difference between the inner man and the outward man. It is one of the profoundest discoveries that we can ever make in our Christian experience. The inner man is the opposite of the body and all its faculties and functions. It is this other man that is apart from them, the innermost part of our being, the spiritual part of our being. It includes the heart, and the mind, and the soul, and the spirit of the regenerate man, the man that is 'in Christ Jesus'.

The ultimate trouble with the unregenerate, with the non-Christian, is that he lacks this inner man. He knows nothing of the inner man, he does not believe in the inner man; he lives only in the outward part. He lives a life in the flesh only, a life which is really nothing but a life of the body and what you may call the physical part of man. There is nothing spiritual about him. His whole life is bounded by what he is aware of, that is to say, his sensations within himself and in his correspondence with the world of things that can be seen and heard and felt and handled. That is his only life, it is his total life; it is confined to the body and its faculties and its relationships with similar people and things in the world in which he finds himself. It is a soulish life.

That is the tragedy of man in sin, of man as the result of the

Fall. He is no longer aware that he was created a spiritual being. He is not aware that there is something higher than all the senses in man. Man is to him at best a reasoning animal, an animal who happens to have more highly developed faculties than the brute creation; but who still essentially belongs to the same order as the animals. His brain has an extra kink beyond that of the animal, but that is the only difference between him and the animal. He is not aware that in addition to his animal nature there is this other part of man's being, the part that Paul refers to as 'the inward man'.

The final tragedy of the natural man is that he has no inner man to retreat into in times of trouble and stress and trial. Do you know what I mean by 'retiring into the inner man?' Do you know what it is, when your life as a man or a woman in this world is overwhelmed by the things that are happening and you are on the point of falling and of fainting, do you know what it is to retreat into your 'inner man'? That is one of the most blessed experiences you can ever know. Here was the Apostle Paul, old before his time because of his preaching and his travelling and the persecutions and trials that he had suffered and endured, his body failing, an old eye complaint still troubling him, obviously a very sick man. 'Our outward man', he says, 'is perishing'; but he does not sit down in a corner and say, It is the end, I have had a fairly good innings, I have now to give place to others, my time is come, I might as well turn my face to the wall and face the fact that the end is here. Not at all! When he has realized the truth of all that is happening to the outward man, he then retires to the inner man and he says, 'But the inner man is renewed day by day'. As the outward is falling away, the inner is being built up. As the world is taking away the outward life and it is inevitably passing from him, this inner man is receiving accessions of strength from heaven and from glory. He has retired into the inner man.

The man who is not a Christian knows nothing of all this. Poor fellow! He is dependent only upon circumstances, and he is entirely controlled by them. He lives in one realm only, and he knows nothing at all about the other. Therefore he has no comfort, no consolation, and so has to fall back on psychology, or drugs and various tricks that he does to himself. He rushes off into pleasure just to forget his troubles for the nonce, and so on. He really cannot face life because he lives only in one dimension, and when that goes everything has gone. He becomes depressed and disconsolate and wretched and hopeless. But when we become Christians, and receive the gift of the new birth and the new life, a new man is put into us, a new order of life begins, and we enter a new realm, a spiritual unseen realm. This is not the temporal, the physical, the vanishing, but something which is of God. We are made partakers of the divine nature, a seed of divine life is implanted in us; it grows and develops, and trials and tribulations often stimulate it to grow in a most glorious manner.

Because of this inner man that is in us we are enabled to have great victories over the devil. He attacks us in many ways, but he sometimes goes too far and makes a mistake, and unintentionally reminds us of our position in Christ. More ordinarily he simply keeps us in a general state of depression. He may use the weather, for instance, or take advantage of our particular constitution or bad circulation. He makes us feel slack, we cannot think or do anything, and then he discourages us with evil thoughts, and makes us feel hopeless. But suddenly we see in the case of someone else who is in a similar condition that it is plainly an attack of the devil; and in seeing what he does to this other person we are suddenly awakened to the fact that it is he who is really attacking us. So the inner man is revived even by problems from the outside, and we overcome the devil and are made 'more than conquerors'.

Do you know about 'the inner man?' Do you know that you have an 'inner man?' Is there this other that you are aware of and into which you can retire? Do you know that while the outward man is falling and collapsing and decomposing, the inner man is being renewed day by day, and is being built up, and has a vision of a glory which is 'incorruptible and undefiled and that fadeth not away'? Our secret as Christians, as the Apostle reminds us, is that we have an inner man, and when that inner man has been strengthened by the Holy Spirit, what happens round and about us and even to the outward man himself is comparatively unimportant. May God give us the assurance of the possession of the inner man, the spiritual man, the new man in Christ Jesus.

IO

'Strengthened with Might'

'That he would grant you, according to the riches of his glory, to be strengthened with might by his Spirit in the inner man.'

Ephesians 3:16

The Apostle now tells us that he is praying that the inner man may be strengthened with might by the Holy Spirit. I must emphasize that this prayer is offered for those who are already Christians. He is praying for the people whom he has been describing in the first and second chapters, where he said some very remarkable things about them, such as, 'In whom ye also trusted, after that ye heard the word of truth, the gospel of your salvation; in whom also, after that ye believed, ye were sealed with that Holy Spirit of promise, which is the earnest of our inheritance until the redemption of the purchased possession'. Not only so! The Apostle has already offered a great prayer for them in chapter 1, namely, 'That the God of our Lord Jesus Christ, the Father of glory, may give unto you the spirit of wisdom and revelation in the knowledge of him'. But still he is not satisfied. He goes on praying for them, and he lets them know that although he is in prison and far away from them, he is bowing his knees, he is praying in the presence of God, he is looking into God's face on their behalf, and he is praying that in the inner man they may be strengthened with might by the Spirit of God.

I emphasize the fact that he offers this prayer on behalf of Christians because the experience of forgiveness and of salvation is merely the beginning of the Christian life. It is only the first step, an indication of entry into the Kingdom of God. Unfortunately there are many Christians who stop at that point; they are concerned only about their personal security and safety;

their sole concern is to belong to the Kingdom of God. They are anxious to know that their sins are forgiven, that they will not go to hell, and that they have a prospect of going to heaven. But the moment they have had this initial experience they seem to rest upon it. They never grow, and you cannot detect any difference in them if you see them fifty years later. They are still where they were. They think they have everything, and there is no indication whatsoever of any development.

Now that is very far removed indeed from what we find here about the Christian. There are great and glorious possibilities for Christians. One of them is 'that Christ may dwell in your hearts by faith' and that they may come to know something about God's love in its 'breadth and length and depth and height'; indeed that they 'might be filled with all the fulness of God'. These words indicate something of what is possible for the Christian; and we must underline the fact that it is possible for *all* Christians. The Apostle is not writing a circular letter to apostles, he is not concerned here only with some very exceptional persons; he is writing to the ordinary church members of the Church of Ephesus. We do not know their names, we know nothing about them; they are people whom we describe (if there is such a thing) as ordinary Christians. Yet Paul is praying for them, and he prays that they may experience all these blessings, leading to the almost incredible climax, 'that ye may be filled with all the fulness of God'.

This is not only a possibility for all Christians, it is the duty of all Christians to be in this position. The great Charles Haddon Spurgeon, dealing with this matter, once said, 'There is a point in grace as much above the ordinary Christian as the ordinary Christian is above the worldling'. In other words, there is a stage in the Christian life, in the development of the Christian, 'which is as much above the ordinary Christian as the ordinary Christian is above the worldling'. That states the matter in a very striking and strong manner, but it is right and true. We all know the difference in level between the non-Christian and the Christian. The Christian is on a higher level, a higher plane than the non-Christian. But Spurgeon reminds us that there are higher reaches in the Christian life which are as much above this ordinary Christian level as the Christian is above the non-Christian. We must accept that, if we really believe that Christ can dwell in our hearts, that we can know this love of God and of Christ in all its dimensions, that we may be filled with all the fulness of God. Clearly, that is as much above the ordinary Christian level as that level is above the non-Christian.

The question we must face therefore is: Have we reached this level to which Spurgeon refers? Do we conform to the description which the Apostle gives here of what is possible to the Christian? Is Christ dwelling in our hearts by faith? Have we looked into this great 'cube' of God's eternal love? Have we been staggered as we have looked at its dimensions? Do we know what is meant by being 'filled with all the fulness of God'? Do we know the God who is able to do for us exceeding abundantly above all that we either ask or think? Have we reached that level, that height? Are we dwelling there? Or are we still down on the ordinary Christian level? There is always the danger of imagining that because we have been converted we can rest upon our oars, or simply become active, busy workers always rushing into activities.

Having dealt with this matter we must obviously go on to the next question. If we feel that we are still on this ordinary level, how can we reach the higher level? There is but one answer to that question, it is the answer given by the Apostle's prayer. We must be 'strengthened with might by (God's) Spirit in the inner man'.

* * *

Why does our inner man need to be strengthened?

The first answer is that initially the Christian is only a babe. That is the New Testament term. Paul, writing to the Corinthians says, 'I could not speak unto you as unto spiritual, but as unto carnal, even as unto babes in Christ' (1 Cor 3:1). A babe has only started to live; he has not developed fully, and he needs to be strengthened. He is weak, he is ignorant, he is innocent of many things in the world that is round and about him, and he does not have an immunity against the things that are liable to attack him. That is always the characteristic of infancy. That is why the child has to be protected by the parents; obviously he does not know, he does not understand. He takes everybody at their face value, he takes the world as it is, and sees everything superficially. He does not know of its ugliness and the foul things that are in it. It is only as we grow that we begin to understand these things. I am not saying that the babe is without sin, or that he is innocent. I do not agree with Wordsworth's idea that we come into this world 'trailing clouds of glory', and that later 'shades of the prison-house begin to close upon the growing boy'. I am saying that a child, because of his ignorance, is not aware of the dangers, and therefore needs to be protected.

The same is true of the new man in Christ Jesus. However old a man may be when he is converted, he is at first a babe in Christ. And as a babe he feels at first that everything is solved, that he will never have another difficulty. Quite frequently evangelists are responsible for such thinking; they give him that impression. In his utter innocence the babe imagines that there will never be another cloud in the whole of his life. But alas, the clouds come, difficulties arise, problems come across his path; and he is bewildered, and often he falls. He may even become a backslider. This is largely because he was a babe and was not aware of the facts. So the babe needs to be strengthened. The Apostle John in his First Epistle writes to 'little children', 'young men', and 'fathers', because there are these gradations in the Christian life, which is a process of growth and of development.

A second reason for the need of this strengthening of the 'inner man' is the existence of the devil, the adversary, the accuser of the brethren. Anyone who has not realized that he is confronted with this power is the merest tyro in the Christian life. The Apostle emphasizes the matter in the last chapter of this very Epistle, saying, 'We wrestle not against flesh and blood'. The problem is not only that we have to struggle against our own flesh and blood, that is, our bodies. Neither is it merely a struggle against other men. The real problem, says Paul, is the struggle against 'the principalities and powers, the rulers of the darkness of this world, the spiritual wickedness in high places'. The inner man needs to be strengthened because this power is not only great in might, but also in subtlety and in cunning. This same apostle tells the Corinthians that the arch-enemy is so powerful that he is able to 'transform himself into an angel of light' (2 Cor 11:14). He can quote Scripture, he can reason with you, he can put up arguments and present cases, and he can confront you with an appearance of truth which sounds right and truly Christian, but which is false; and he can lead you astray and into snares which will trap you. There is no more powerful reason for the need of strengthening with might by the Spirit in the inner man than the fact of the devil.

The devil always makes a special target of this inner man. I have often had to deal with people who were in trouble and difficulties in their spiritual life simply because they had not realized his existence and his cunning. They seemed to think that the only sins were the sins of the flesh. They were watching and on guard against these, and they had reached a point at which they were comparatively free. So they thought that that was the only line on which the devil attacks, and they were not aware that with great subtlety and as an angel of light he can make direct attacks upon the inner man, and insinuate there his evil thoughts and ideas, his innuendos and suggestions. Being unaware of this they suddenly found themselves unhappy and wretched and wondering whether they had ever been Christians at all. This was entirely due to the fact that the devil in his subtlety had ignored the outward altogether and had concentrated all his attention upon the inner man. Hence the exhortation in the Old Testament: 'Keep thy heart with all diligence; for out of it are the issues of life' (Prov 4:23).

A third reason why we need the strengthening of the inner man is the very greatness of that which is offered to us, and which is possible for us. This possibility is 'that Christ may dwell in our hearts by faith', and that we may know the love of God and may 'be filled with all the fulness of God'. The very greatness of what is offered to us demands that we be strengthened in order to receive it, lest we might be shattered by it. This is a most important point, and one which is often misunderstood; many Christians do not appreciate its significance.

An illustration of what I regard as a complete failure to understand this point occurs in some words written by the saintly Bishop Handley Moule. He writes, 'And why do we need a supreme empowering just in order to receive our Life, our Light?' He thinks that it is odd to say that we need to be strengthened to receive Jesus Christ who is our life and our light. He asks,

'Does the hungry wanderer need power in order to eat the food without which he will soon sink? Does the bewildered mariner need power to welcome on to his deck the pilot who alone can steer him to the haven of his desire? No!' The very suggestion, he suggests, seems quite ridiculous. But, in my view, this sounds quite wrong. Paul prays that we may be strengthened with might by His Spirit in the inner man in order that we may receive Christ. But, says the good bishop, Christ is our strength. In what way do I need strength in order to receive strength? After giving his two illustrations he goes on to say that Paul must be referring to a tendency within us to dread the thought of Christ's 'absolute indwelling' of our hearts, and to be afraid of it, and to wonder what it might do to us. While there is an element of truth in that statement I reject it as an exposition of this particular verse. The bishop says that we need to be strengthened by the Spirit because, left to ourselves, we are afraid to receive Christ in His fulness.

There is a very definite fallacy in Bishop Moule's argument, and a fallacy even in terms of his own illustrations. He asks the question whether a man who has been without food for a long time needs strength in order to take the food which is going to give him strength. He says, No! I venture to suggest, with great respect, that the answer may be Yes! Let me explain. Some of us have probably read about men who, during the last war, were torpedoed and who had spent many days on rafts or in boats upon the ocean; or of men who had been in concentration camps where they had been brought to the verge of starvation. Eventually these men were rescued or set at liberty. One's natural tendency would be to set them down at a table and put a great square meal before them. But to do so might very well kill them. The explanation is that the man is not strong enough to take such food. Before he is in a fit condition to take a heavy meal he must regain his strength. In order to do so you have to inject glucose into his veins, into his blood; you may have to give him various meat extracts, or a very lightly boiled egg which has but little nutriment in it. He has at first to be put on a very light diet. A man who is weak and exhausted simply cannot take strong food; it is dangerous for him to do so. I argue therefore that in terms of his own argument the bishop's case is quite wrong. It certainly misses the spiritual intent of the Apostle's prayer at this point, which, I suggest, is that what we are going to receive is so potent, so mighty, so strong, that we need to be strengthened in order that we may receive it.

Let me support my argument by referring to what Paul wrote to the Corinthians: 'I have fed you with milk, and not with meat, for hitherto ye were not able to bear it, neither yet now are ye able' (1 Cor 3:2). Correspondingly, the author of the Epistle to the Hebrews writes: 'Strong meat belongeth to them that are of full age' (5:14), that is to say, to those who have grown and developed. If you gave a baby red meat, strong meat, it will give him acute indigestion and cause him great sickness and illness. You do not give strong meat to babes; you give them milk. Strong meat is only appropriate to those whose senses have been exercised by use, who have developed, who are strong enough to take it. Indeed the Apostle Paul has said the same thing to the Corinthians in the First Epistle, chapter 2, verse 6: 'Howbeit we speak wisdom among them that are perfect'. He had not taught 'wisdom' to them because they were yet carnal, in fact, mere babes in grace. He had given them the food that was appropriate for them. Before they could receive 'wisdom' they needed to be strengthened.

All this is fully substantiated by what we find in the experiences of many saints of God. There is a well-known story of an experience that came to D. L. Moody as he was walking down Wall Street in New York City one afternoon. Suddenly the Holy Ghost came upon him; he was baptised with the Holy Ghost. He tells us that the experience was so tremendous, so glorious, that he really began to wonder whether he could stand it in a physical sense; so much so that he cried out to God to hold his hand lest he should collapse on the street. This was because of the transcendent glory of the experience. When Christ enters the heart the glory is such, the power is such, that the very physical frame seems to collapse beneath it, and we are made to tremble and shake. The same can be found in the experiences of men like Jonathan Edwards and David Brainerd. When Christ comes and dwells in the heart by faith, and when we are filled with the whole fulness of God, we need to be strong. It is a shattering, overwhelming experience. So the Apostle prays that these Ephesians may be strengthened with might by the Spirit in the inner man. The greater the power, the greater is the strength that is needed to contain it.

* * *

How then does this weakness of the inner man show itself? First of all, in a spiritual sense the mind needs to be strengthened. This is so because we are assailed by doubts. Some of the greatest saints have reported that they were assailed by doubts even at the end of their lives. They have not believed the doubts, but the doubts have presented themselves and have troubled them for a while. Then there is the problem of depression. Depression is very difficult to define. You may wake up in the morning and find your mind in a depressed condition. The mind that may have been working perfectly yesterday does not seem to be functioning happily today. We are conscious of a kind of dullness and slowness and inability to think clearly. The mind seems to need to be strengthened. Or we may be troubled by evil thoughts that come and attack the mind. They seem to be thrown at us. Paul talks later in chapter 6 about 'the fiery darts of the wicked one'. The devil hurls them into the mind. They start when you wake up in the morning before you have had time to think. So the mind needs to be strengthened. Another problem is that of wandering thoughts. We all experience this. You find that you can read light literature or a newspaper with no difficulty in respect of concentration. But when you try to read the Bible your mind seems to wander in all directions and you cannot concentrate. You are looking at words, you are reading the verses, but your mind seems to be elsewhere.

We need to be strengthened in the mind also because of the nature of Christian truth. While the gospel of the Lord Jesus Christ is in one sense gloriously simple, it is also true to say that it is the profoundest truth in the world. This Epistle to the Ephesians is not simple. You cannot understand it in a casual manner and without effort. You cannot gallop through it. There is profound truth here and subtle argumentation. There are 'immensities and infinities', to quote Thomas Carlyle. You cannot take these things 'at a run'. Born again people, Christian people, when they read this Epistle to the Ephesians may well say,

[137]

'I do not understand it'. So the mind needs to be strengthened. We are meant to apprehend truth; and we cannot do so and realize what it means, and what it is telling us, unless our minds are strengthened.

Alas, there are many Christians who do not know this, and completely fail to realize it. Not only do they not know it, they do not want to know it. Such is the Christian who says: 'I am a simple Christian, a plain man; I can give my witness and my testimony. I can do practical work. But these things are too hard for me, I cannot grapple with them. I am not concerned about doctrine and theology; I believe the simple gospel'. But no Christian has the right to speak in that manner. If you are making no real effort to understand this Epistle to the Ephesians, or all the other profound teaching in the New Testament, you are guilty of sin. This Epistle was written to ordinary Christians. We are all meant to understand these things; and we have no right to contract out of our responsibilities and say that we want a simple message, a plain gospel. For a Christian to say that he cannot be bothered, that it means too much of an effort, that his mind is tired, and that he is busy with affairs and has many problems in daily living, that he is not a natural reader or thinker, and that he is not prepared to make an effort to understand, is to deny the Scripture. The Apostle Paul prays that the minds of these Ephesians might be strengthened in order that they might realize these higher possibilities of the Christian life and experience them, and rejoice in them, and so be able to bear a powerful witness and testimony to the glory of God. Intellectual lethargy is undoubtedly the greatest sin of many Christians today. They never grow in knowledge, they end where they began. They are always talking about their first experiences, but they have never entered into these riches to which Paul refers; they have never climbed the mountain tops and breathed the pure air of God's holy truth. They are content with the ordinary level; they are ignorant of the more advanced teaching because it demands an intellectual effort.

In exactly the same way the heart needs to be strengthened because we are attacked by fears and by imaginations. We are subject to discouragement. We tend to indulge in evil forebodings. Even when all is going well with us our hearts begin to say, Ah! all is right at the moment, but you never know what is coming! And immediately we are depressed. Have we not all experienced this? How treacherous the heart can be! It can conjure up possibilities; and we go to meet them in imagination: What if this happens? what if that happens? what if this child dies? what if I lose my loved one? and so on. Thus we can make ourselves feel wretched. Nothing is actually happening, we are only imagining what we would be like if it did happen. Thus these fears and forebodings and discouragements and evil imaginations often play havoc with the Christian. There are some Christians whose whole course is 'bound in shallows and in miseries' because they have never realized the need of having their heart strengthened by the Holy Spirit.

In the same way the will needs to be strengthened. Our wills are feeble and irresolute as the result of sin and the Fall. We honestly resolve and propose to do certain things: and we really desire to do them. Then at the last moment, we are afraid, or we give up. Because of questions such as: What if I do, or what will happen if I do? the will seems to be paralysed or made irresolute, and we fail to do the thing we know we should do. How often we fail at the very last moment!

The moment you begin to look into this inner man, and to analyse him, you see that he is very weak, very feeble, and needs to be strengthened. Were it not that we can offer for ourselves the prayer that Paul was offering for the Ephesians we should every one of us fail and falter. How often have we done so in mind or in heart or in will! If we were left to ourselves there would be no hope for us, and there would be no one to recommend the gospel. But thank God there is this way whereby we can be strengthened. The Apostle states it perfectly for us here. So that however weak you may feel yourself at this moment, however much you may have failed, this is the way. The Apostle's prayer is that 'the Father of our Lord Jesus Christ, of whom the whole family in heaven and earth is named', would strengthen them in the inner man. May we not then say, All is well: I can be reinforced by God? I cannot make myself strong: I cannot put this iron into the walls of my soul; do what I will, I fail. But here is strength from God. He is all-sufficient!

The next term reads, 'may *grant* you'. What a blessed word is this word 'grant'! God makes me a grant; He gives me this. It is a free gift; you do not have to earn it, you do not have to purchase it. You simply ask for it and receive it. 'That He may grant you . . .' The feeblest saint can lift up his face even when he cannot stand on his feet. He just looks and says – 'Lord have mercy upon me', 'God strengthen me'. And He will 'grant' you the strength you need.

But, and yet more wonderful, Paul says, 'that He would grant you *according to the riches of His glory*'. The glory of God is the sum, the summation, of all the attributes of God, His might, His majesty, His holiness, His purity, His righteousness, His justice, God in the totality of His being. The glory of God! And it is according to the riches, the fulness of that glory, that God is able to strengthen us with might.

God does this *by His Spirit*. It is the special function of the Holy Spirit to do this. It was the same Holy Spirit who convicted us of sin, and who gave us the gift of faith that enabled us to believe. We could never have believed without Him, because 'the natural man receiveth not the things of the Spirit of God: for they are foolishness unto him: neither can he know them, because they are spiritually discerned' (1 Cor 2:14). But God has given unto us of His Spirit, and it is by the Spirit we believe, and by Him that we are made spiritual men. The same Spirit can also strengthen us in the inner man. The Apostle in chapter 4 of the Epistle to the Philippians says: 'In nothing be anxious'. When things go wrong we tend to become anxious, and especially in our hearts and minds. There is only one way of getting rid of anxiety. It is, 'In all things by prayer and supplication with thanksgiving let your requests be made known unto God' (vv. 6–7). If you do so, says Paul, 'the peace of God that passeth all understanding shall keep your hearts and minds through Christ Jesus'. The circumstances are not changed, they remain exactly what they were. Whence then comes the peace into heart and mind? It is from the Holy Spirit who has strengthened your heart and your mind so that you can resist everything that is against you; and you are safe.

Such then is the prayer the Apostle offers. We are living in days when we are constantly hearing about the reinforcing of materials. They reinforce concrete and there is ferro-concrete. Concrete is very strong, but, if you put some iron into it, it will be stronger still. And as new massive buildings are erected something is needed to support and to hold the weight that they will have to bear. That is the principle behind what the Apostle says here. If you and I are to contain the Lord Jesus Christ within us, and be 'filled with all the fulness of God', we must be reinforced in the inner man by the Holy Spirit. And if we realize that these are possibilities for us, and desire them, and ask God 'according to the riches of his glory' to reinforce us by His Spirit, He has promised to do so, and Christ will dwell in our hearts by faith.

Are we as much above the level of the ordinary Christian as the ordinary Christian is above the level of the man who is not a Christian at all? To be such is a wondrous, glorious possibility for every one of us at this moment, in Jesus Christ, by the grace of God.

11

Christ in the Heart

'That Christ may dwell in your hearts by faith.'
Ephesians 3:17

We are here face to face with the highest heights of the Christian life and of what is possible for us as Christian people. It is therefore not an easy portion of Scripture. But there is nothing which is more glorious. People who climb mountains tell us that the higher you get the more difficult it is to climb; and yet it becomes more and more exhilarating and wonderful. The same applies to the Scriptures. And here we are certainly on the very mountain top of Christian experience.

But let us remind ourselves afresh that this is something which is meant for all Christians. The Apostle writes to all the members of the church at Ephesus and he obviously meant them to understand it; indeed he assumes that they will be able to understand it. I say that for the reason that there are so many Christians today who do not attempt to understand anything which is at all difficult. But that is deliberately to ignore the plain teaching that we are meant 'to grow in grace and in the knowledge of our Lord and Saviour Jesus Christ' (2 Peter 3:18). As the Apostle says in the next chapter, we are not to be children, not to remain children, and 'to be carried about with every wind of doctrine'. And these words, let us never forget, were written to people who were probably slaves, and who had received no education at all, and had none of the advantages which we enjoy. So, to use the language of the Apostle Peter, we must 'gird up the loins of our mind'. We have to make an effort to discipline ourselves as we enter this rarefied atmosphere. We need to move with precision and with all our might and power. But above all we must pay attention to the Apostle's petitions.

The first petition, as we have seen, is that we might be 'strengthened with might by God's Spirit in the inner man'. When we are strengthened 'according to the riches of God's glory' by the Holy Spirit we shall be able to climb and to attain to this great height. We can test ourselves at this point by asking ourselves one simple question – Am I looking forward to the ascent? Am I thrilled with expectancy as I consider these glowing phrases which the Apostle puts before us?

We now come to the petition, 'that Christ may dwell in your hearts by faith'. There has been much discussion as to how this, and the former two petitions, are to be taken. Are they saying the same thing in a different way, or does the Apostle put the petition about being strengthened first because it is an essential preliminary to this further petition? I have no doubt myself but that the latter possibly is the true one, although there is a sense in which it is equally true to say that these things always more or less merge together and cannot be divided in any ultimate sense. The Apostle puts them in this order – the strengthening first and then 'that Christ may dwell in your hearts by faith'.

As we approach this staggering statement – and we must walk, as I have suggested, warily, carefully, and circumspectly – it is essential that we remind ourselves yet once more that this prayer is offered for believers. I emphasize the matter because a phrase has gained currency in connection with evangelism which has often caused confusion with respect to this particular verse. In giving their experience and talking about their conversion people often say, 'It is now many years since I first received Christ into my heart'. Evangelists often put their message in that way, and ask people whether they will receive Christ into their hearts. But this is not a scriptural expression and it can be most misleading, particularly when we meet with a phrase such as the one which we are now studying. It is for this reason that I remind you that the Apostle is offering this prayer for people who are already believers. They were people who once were afar off but who have now been made nigh, brought nigh, by the blood of Christ. They are already believers, they are already united to Christ their Head, they are already members of His body which is the Church. They are 'in Him' and He is in them.

In other words, the Apostle is not praying that these people may become Christians, He is praying that Christ may dwell in their hearts by faith, although He is already present. Paul is not praying for their conversion, or their salvation, or their justi-fication. All that is taken for granted; it has already taken place. To remove any possible doubt or confusion concerning this, let us remind ourselves again of the Apostle's statement in the Second Epistle to the Corinthians, chapter 13 verse 5, 'Know ye not your own selves, how that Jesus Christ is in you, except ye be reprobates?' He says that to be believers, to be Christians at all, means that Jesus Christ is in us. You cannot be a Christian at all without Jesus Christ in some sense being in you. Likewise there is the statement in the Epistle to the Romans, chapter 8 verse 9, 'If any man have not the Spirit of Christ he is none of his'. That was true of these Ephesians; they are already Christians. Indeed it is because they are Christians he goes on to offer this prayer for them, that Christ may dwell in their hearts by faith.

What then is the difference between this, and the normal state, the invariable state, of all who are truly Christian? The answer is to be found primarily in the word 'dwell'. It is a compound word which basically means 'to live in as a house'. But when a prefix, meaning 'down' is added, the word comes to mean 'to settle down and be at home'. The Apostle deliberately chooses to use this word to emphasize the idea of taking up your abode, of settling down, of making your permanent home, as distinct from merely paying a visit or as being in a place in some general sense.

Light is thrown on this conception by what we read in the third chapter of the Book of Revelation in the message to the church of the Laodiceans, and especially in verse 20. The risen Lord says, 'Behold, I stand at the door, and knock: if any man hear my voice, and open the door, I will come in to him, and will sup with him and he with me'. I sometimes think that there is no single statement of Scripture which is more frequently mis-understood, and more misused and abused, than that particular statement. It is taken almost invariably in an evangelistic sense. Christ is depicted as standing outside the shut door of the sinner's heart, and as entreating the sinner to give him admittance and to receive Him into his heart. But that is a completely false interpretation of Revelation 3:20. The letter to the Laodiceans is, of course, a letter to a church; it is 'what the Spirit saith to the churches'. Its words are not addressed to unbelievers, but to those who are already Christians and within the Christian Church. The whole of chapters 2 and 3 of the Book of Revelation, we must always remember, are addressed to Christian people, to believing people, to people who have already believed on the Lord Jesus Christ and who are joined to Him, who are in Him and He in them. And yet the message of the knocking at a closed door is addressed to them, in particular to the Church of the Laodiceans. They were Christian people; but they were in a bad condition, 'neither hot nor cold'; they thought that they were rich and had everything, whereas in reality they were poor, and naked, and blind, and empty. It is to such Christians that our Lord says, 'Behold, I stand at the door and knock: if any man hear my voice, and open the door, I will come in to him, and will sup with him, and he with me'.

These words then are addressed to Christians who have spiritual life, but who are in a very poor and immature condition. There is a sense in which they know the Lord Jesus Christ, but in a deeper sense they do not know Him. They are in a relationship to Him, but they are not controlled by Him. They are certainly in a position in which they are having dealings with Him; but He is not in the centre of their lives. He is not really in their hearts, He is not 'dwelling' there, He has not 'settled down' there, He has not 'taken up His abode' there.

The letter to the church of the Laodiceans supplies us with the key to the understanding of the petition which is being offered by the Apostle Paul on behalf of the Ephesians. He thanks God for all that has happened to them; but he longs for them to realize what is yet possible for them, and especially this further intimacy with the Lord Jesus Christ Himself. This cannot happen until they have been strengthened by the Spirit. We have to be prepared for this, as a home has to be prepared for some great and distinguished guest. As Paul has already told them, the church is made to be, and meant to be, 'a habitation of God through the Spirit', and individually they are to be habitations for Christ through the Spirit. This had not yet happened to the Ephesian Christians, but Paul desires it to happen.

The Apostle longs for this to happen to them because he himself knew exactly what it means to experience it. This is a man who is able to say in writing to the Galatians: 'I live, yet not I, but Christ liveth in me: and the life that I now live in the flesh I live by the faith of the Son of God, who loved me and gave himself for me' (2:20). He was in a position in which he could say without any doubt or hesitation, 'I live; yet not I, but Christ liveth in me'. So he prays that the Ephesians may have, and may enjoy, a like experience.

We can look at Paul's petition also in terms of a passage in chapter 14 of John's Gospel. Our Lord, on the very eve of His crucifixion, turns to these men who were so wretched and unhappy and crestfallen because He has just told them that He is going to leave them, and says, 'Let not your heart be troubled, neither let it be afraid' (v. 27). He says that in one sense He is going to leave them, but that in another sense He is going to come to them. Then He introduces the truth concerning the Holy Spirit and His coming, and tells them that as the result of the coming of the Spirit He Himself will come back to them, in order to 'dwell' and 'take up His abode' in them. He further told them, 'At that day ye shall know that I am in my Father, and ye in me, and I in you' (14:20). They did not know it at that time; so He says, 'at that day' ye shall know it.

When the Lord was speaking to them they were already Christians, and so He proceeds to say to them, 'Now ye are clean through the word which I have spoken unto you' (15:3). He also differentiates between them and the world in chapter 17 when He says: 'I pray for them: I pray not for the world . . .' (v. 9). They are Christians; but they do not yet realize that they are in Him and that He is in them. Or take verse 21 in that same chapter 14 of John's Gospel. The Lord is talking about the Christian man to whom the Spirit shall have come and who is keeping His commandments. He says, 'I will love him and will manifest myself to him'. He emphasizes that He will not manifest Himself in that way to the world but only to the man who is already a Christian. This cannot refer to the general revelation which we have in the Scriptures because the disciples had already believed it. This is something further, as is made yet more clear when the Lord goes on in verse 23 to say, speaking of Himself and the Father, 'We will come unto him and make our abode with him'. The word 'abiding' is a characteristic of John's Gospel. It conveys this same idea of 'settling down', 'taking up permanent residence', not just occasionally being present, but being there permanently.

*   *   *

Quite clearly, this is something entirely beyond simple believing; it is entirely beyond justification; it is entirely beyond salvation in the sense of the experience of the forgiveness of sins. We might well refer again at this point to Spurgeon's words about there being a point in the experience of the Christian which is as much above the experience of the ordinary Christian as the experience of the ordinary Christian is above the experience of the man who is not a Christian at all.

What then is the Apostle really praying for here? We must look at one other word before answering the question. The word 'dwell' really conveys all, but the Apostle underlines it, as it were, by saying, 'That Christ may dwell in your *hearts* by faith'. In Scripture the word 'heart' generally means the very centre of the personality. It does not mean the seat of the affections only; it also includes the mind, the understanding and the will. It is therefore the very citadel of the soul. So what the Apostle desires for the Ephesians is that Christ may dwell in their minds; not only in their intellects but also in the very centre of their personalities. He was already in their minds, for they had already believed; but there is a great difference between being a believer in Christ and having Christ dwelling in your heart. Such is the distinction which Paul is clearly drawing here in the case of Ephesian Christians.

It is vitally important that we should apply this to ourselves. To believe in the Lord Jesus Christ is not the end of Christianity, it is but the beginning. To believe the truth about His person and about His work is absolutely essential, and if we do not subscribe to these truths we are just not Christians at all. No man can be a Christian unless he believes on the Lord Jesus Christ in that sense. But that is not what the Apostle has in his mind here. You can have Christ in your mind and in your intellect and still not be able to say 'I live, yet not I . . .' Paul's desire is that Christ may also dwell in their affections, that Christ may dwell in their will, that Christ may be the dominating factor in the whole of their life, controlling it and directing it. Christ is to be the very heart of their hearts, He is to be at the very centre of their lives.

It is here then we come into that rarefied atmosphere to which I have referred. If Christ is in your heart, then Christ has manifested Himself to you. And when Christ manifests Himself to us it is not merely a figure of speech, it is real, it is actual. It is so definite that there is no doubt at all about it. As you read the experiences of some of the saints of the past you find that they are very careful to draw this distinction. They say that there was a time when they came to believe in Him and when they had an assurance that their sins were forgiven. They knew that they were related to Him, that they were in Him, and that they had found peace and rest for their souls. They also say that for a while, sometimes for years, they thought that that was the whole of Christianity. But then they began to discover that there was something altogether vaster and greater, which they had never known at all. They came across the Lord's promise expressed in the words, 'I will manifest myself to him' (John 14:21), and they began to wonder whether Christ had manifested Himself to them. They were not sure as to its meaning. They believed on Him and were aware of His general influence upon them; but this statement about His manifesting Himself to His own seemed to be such a specific statement. Then they began to realize that they had never known it.

When Christ manifests Himself to us He becomes real to us as a person. We get to know Him in a personal sense. In other words, such an experience is the fulfilment of all that the Lord promises in chapter 14 of the Gospel according to St John. Let me ask a very personal question: Do you really know the Lord Jesus Christ personally? Do you know Him as a person? As a person is He real to you? Has He manifested Himself to you in that sense? It is clear that that had happened to the Apostle Paul. Not only had he seen Him actually on the road to Damascus, not only had he had a vision later in the temple; in addition to that, and above that, he says in writing to the Galatians, 'It pleased God to reveal his Son in me'. He says 'in' me and not 'to' me. It is an inward manifestation of the Son of God in which He is made as real to us as any other person, even more so. I cannot do anything better at this point than to quote a little verse which Hudson Taylor used to pray for himself every day of his life:

Lord Jesus, make Thyself to me
A living, bright Reality;
More present to faith's vision keen
Than any outward object seen;
More dear, more intimately nigh
Than e'en the sweetest earthly tie.

That is what the Apostle was praying on behalf of the Ephesians. He seems to say: I know that you are Christians, I know that there is a sense in which Christ is in you, for you cannot be Christians without being united with Him as your Head, I know that you are in Him and that He is in you; but beyond that, do you know Him? Is Christ Himself at the centre of your life; is He actually real to you and known to you? Or is He someone who is vaguely in the distance, someone whom you approach only in terms of belief? Has he really manifested Himself to you?

There is a further element in Paul's statement which makes this exposition still more sure. The tense of the verb which he uses in connection with 'dwelling' is the aorist, which carries the meaning of something that happens once and for ever. Here, therefore, he is praying for a specific and not merely for a general blessing upon the Ephesians, a blessing which leads a man to say: 'Up to this moment I have not really known Christ personally, but now He has manifested Himself to me and I know Him. He has become real and living to me. It is a supreme moment of my life.' It is not a question of visions or of trances, but of a spiritual knowing of Christ. The Holy Spirit brings Him to us, and through the Spirit He manifests Himself so that He becomes real and living and true to us. In his great hymn J. Caspar Lavater prays for this very thing when he asks, 'O Jesus Christ, grow Thou in me, And all things else recede'. In a later verse he prays that Jesus Christ may become more real, more dear, the passion of his soul. That only becomes true when one has this personal knowledge of the Lord Jesus Christ.

This, in turn, leads to a conscious sense of fellowship with the Lord and an enjoyment of Him. Do we know what it is to enjoy a conscious fellowship with the Lord Jesus Christ? Let us be clear about this; you can be a Christian without it. Thank God for that! You can be a Christian without enjoying conscious fellowship with Him. You can be in the position in which you are relying upon Him, relying upon His perfect work on your behalf, and you can even be praying to Him, and yet not have a conscious fellowship, a conscious realization of His nearness and a conscious enjoyment of Him. That is what the Apostle desires for these Ephesians, 'That Christ may dwell in your hearts by faith'. And when this is true, of course, He obviously controls everything in our lives.

We can sum it up by repeating words used by the Apostle Paul elsewhere. It is when Christ is thus known to us, and in our hearts, that we can say honestly and truthfully, 'I live, yet not I' (Gal 2:20), and 'I can do all things through Christ which strengtheneth me' (Phil 4:13). The Apostle is not boasting when he writes such things. There is always the danger when we read his epistles that we may regard him as some literary man who indulges in hyperbole. But that is not the case. When the Apostle uses these phrases he is being strictly accurate, he is stating his experience, it was all true of him. He knew the Lord Jesus Christ so well that he can say, 'I can do all things through Christ which strengtheneth me' and 'I know both how to be abased and how to abound' (Phil 4:12), how to be rich and how to be poor. It does not matter what happens, says Paul, as long as He is with me He strengthens me, and I can do everything. I am not alone. This is indeed most elevated doctrine.

But we must go one step further. This presence of Christ in the heart is something real. It does not only mean that He is present through the Spirit, or present in the sense that He is influencing us in a general manner, and giving us graces and enabling us to feel certain of His influence. It goes beyond that. It means that He Himself in some mystical sense that we cannot begin to understand really does dwell in us. This is what the Apostle has in mind when he reprimands the Corinthian Christians for being guilty of certain bodily sins of the flesh, and says: 'Know ye not that your body is the temple of the Holy Ghost which is in you?' (1 Cor 6:19). This not only means that the Holy Spirit is influencing us generally. When Paul says 'body' he means 'body', flesh and bones and sinews; he means our physical frame.

This refers, not to His influence, but to the fact that He Himself is in you. That is why to sin with your body is so serious; and it is in this way that the Christian should face sin. He is not only to look at the particular sin and confess that he has done wrong and should not have done so; the Apostle teaches that we have to realize that the Holy Spirit is resident in our bodies and that we are not to use the temple of the Holy Ghost in an unworthy manner.

Similarly, as the Holy Ghost dwells in our bodies, the Lord Jesus Christ enters in the same manner. He is standing and knocking at the door of the heart of the Christian who does not know Him, and He says in effect, I would like you to know me. If you but open that door I will come in and I will manifest myself to you, and I will sit down, and I will sup with you and you with me. You will then know Me with an intimacy that you have never yet experienced. I will come into you, and I will dwell within you. It is as real as that!

We must note that all this becomes possible by faith – 'That Christ may dwell in your hearts by faith'. 'By faith' means that it is faith that reveals this possibility to us. Had you realized that this was a possibility for you? It is possible for us to read the Scriptures with much intellectual understanding, but without faith it is possible to read over these great words without understanding their real meaning. You may have read this third chapter of the Epistle to the Ephesians and many times have said 'Marvellous! Wonderful! How eloquent the Apostle is!' But had you realized that it means that Christ will come right into your heart and that you will know Him in a living and in a real sense? It is faith which reveals this possibility to us.

It is likewise faith also that enables us to believe that the indwelling of Christ in the heart is a reality and not just a phrase. The man who lacks faith will never believe it. I can imagine a man hearing or reading this and saying, 'What is all this about? I really have no idea what the Apostle has been talking about. It seems to be up in the clouds somewhere. I am a practical man, and I have to fight against temptation and sin, and I am living in a world in which I am surrounded by problems – what is all this?' A man who speaks in that way is saying that he has not got faith; in consequence he will never know this truth, for it is known 'by faith'. Faith reveals it as a reality.

I can take the matter still further. Faith reveals it as a reality for me personally. Faith enables you to say to yourself as you read it, or as you hear it, That is God's word, which says that it is possible to any Christian, to all Christians; well therefore, it is possible for me. It is possible for me to know the Lord Jesus Christ in this intimate manner. Faith lays hold upon the promise, personally and individually. It is faith alone that enables a man to believe God's word, to accept it fully, and to rely upon it. And after coming to believe it he then begins to pray for it. The Apostle himself believing it, and experiencing it, was praying without ceasing for the Ephesian Christians. He 'bows his knees' before the Father and he prays that they may be strengthened in order that this may happen to them. And if you and I believe it we shall begin to pray this for ourselves from this moment. We shall say, I do not know Christ in that intimate manner, and I want so to know Him. I believe it is possible, and I am going to ask for it. So you go to God in faith, with confidence, with boldness, and with assurance, and you say 'I know that this does not depend upon me, but I pray that YOU would strengthen me with might by the Spirit in my inner man, that I may get this knowledge, that Christ may manifest Himself to me. I want to know Him, I want Him to live in my life and to control the whole of my being'.

So you begin to pray, and you go on praying thus in faith until some marvellous moment comes and suddenly you find yourself knowing Christ. He will have manifested Himself to you, He will have taken up His abode in you, and settled down in your heart. And you will say with amazement: How could I have spent so many years being satisfied with the mere beginnings of Christianity, the mere portals of the temple, when it was so wondrously and gloriously possible for me to enter into 'the Holiest of all'?

> O Jesus Christ, grow Thou in me,
>   And all things else recede;
> My heart be daily nearer Thee
>   From sin be daily freed.

Each day let Thy supporting might
  My weakness still embrace;
My darkness vanish in Thy light,
  Thy life my death efface.

More of Thy glory let me see,
  Thou Holy, Wise, and True!
I would Thy living image be,
  In joy and sorrow too.

Make this poor self grow less and less,
  Be Thou my life and aim;
Oh, make me daily, through Thy grace,
  More meet to bear Thy Name!

(Johann Caspar Lavater)

12

Truth Begins to Shine

'That Christ may dwell in your hearts by faith; that
ye, being rooted and grounded in love,'

Ephesians 3:17

As we continue our study of this great statement we need to pray
for ourselves, as the Apostle prayed for these Ephesians, 'that we
might be strengthened with all might by his Spirit in the inner
man'. It would be foolish to pretend or assume that this great
prayer is easy to understand or easy to expound. Of necessity it
is not so and cannot be so, and is not meant to be so. The
Christian faith, the Christian message, can be compared to a great
ocean. A little child can paddle at the edge of the ocean, but out
in the centre in the depths, the mightiest Atlantic liner is but like
a cork or a bottle. It is illimitable. We enter into the Christian life
as children, and begin to paddle; but we must go on and out into
the depths. That is what we are doing as we consider this great
prayer, and as we return to the seventeenth verse. One cannot
just make a few comments on these mighty phrases and then pass
on feeling that you have dealt with them, and pass on to something
else. These phrases are all so full of matter that it is our business
and our duty to pause and to ponder them deeply, and to spend
much time with them.

Furthermore, great and profound truth is always liable to
misunderstanding. When we handle truth of such profound
character we are incapable of the precision which we can exercise
when we are dealing with the beginnings of the Christian faith.
There should be little difficulty in stating the doctrine of Justi-
fication by Faith clearly. One who cannot do so should never
stand in a pulpit. In such a matter there should be exactitude and
precision; but when we come to statements such as we find in

this paragraph the position is very different. The very nature and character of the truth makes that quite impossible. An element of incomprehension and difficulty is to be expected. Indeed there is a sense in which that is as it should be. You cannot dissect an aroma, you cannot analyse love. And that is what we are dealing with here – the love of Christ and of God. We can but go forward, and go as far as we are able in our attempt to bring out the truth in its richness and to elucidate it as far as possible. But we do so with 'fear and trembling'.

I confess freely that I do not recall in my preaching ministry having dealt with anything in the Scripture where I have been so conscious of my own inadequacy and inability as with this particular passage. I do not claim to be able to make authoritative statements, but, by the grace of God, I regard it as a great privilege just to hold these things before you, and to beseech you in a spirit of humility to look at them, and to ponder them, and to pray about them; not in an argumentative spirit, not with a desire to have everything exactly labelled, but with a desire to enter into that position where, coming face to face with God and the Lord Jesus Christ through the Holy Spirit, we may well find ourselves to be speechless because of the transcendent glory with which we are confronted.

There are two great principles which we must continue to bear in mind. The first is that this petition is offered for those who are already believers. It calls us to compare and contrast ourselves, not with unbelievers or with immature Christians, but with well-established saints, and with the possibilities indicated here. We must realize that we have not received all, and that our business is not merely to maintain the position at which we have arrived. We must press on unto perfection. We must forget the things that are behind and press onwards towards the mark, the high calling, the prize that is in Christ Jesus.

But, again, and for our encouragement, let me emphasize the second principle which is that the Apostle offers this prayer for all Christians. It is not merely a prayer for certain exceptional people. The New Testament, unlike the Roman Catholic Church and other forms of Catholicism, does not divide believers into 'religious' and 'laity'. There are no specialists in the Christian life. These things are possible for all Christians, even for Christians whom the Apostle has to remind later that they must not continue to steal, to commit adultery, to talk foolishly and make unworthy jests and jokes, and must not continue to be liars. They had been brought out of all these sins, and although this had only recently happened to them, the Apostle holds before them this tremendous possibility. It is because it was possible for them that he thus prays for them.

We must remind ourselves, therefore, that it is wrong and sinful for us to say that such deliverance is not for all of us, but is only for some exceptional Christians. We must never be satisfied until we are in this position, and know it experimentally, and are able to rejoice in it. I imagine that there will be nothing more humbling at the Day of Judgment, when we shall see our Lord face to face, than to realize what had been possible for us in this life, to realize that we never concerned ourselves about it, but simply skimmed over these great phrases without ever delving into them and trying to discover what they meant and in what ways they applied to us.

*   *   *

As we attempt therefore to explain yet further our definition of what Christ dwelling in our hearts by faith means, let me start by asking a particular question. What is the relationship of this indwelling to the 'sealing of the Spirit'? Some teach that it is identical with the sealing of the Spirit. But obviously that cannot be the case. The Apostle has already reminded the Ephesians in the thirteenth verse of the first chapter that they have already been 'sealed with the Spirit': 'In whom ye also trusted, after that ye heard the word of truth, the gospel of your salvation: in whom also after that ye believed (or, having believed), ye were sealed with that holy Spirit of promise'. He is offering this petition, that Christ may dwell in their hearts by faith, for those who had already been sealed with (or by) the Spirit.

One can well understand how confusion arises. As we have seen, in this realm it is very difficult to catalogue spiritual things, and to put labels upon them as distinct and separate things, for the reason that every experience, and especially every high experience, in the Christian life is of necessity related to both the Holy Spirit and to the Lord Jesus Christ. As we have emphasized previously, you cannot be a Christian at all unless Christ is in you, and the question arises, If Christ is in all Christians what does the Apostle mean by praying that Christ may dwell in their hearts? We have answered the question; but still to many there seems to be a confusion at this point. That is because of the inadequacy of language, and of the glorious nature of the truth. And the same applies with respect to the Holy Spirit: 'If any man have not the Spirit of Christ, he is none of his' (Rom 8:9). Yet that is different from being 'baptised by the Spirit', or being 'sealed by the Spirit', as we have seen. In a sense we are still using the same terms, we are still talking about the Lord Jesus Christ, and about the Holy Spirit; and yet there is a difference. These Ephesian believers had been sealed already, and yet Paul prays that what he mentions here may be their portion.

What then is the difference between this and the sealing of the Spirit? I suggest the following answer: the sealing with the Holy Spirit is primarily a matter of assurance of salvation. It is that which gives us a direct and immediate assurance that we are the children of God, and heirs of God, and that the inheritance is ultimately to be ours. But what the Apostle has in mind here in this third chapter is not primarily a matter of assurance. It is mainly a question of communion with the Lord. The sealing assures me that I am related to Him. This further experience brings me into fellowship and communion with Him in a deeper and in a greater sense. Obviously both are great experiences, and, as we have seen, when a Christian is sealed with the Spirit he has a consciousness of Christ and is aware also of the power of the Spirit. But here we are dealing with something which goes beyond that and is still deeper.

I suggest, secondly, that this experience is more permanent than that of sealing. The sealing is something which can be often repeated. This is seen clearly in the lives of many saints, as well as in the Book of the Acts of the Apostles. But here we have something which is more permanent. The very word 'dwell' emphasizes that this is a 'settling down', a 'taking up of an abode in'. This must not be pressed too far, but it is a real distinction. There is a greater element of permanence here.

Furthermore I would add that in this experience there is less of what may be called the ecstatic element than in the sealing. In connection with the sealing, what one is conscious of is the immediacy, the luminosity; everything suddenly becomes clear; whereas here it is something on a deeper level, more permanent, and therefore more ecstatic. Let me illustrate what I mean.

I remember hearing of what an old preacher said during the revival in Wales in 1904–1905. In that revival large numbers of people were suddenly experiencing the baptism of the Spirit, and it was often accompanied by great ecstasy and joy and much praising. Some of the younger people were rather surprised at this old minister who had been in a similar revival in 1859 when he was a young man. They expressed surprise that he did not seem to be having the ecstatic joy which they were experiencing. They could not understand this, and felt that there was something wrong with him, so they went to talk to him about it. He received them kindly and patiently and answered them in the following fashion. He pointed out to them that there is a difference between a first falling in love with the one who becomes your wife, and living with your wife in a state of love throughout the years. That first ecstatic excitement does not continue; but it does not mean that there is less love. There is less excitement in connection with it, there is less fuss and less of the demonstrative element, but it does not mean that there is any diminution in the love. Indeed it may well mean the exact opposite, that it is a deeper love. I suggest that the same principle here applies to explain the difference between the sealing with the Spirit and Christ dwelling in the heart. This is a greater love, a greater knowledge, a greater intimacy, a deeper fellowship; but it is not accompanied by the thrilling element which the first experience of the power of the Spirit invariably brings.

Let me also attempt to describe yet further the nature and the character of this experience of the knowledge of Christ dwelling in the heart by faith. It is the difference between knowing Christ 'for' you and knowing Christ 'in' you. In the beginning of the Christian life, of necessity we have to concentrate on Christ 'for' us. The beginning of the Christian life is generally mainly objective. In other words, what makes us Christian is that we realize certain things about the Lord Jesus Christ and His work for us and His relationship to us. That is objective truth. We look at Christ outside us; we look at Him coming into the world, and being born as a babe in Bethlehem. We watch Him growing up; we listen to His teaching; we observe His miracles; we see Him dying on the Cross and then rising from the grave. We look at all these things and we ask: What is happening there, why did He come, what is He doing on the Cross? And we say: He is there bearing my sins, He is dying for my sake: Christ 'for' me. I am looking at Him and what He has done for me and on my behalf objectively. But Christ dwelling in the heart is not objective, but subjective; it follows on, and results from the objective.

But someone may argue that there is a definite subjective element in the initial believing. Of course there is! I repeat that we must not draw these distinctions too sharply. If there is no subjective element you are not a Christian at all; you may only be giving an intellectual assent to truth. But, speaking broadly, the first believing is mainly objective, whereas this is mainly subjective. The objective element remains but it is included in something greater. We have advanced to a position in which we are mainly concerned about Christ, not as the One who died for us, but as the 'Christ who is our life', Christ as the One who lives within us and who takes up His abode within our lives and within our consciousness.

Words spoken by the Lord Himself help us to understand this. They are found in the Gospel according to John. 'Verily, verily, I say unto you, Except ye eat the flesh of the Son of man, and drink the blood, ye have no life in you. Whoso eateth my flesh, and drinketh my blood, hath eternal life; and I will raise him up at the last day. For my flesh is meat indeed, and my blood is drink indeed. He that eateth my flesh, and drinketh my blood, dwelleth in me, and I in him. As the living Father hath sent me, and I live by the Father: so he that eateth me, even he shall live by me' (6:53–57). That is a profound saying and one which is difficult to understand. We read later, 'Many therefore of his disciples, when they had heard this, said, This is a hard saying; who can hear it?' Indeed the passage goes on to say that many of them 'went back and walked no more with him' (vv. 60, 66). They could not follow this teaching, this had gone beyond their understanding, so many who had been following him left Him.

We are in a realm here which tests and strains our understanding, but we must persevere and try to grasp it. It is Christ dwelling within the believer – not as an influence, not as a memory, not merely through His teaching, not merely through the Holy Spirit. It is Christ Himself dwelling within him in a mystical relationship. I have to use the term 'mystical' because nothing else and nothing less does justice to the teaching of the New Testament concerning this matter. Take the passage in chapter 6 of John's Gospel; or the statements in the later chapters of that same Gospel to which we referred previously, where Christ says that He would manifest Himself to His disciples, where He says that He would come and take up His abode in them, that He and the Father would take up their abode. The Lord's high priestly prayer in the seventeenth chapter of John's Gospel makes similar statements. Or take the Apostle's expression in the Epistle to the Colossians: 'Christ in you, the hope of glory' (1:27). It is not Christ 'among you', but Christ 'in you', the hope of glory. Or again, 'I live, yet not I, but Christ liveth in me' (Gal 2:20). All these statements and terms describe a mystical relationship.

I express it thus because someone may say, 'What do you mean by saying that Christ dwells in me? I cannot understand it'. My answer is, 'Of course you cannot; I do not understand it; nobody can understand it. It is a mystical statement and experience that is beyond understanding. Our bodies, we are told, are 'the temples of the Holy Ghost which dwelleth in us'. The Holy Ghost is in heaven; but He is also in me. The Lord Jesus Christ is in heaven but He is also in me. This can only be described as a mystical relationship. We must not minimize it, we must not scale it down. We must give it its full weight. If we fail to do so we are not doing justice to the Scriptures.

Furthermore, we not only fail to do justice to the Scriptures, we also fail to do justice to the great experiences the saints of God have known throughout the centuries. Take the hymn which includes the stanza

> *Jesus, Thou Joy of loving hearts,*
> *Thou Fount of life, Thou Light of men,*
> *From the best bliss that earth imparts*
> *We turn unfilled to Thee again.*

Is He that to you? Is that true of you? It is possible to believe in His work for you. You can be a Christian and can be saved by

Him without being able to say quite honestly that He is 'the joy of your heart'. The people who wrote these hymns meant what they said; they were being honest and were relating their experiences, It is not mere poetry.

But consider another hymn of Bernard of Clairvaux which says:

> *Jesus, the very thought of Thee*
> *With sweetness fills the breast*

Is this true of you? Can you honestly use these words? My argument is that these men are expressing their experiences in these hymns. It is not a theory. These men had read the Scriptures, had realized their application to themselves, and had sought this experience and obtained it. But let us continue with this great hymn:

> *O Hope of every contrite heart,*
> *O Joy of all the meek,*
> *To those who fall how kind Thou art,*
> *How good to those who seek!*

> *But what to those who find? Ah, this*
> *Nor tongue nor pen can show;*
> *The love of Jesus, what it is*
> *None but His loved ones know.*

'His loved ones know'. They cannot tell us much about it in an exact or logical manner, but they *know* it, they are rejoicing in it.

Take yet another expression of this in another hymn attributed to Bernard –

> *O Jesus, King most wonderful,*
> *Thou Conqueror renowned,*
> *Thou Sweetness most ineffable,*
> *In whom all joys are found.*

There is much to be said for the view that we should not sing certain hymns in public. We can often be dishonest as we sing hymns. We have often sung this hymn, but is it true of us? We claim to be singing experience – 'Thou Sweetness most ineffable, In whom all joys are found'. Is that true of you? These men had found it so; that is why they sing thus. They are not dishonest;

they are relating their experience. The writer of that hymn goes on to say:

> *When once Thou visitest the heart*
> *Then truth begins to shine;*
> *Then earthly vanities depart;*
> *Then kindles love divine.*

Here we are in a different, an altogether higher realm than that of intellectual apprehension. Here you know the luminosity, the shining of the truth. That is what happens when Christ dwells and settles in the heart.

Next let us turn from a writer of the twelfth century to an eighteenth-century writer. Charles Wesley says,

> *Thou, O Christ, art all I want,*
> *More than all in Thee I find.*

Is that true of us? Can we say it? That is the language of a man in whom Christ has taken up His abode, in whom Christ dwells.

I could have mentioned from the seventeenth century the saintly Samuel Rutherford. In his letters, and the accounts of his life, you will find that this element of 'Christ-mysticism' was prominent in his experience. He was a Calvinist who knew Christ, who loved Him, and loved to speak about Him and to dwell upon Him and His love. The same note is to be found in all centuries and in men who belonged to different theological schools. We find Count Zinzendorf, a Moravian of the eighteenth century, saying, 'I have one passion; it is Christ, and Christ alone'. Now this is not the language which what we may call the *average*, the *ordinary* Christian can employ. You can be a Christian and yet not be able to say such things. This explains why the Apostle was offering this prayer for the Ephesians. They had believed, they had been sealed by the Spirit, but they could not use this kind of language; they did not know Christ in this way; He had not 'settled down' in their hearts. As I have said repeatedly, it means that Christ dominates the life, it means that He rules over the whole of our activities. He is the Lord of our life in a real, practical sense. We are dominated by Him; it is some kind of 'Christ-intoxication'.

I have quoted these various statements because it seems to me that that is the best way to convey this precious truth. But ordinary men and women throughout the centuries, as well as exceptional people, have been able to sing such hymns honestly. Search your hymn books, and especially the sections on the Lord Jesus Christ, and particularly those that express joy and peace, and love to God and to the Lord Jesus Christ. Look also at the sections on consecration and holiness, and you will find that hymn-writers throughout the running centuries have dealt with this theme of Christ in the heart. It was this that made them write, it was this that inspired their magnificent poetry and produced their elevated, exalted thought.

* * *

But to end on a practical note: How does all this become possible for us? What have we to do in order to arrive at the position where we can really appropriate these statements honestly and make them the language of our own hearts and the expression of our own experience? My answer is that we should repeat verses 16 and 17 of this chapter and we should be careful to take them in the right order. The Apostle prays first that God would grant them, 'according to the riches of his glory to be strengthened with might by his Spirit in the inner man'. Without that there is no hope. The Holy Spirit must first work upon our minds and our hearts and our wills. Do you feel that your mind needs to be strengthened as you confront such a truth as this? How much easier it is to understand history, or literature, or geography, or geometry, or law, or medicine! Have you not felt as we have been looking into these great depths of truth that your mind needs to be strengthened, and must be strengthened, otherwise it all seems impossible? We all tend to feel, by nature, as did the people who were listening to the Lord when He talked about eating His flesh and drinking His blood; they said, This is a hard saying; who can follow this sort of preaching? And they left Him. We need to have our minds strengthened in order that we may not stagger when we are confronted by something so marvellous and transcendent. Our minds cannot comprehend such truths; we cannot take hold of them easily and say, 'I have grasped them'. They always seem to be eluding us and going

[163]

beyond us. So the mind needs to be prepared, and thanks be to God, the Holy Spirit can perform this work.

Recall how the Apostle in writing to the Corinthians, says that 'The princes of this world' did not know Him and the truth concerning Him; 'but God hath revealed them unto us by his Spirit; for the Spirit searcheth all things, yea, the deep things of God' (1 Cor 2:8, 10). Do not despair if you find these truths hard and difficult to follow; remember the power of the Holy Spirit, and pray that He may strengthen your mind.

Our hearts also need to be strengthened, because while we love ourselves, Christ will not come into our hearts. We have to be rid of the love of self. That is the most difficult of all tasks in our experience. The ultimate battle in the Christian life is to get rid of self and of self-love. And of ourselves we cannot do this. You drive it out as it were by one door of your house, but it soon returns by another, or through some window, or by the chimney. To get rid of self-love seems impossible. But Christ will not come into our hearts until there is room for Him. We cannot create love, we cannot 'work it up'. Nothing is so foolish as to try to do so. Love is a gift of God through the Spirit; so we must pray that He will strengthen our hearts to receive this pure love, which is so strange to us as natural men and women.

Likewise the will needs to be strengthened. Is not this your experience? You hear or read a passage such as the one before us, and you say, 'I would cut off my right hand if I could but have that; I am going to seek it: I must have it'. But by tomorrow night you may well have forgotten all about it. You will be interested in something else, in some worldly interest. You were fully resolved at the time, you were determined to seek this; but you enter into an argument, and talk about trivialities, and soon you have forgotten all about it. You return to it again, or your attention is called to it, and you say. 'Ah, I thought that by now I would have known it'. But you have not applied yourself; your will is too weak. The wills of all of us are weak; we are always proposing, we are always resolving. But we do not keep our resolutions, we fail to give effect to them. The will needs to be strengthened.

We must therefore pray that the Holy Spirit will strengthen us in all these respects. The Apostle prayed constantly for the

Ephesians. It is the business of any one who is called to minister
to men and women to pray for them. God forgive us for our
failure! But you must also pray for yourself. If you realize that
this experience is a possibility for you, then pray for it until you
know it. Pray that you may be strengthened with this power,
this might of the Spirit in your inner man. As the experience
comes to you, certain results will follow. You will begin to see
your sin and your sinfulness in a way that you have never seen
them before. You thought that you knew about sin; you will
discover that you knew but little about it. You will discover a
vileness in yourself that you could not even have imagined;
you discover that evil is in your very nature.

You will then begin to act, and 'to mortify the flesh'. You will
try to cleanse your heart and your hands, you will attempt to
'purify your flesh and your spirit', as Paul exhorts the Corinthians
to do. Your reason for doing all this can be understood in the
following way. Whenever you invite a guest to come to stay in
your home you always begin to tidy up the house; you want the
place to look nice, and at its best. It would be insulting to your
guest not to do so. In so doing you are paying your guest a very
subtle and delicate compliment. If you have some great personage
coming to stay with you, you redouble your efforts; there is
nothing you will not do. What we have been considering is the
possibility of the Lord Jesus Christ, the Son of God, coming to
dwell with us; not only to pay a visit, but to make His home
within us. This needs preparation, but preparation beyond our
natural capacity and capability. So we need to be strengthened by
the Holy Spirit, and as we thus become strengthened, we act, we
get rid of the rubbish, we cleanse and purify ourselves, mortify
the flesh, deliberately keep out things that we know are not
compatible with Him, or which would grieve Him and offend
Him. We do all we can, and we go on doing so. We plead with
Him to come; we yearn for Him.

This is where faith comes in – 'That Christ may dwell in your
hearts through faith'. We believe in the possibility, knowing
that it can become an actuality. This does not mean what is often
called, 'taking it by faith', which simply means that you persuade
yourself that He has come, or go on repeating to yourself that
He has come. No, when Christ dwells in your heart you will not

need to persuade yourself; you will know it as a fact! You will be able to say, 'Thou Sweetness most ineffable, in whom all joys are found'. The pernicious doctrine of 'taking it by faith', I believe, has hindered many people at this point. They say: 'I have opened the door, I have let Him in, I believe by faith He is there'. They do not feel any different; they cannot in honesty use the language we have quoted because He is not 'dwelling' in them. When He dwells within, we know it. Nothing else really matters; it becomes the supreme thing. It is the most glorious thing of all.

Let us then realize this glorious, wondrous possibility. If He has ever visited us, let us plead with Him and say, 'Come and stay; leave me not. Come and make Thine abode and Thy dwelling with me!' 'Strengthened with might by His Spirit in the inner man'. Let us pray in faith, and keep on and on and on, until we can honestly appropriate the language, and say with the Apostle, 'I live, yet not I, but Christ liveth in me'.

13
The Heart Prepared

'That Christ may dwell in your hearts by faith; that
ye, being rooted and grounded in love,'

Ephesians 3:17

We continue our study of the seventeenth verse – the petition
which the Apostle offers for the Ephesian Christians – 'That
Christ may dwell in your hearts by faith'. So far we have considered it in general. We must now look at it in a more practical
sense. Beyond any question we are dealing here with the greatest
truth which can ever confront a human being. Here we are shown
the possibilities for a Christian in this present life in this world of
time. This is true. I repeat that I am not saying that you cannot
be a Christian without being in this position; I am saying, rather,
we are very poor Christians unless we know something about it.
This is what we are meant to be, this is what is possible for us.
Surely, therefore, nothing is more important for us than to know
how we may arrive at this position, and at the same time know
whether Christ does actually dwell in us, and how we may be
enabled to enjoy this supreme privilege and greatest source of
joy.

Let us remind ourselves of what this means in order to whet
our appetites and stimulate our desire for it. For we are not
dealing with a purely theological matter here, but with something
which has been a realized fact in the life of large numbers of God's
people in all ages and places, and often in spite of theological
differences. As we have already seen, there is a common testimony
to this great experience of Christ in the heart. Let us take as a
further example and illustration the testimony found in one of
Charles Wesley's hymns:

Thou hidden Source of calm repose:
Thou all-sufficient Love divine;
My help and refuge from my foes,
Secure I am if Thou art mine:
And lo! from sin and grief and shame
I hide me, Jesus, in Thy Name.

Thy mighty Name salvation is,
And keeps my happy soul above;
Comfort it brings, and power, and peace,
And joy and everlasting love:
To me, with Thy dear Name are given
Pardon, and holiness, and heaven.

Jesus, my All in all Thou art,
My rest in toil, mine ease in pain;
The medicine of my broken heart;
In war my peace, in loss my gain;
My smile beneath the tyrant's frown;
In shame, my glory and my crown:

In want, my plentiful supply;
In weakness, mine almighty power;
In bonds, my perfect liberty;
My light in Satan's darkest hour;
My help and stay whene'er I call;
My life in death, my heaven, my All!

I ask a simple and obvious question, Is this your experience? Can you adopt these words and use them? Does Christ mean this to you? That is what happens when Christ dwells in the heart. Observe the intimacy of the relationship, the fulness of the satisfaction. Christ is his 'All in all', his everything, whatever the circumstances and conditions. This is experimental, experiential; it is not held in the mind only; it is not theory. Charles Wesley found his complete satisfaction in Christ. He had proved the truth of the words spoken by our Lord Himself when He said that if any man came to Him he would 'never hunger', if any man believed in Him he would 'never thirst'. He had within him 'a well of water springing up into everlasting life'.

I repeat that this is essential Christianity. It is what we are offered, and it is to the extent that we know this experience and can testify to it that we are likely to attract others to the Christian faith. Non-Christian people are entitled to watch and observe us, and they do so. We make the tremendous claim that God has done something unique, that He has sent His only Son into the world. We believe in the Incarnation, in the power of the Spirit; but what does it lead to in practice? And if as Christian people we appear to be miserable, if in times of stress and strain we seem to have no consolation or reserves to fall back on, the world is fully entitled to ask, What is the value of your Christianity? what is there in it after all? In an age such as this, when the hearts of so many people are failing for fear, they tend to look at us. So not only for our own sakes, but for the sake of God and His glorious salvation, for the sake of the Son of God who came and endured so much that we might come to this position, it behoves us to be able to testify to this great fact of Christ dwelling in our hearts from day to day.

*   *   *

We come, then, to this most practical and essential question: How does this become possible? How may the longings of those who say that they would give the whole world if they could but use those words of Charles Wesley honestly be satisfied? The Apostle answers, 'By faith' – 'That Christ may dwell in your hearts by faith', or, 'through faith'. This phrase is one which is frequently misunderstood. We can consider it in terms of the picture to which we referred earlier, in Revelation 3:20, where Christ says, 'Behold, I stand at the door and knock: if any man hear my voice and open the door, I will come in to him, and will sup with him, and he with me'. What is meant by 'opening the door'? and how is it related to faith?

To answer these questions in a practical manner we must start with verse 16; 'That he (the Father) would grant you, according to the riches of his glory, to be strengthened with might by his Spirit in the inner man'. This is something of which no man in and of himself is capable. But at this point the danger arises of thinking that, because of this emphasis and stress upon the primary work of the Holy Spirit, we simply have to remain passive and wait for something to happen to us. But that is an entire fallacy. The truth about this matter is expressed once and for ever in the Epistle to the Philippians, chapter 2, verses 12 and 13, where the Apostle says, 'Work out your own salvation with fear and trembling. For it is God which worketh in you both to will and to do of his good pleasure'. There we have the right balance and the right sequence. The Apostle starts with an exhortation, almost a command: 'Work out your own salvation with fear and trembling'. There is the imperative; there is something you and I have to do. But immediately he adds, 'For it is God which worketh in you'. Though the order there is the reverse of what we have here in Ephesians 3:16 it is saying the same thing. Were it not for the fact that God 'works in us both to will and to do', we could never do anything at all. Our wills, as we have seen, need to be stimulated and to be strengthened; we need the power. And it is because God 'works in us both to will and to do' that we can 'work out our own salvation with fear and trembling'. Verse 16 does not therefore teach any kind of passivity in which we simply wait and do nothing.

Next, the Apostle goes on to say that this is something which happens 'by faith'. What does that mean exactly? Once more we come across a type of teaching which has caused many to stumble and has kept them from the living experience we are considering. 'By faith' does not mean (I use the current phrase) 'take it by faith', to which we have already referred briefly. This teaches, concerning this or any other experience in the Christian life, that it is 'quite simple', you 'just take it by faith'; you just 'open the door to Christ', and He is in your heart immediately. Though you may feel nothing at all, you must convince yourself that because the Word says that if you open the door He will enter in, therefore, if you have opened the door, He must have entered! That you feel nothing is quite immaterial; they say you must go on 'reckoning' and assuming that He has entered because He says He will do so.

Such teaching is completely wrong. No teaching is so calculated to rob us of the most exalted experiences in the Christian life; and for this reason, that it is nothing but a form of self-persuasion, the putting into practice of the psychological principle of auto-suggestion. What makes it particularly wrong in this connection is that we are not dealing here with an influence, but with a Person: 'that *Christ* may dwell in your hearts by faith'. When Charles Wesley wrote the hymn we have quoted, he was not persuading himself, but writing his experience of what Christ actually was to him. He does not say that he had no feelings whatsoever, that he was left to himself, and had to persuade himself that these things are so, and 'take them by faith'; what he says is that Christ is the medicine of his broken heart, his perfect liberty when in bonds. It was a matter of experience. He was not persuading himself of something, he was experiencing this something. And that, as we have seen, has always been the experience of God's people. It is not something which you have to assume or to take for granted, and then continue on your journey in blind faith. Thank God it is not such; it is a reality, a living reality. The Apostle Paul is not speaking in hyperbole when he says, 'To me to live is Christ'; it was true of him. And when he says, 'I can do all things through Christ which strengtheneth me', he was stating a fact in his experience.

We must therefore reject the teaching which talks about 'taking it by faith'. In any case, there is nothing which is so misleading as to say that it is 'quite simple'. Advocates of this false teaching often use a particular illustration. They ask us to think of a room with drawn blinds, which as a consequence is in a state of darkness, although there is brilliant sunshine outside. They say, 'All you have to do is to let up the blinds, and the sunshine will come streaming in. It is as simple as that!' Such teaching leaves many people in perplexity because they say that they have been trying to practise this advice for years. They have believed that it is 'quite simple', but somehow it does not seem to happen and they still have not had this experience. But faith is not 'simple' in that sense; it is not auto-suggestion, or some kind of 'believism'. Faith is much more active. If you read the biographies of God's people who have known what it is to have Christ in their hearts by faith, you will find that not one of them says that it is 'quite simple'; on the contrary you will find that many of them, indeed most of them, have known a long process of seeking and of searching, of becoming almost desperate and of almost giving up in despair. But they have continued in the quest, they have sought and they have struggled, and at last they have become aware that Christ is in truth and in fact dwelling within them.

*   *   *

Let us turn to the positive answer to the question of what is meant by this expression 'by faith'? We cannot do better than take the description we are given in chapter 11 of the Epistle to the Hebrews, a chapter written in order to give us an account and a description of what the life of faith really is. It is not a passive state, we shall find, but primarily and essentially an activity; and the author of that Epistle sums it up for us in one verse: 'These all died in faith, not having received the promises, but having seen them afar off, and were persuaded of them, and embraced them, and confessed that they were strangers and pilgrims on the earth' (Heb 11:13). In the light of this definition of faith we can now discover the true meaning of the words: 'That Christ may dwell in your hearts by faith'.

The first principle involved is that I must 'see' this – 'having seen the promises afar off'. In other words I must recognize the teaching, and not read it superficially. I must be arrested by it. The men depicted in that eleventh chapter of Hebrews were living their lives in this world, even as you and I are doing, and a message came to them of something very different, something spiritual, something from God. And these men of faith 'saw' it. Most of their contemporaries did not see it, in fact they ridiculed it. Take a man like Noah, for instance. He heard the message that God was about to destroy the world by a flood. He 'saw' that message; and he did something about it. His fellow-men and women did not, they ridiculed him for building his ark. They laughed at him with scorn and derision; the thing seemed to them to be monstrous.

What differentiates the Christian from all others, in the first instance, is that he 'sees' something. So the vital question for us as we consider the possibility of Christ dwelling in the heart is: Do we see this possibility? Or are we inclined to think that it is some kind of mysticism or enthusiasm or fanaticism? 'I believe in being a Christian', says a certain type of believer, 'and I believe in holding to the Christian truth in general in my mind, and leading a good life; but you are now leading us, surely, into a dangerous realm, where strange things may happen to us'. Indeed I am! I am directing you into the realm of the great heroes of the faith. I am leading you into the realm in which the Apostle Paul, and the other apostles, and the first Christians lived. Unless we see this as a concrete reality, obviously we shall never know it or experience it.

But not only did these people see these things, they were 'persuaded' of them. This must be emphasized, because many, when they read this passage and begin to get some understanding of it and to 'see' it, go no further, for they reason as follows. They recognize the type of experience described, and grant that it can be demonstrated out of the Scriptures and the hymn books, and that it has certainly been true of many Christians. But they wonder whether this is only true of rather exceptional people. And does it not depend finally upon one's make up? Some people are naturally mystical, while others are more stolid, more ordinary, more of the mundane type. Is not this experience solely for a certain type of person? There are many who think and argue in that fashion. The devil has come and has suggested to them that this is a perfectly genuine experience, of course, but it was never meant for everybody.

But difficulties may take yet another form. One may say: Of course, this is a very wonderful experience and I enjoy hearing and reading about it; but it is obviously not meant for me; I am a business man and am concerned with the affairs of this life. Or, I am a professional man and am extremely busy. I can see quite clearly that if I had nothing else to do but to spend my days in study, concentrating upon the Christian life, or if I became a monk or a hermit or an anchorite, and could really give myself to the pursuit of this matter, I have no doubt that it would be possible for me. But I am immersed in business affairs and many pressing problems; surely this experience is quite impossible for me?

The simple answer to this plea is that the Apostle Paul regarded it as a possibility for every one of the members of the Christian Church in Ephesus. These early Christians, at least the majority of them, were slaves, not their own masters at all, and were forced to work and to labour and to sweat. They often lacked education and knowledge and culture, and were immersed in the most sordid details of life. Yet the Apostle maintains that this is possible for them.

So it is essential that we should be persuaded about this truth. If you evade it by pleading that your position or your circumstances are such that it is not possible for you, of course you will never know it. But to do so is utterly unscriptural. You are denying the Apostle's teaching, and not only so, you are denying Christian experience in the Church throughout the centuries. I have already warned against that utterly false dichotomy of which the Roman Catholic Church and other forms of Catholicism are guilty when they divide Christians into 'saints' and ordinary Christians. According to the New Testament every individual Christian is a saint. All the members of the Church at Corinth were 'called to be saints', and are regarded as saints by the Apostle. So we must be persuaded by the teaching that this experience is possible for every one of us. As we all enjoy the same salvation by the blood of Christ, and are given the same gift of life, and are meant to experience and to live the same life, to die in the same knowledge of the resurrection, and to go to the same heaven, so we are all meant to enter into this experience. And it is a sheer fact of history that the most ordinary kind of individual has had this blessed experience and has been able to testify to it. It is not confined to outstanding people; it has been the experience of the most ordinary as well as the extraordinary people, because finally it does not depend upon anything in us but upon the Lord Himself. What we have to do is to believe in it, to see it, and to be persuaded of it. If we are not persuaded of it as a possibility for us, obviously we shall not seek it.

The next term in Hebrews 11:13 states that believers *embraced* the promises. Each term takes us a step further. The moment these people were persuaded of the promises they desired to lay hold of them; they began earnestly to desire their fulfilment. Now this is what our Lord said in the Sermon on the Mount, in one of the Beatitudes, as recorded in Matthew's Gospel; 'Blessed are they which do hunger and thirst after righteousness; for they shall be filled' (5:6). Embracing the promises means hungering and thirsting after them. Being persuaded that they were intended for themselves, they now begin to hunger and thirst for them and then to lay hold of them.

The logic of this argument is familiar to us in ordinary life. Are we too busy to be persuaded of, and to embrace, things that we desire in life in this world? Have we no time to cultivate our interests and our tastes? Does a business man or a professional man who tells us that he is too busy to seek Christ in this way also tell us that he is too busy to seek a wife? In that respect he is able to find time indeed, he 'makes' time. We must act likewise with this possibility in the Christian life. We must 'embrace' it. An excellent statement of this is found in a hymn by Gerhard Tersteegen, a saintly eighteenth-century Prussian (though with Dutch associations), who had himself experienced these things. He had not only 'seen' this, he was persuaded of it, and he embraced it.

> *Thou hidden Love of God, whose height,*
> *Whose depth unfathomed, no man knows,*
> *I see from far Thy beauteous light,*
> *Inly I sigh for Thy repose;*
> *My heart is pained, nor can it be*
> *At rest, till it finds rest in Thee.*

He had not only seen it as an intellectual possibility, it had become a spiritual reality to him. He continues:

> *'Tis mercy all, that Thou hast brought*
> *My mind to seek her peace in Thee;*
> *Yet, while I seek but find Thee not,*
> *No peace my wandering soul shall see;*
> *O when shall all my wanderings end,*
> *And all my steps to Thee-ward tend?*

Have we seen the possibility? Do we desire it? Have we sought it, and have we felt that while we cannot find it there is no peace? Have we seen it so clearly that we can say that we shall never be happy again until we have it? Tersteegen did not find it 'very simple', he did not say that it was just a matter of lifting up the window-blind! There is no glibness about this; the people who have experienced this have never been glib. I repeat what I have often felt and said, that there are many people today who have taken so much by faith that they have nothing. Tersteegen had to struggle; he sought, he felt it seemed to be eluding him, and then he cries out in the agony of his soul – 'O when shall all my wanderings end?' Have you sought Him in that way? Have you tried to embrace the promise in that particular manner?

The next term in Hebrews 11:13, is a vitally important one. They 'confessed that they were *strangers* and *pilgrims* on the earth'. This is the point at which they began to act. If we fail to act on what we have embraced, all is in vain. There are certain things which we have to do if this is to become a fact in our experience. In the case of the mighty men of faith referred to in Hebrews chapter 11, we find that their whole life and outlook was determined by this and was controlled by it. The story of each one of those men emphasizes this as their chief characteristic. When Abraham embraced this promise he left his country and went out, 'not knowing whither he went'. He confessed, he acted, his whole life became a testimony to the reality of God. When Noah saw it he separated himself from others and began to build the ark. Once we see this, and are persuaded of it, and embrace it, this becomes the controlling motive of our life and the centre of our being. To desire Christ in the heart makes us ready to give up everything until we have Him.

*   *   *

To this end, the first practical step we have to take is to keep this matter constantly in our minds. You may have been attracted by the possibility many times; the hymns you have read and sung may have caused you to desire it. But how difficult it is to keep this feeling and desire in the mind! The only way to do so is to read your Bible, and especially passages such as this and similar ones, and then to meditate upon it, to think about it frequently and deliberately cause your mind to turn to it. Another invaluable practice is to read the experiences of the saints, as we have it in our hymn books and in the biographies of saintly men of God. Observe how they sought it, and what they did about it. And as you do so you will be keeping it before your mind. We have to do this deliberately, and to be ruthless with ourselves.

Above all we have to remind ourselves constantly that a personal relationship with the Lord Jesus Christ is involved.

That is quite central. We are not dealing with some 'It', or some experience as such; we are talking about Him, Christ in the heart, and the experience which flows out of an intimacy with Him. We therefore have to ask ourselves deliberately whether Jesus Christ is real to us. We believe on Him, we have accepted the Christian faith; but do we know Him in this sense? can we speak of Him as Charles Wesley has done? You have to keep on questioning yourself and holding the Lord's Person before you. That is the first and the most important matter.

The next thing we have to realize is that certain things are quite incompatible with this experience. If Christ is in our hearts then certain other things must not be, and cannot be, in our hearts. A very clear statement on this aspect of the experience is found in 2 Corinthians, chapter 6, where we read: '. . . what fellowship hath righteousness with unrighteousness? and what communion hath light with darkness? and what concord hath Christ with Belial? or what part hath he that believeth with an infidel? And what agreement hath the temple of God with idols? for ye are the temple of the living God; as God hath said, I will dwell in them, and walk in them; and I will be their God, and they shall be my people' (vv. 14–16). There is no need to argue about this. Certain things are incompatibles. There is no concord between Christ and Belial. If Christ is in my heart there are certain things that have to go out of my heart. He will not dwell with them. He is the Son of God; He is holy and sinless.

If then we truly seek this experience and *embrace* it, we have to take action in this respect. 'Love not the world, neither the things that are in the world', says the Apostle John in his First Epistle (2:15). You cannot have the love of the Father and the love of the world at the same time. Therefore, if you want Christ in your heart, get rid of the world and its mind and its outlook and its actions and its behaviour. But having got rid of them, you will find that another enemy still remains, and he is the most subtle of all, namely, self. If you get rid of all other objectionable things in your own strength, you will end by praising yourself, and will become proud of yourself and your holiness. Christ and sinful self cannot dwell in the heart at one and the same time. If He is to occupy I must abdicate. Here again we are aware of a danger to which many of the saints have testified. Let us take an example out of the experience of a French Protestant saint, Theodore Monod:

> *O the bitter shame and sorrow,*
> *That a time could ever be,*
> *When I let the Saviour's pity*
> *Plead in vain, and proudly answered:*
> *'All of self, and none of Thee!'*
>
> *Yet He found me: I beheld Him*
> *Bleeding on the accursèd tree,*
> *Heard Him pray: 'Forgive them, Father!'*
> *And my wistful heart said faintly:*
> *'Some of self, and some of Thee!'*

Even after he had become a Christian and had ceased to say, 'All of self, and none of Thee', there was a stage in which he said, 'Some of self, and some of Thee!'

But he continues –

> *Day by day, His tender mercy,*
> *Healing, helping, full and free,*
> *Sweet and strong, and ah! so patient,*
> *Brought me lower, while I whispered:*
> *'Less of self, and more of Thee!'*

Then he reaches the pinnacle:

> *Higher than the highest heaven,*
> *Deeper than the deepest sea,*
> *Lord, Thy love at last hath conquered;*
> *Grant me now my supplication:*
> *'None of self, and all of Thee!'*

Do we know something about these stages? Do we know the subtlety of the devil? It has to be either Christ or self. While you and I are in control of our lives Christ is not in control; so not only do evil things have to go out, self must go out as well.

But we must not only recognize that all this is true, we must proceed to act on it. 'Wherefore come out from among them and be ye separate, saith the Lord, and touch not the unclean thing'.

It is not 'quite simple', is it? It is not simply a case of letting up the blinds. No! you have to be very active. 'Touch not the unclean thing'. It is then that the promise comes, 'And I will receive you, and will be a Father unto you, and ye shall be my sons and daughters, saith the Lord Almighty'. It is not surprising that in 2 Corinthians 7:1 the Apostle argues, 'Having therefore these promises, dearly beloved, let us cleanse ourselves from all filthiness of the flesh and spirit, perfecting holiness in the fear of God'. The Spirit is already strengthening us with might by His power in the inner man, and it is because He does so that we have got to do these things. If you truly desire Christ in your heart then you have to put this exhortation into practice. There is no other way. 'If any man will come after me, let him deny himself, and take up his cross and follow me' (Matt 16:24). 'They that are Christ's', says Paul, 'have crucified the flesh with the affections and lusts' (Gal 5:24).

Then the next step is the step of prayer. We must realize our utter dependence upon the Lord. If you think that mutilating the body or mortifying the flesh, or doing various other things which some of the mystics have done erroneously, are going to lead to this desired end, automatically, you are greatly mistaken. We must heed the exhortation, 'Work out your own salvation with fear and trembling'; but we must also realize our utter dependence upon Him. I come back again to Tersteegen. Having realized what he needs and having failed to find it, he continues:

> *Is there a thing beneath the sun*
> *That strives with Thee my heart to share?*
> *Ah, tear it thence, and reign alone,*
> *The Lord of every motion there!*
> *Then shall my heart from earth be free,*
> *When it hath found repose in Thee.*
>
> *O Love, Thy sovereign aid impart*
> *To save me from low-thoughted care;*
> *Chase this self-will through all my heart,*
> *Through all its latent mazes there:*
> *Make me Thy duteous child, that I*
> *Ceaseless may 'Abba, Father' cry!*

Each moment draw from earth away
  My heart that lowly waits Thy call;
Speak to my inmost soul, and say,
  'I am thy Love, thy God, thy All!'
To feel Thy power, to hear Thy voice,
To taste Thy love, be all my choice.

Do you pray in this way to the Lord? This is the prayer of a man who is truly embracing these things and confessing them. He spends his time in talking to Christ, in asking Him to come. He tries to cleanse and to purify himself but he realizes that he needs the strength that Christ alone can give. So he pleads for it, he yearns for it, he asks Him for it. Prayer is essential.

Finally there must be perseverance. We must continue and persist. There will be many discouragements. You may well feel much worse than you did before. You may find things in your own heart such as you had never imagined were there. You may feel that you are going further from God. But go on, continue, persevere. It is His process, He is leading you on. And we have His definite promise and assurance, 'Him that cometh unto me I will in no wise cast out' (John 6:37). This is His desire for us. But, knowing us as He does, He knows that those other things have to take place first. Thus it generally happens that the first step in the coming of this experience of 'Christ in the heart' is that we are given a vision of the blackness of our hearts, the horror of self, and of the self-seeking life which daunts us and makes us feel utterly desperate. But that is precisely what He wants us to feel. It is only when we are utterly desperate, and feel quite hopeless, that we look to Him and realize our need of the strengthening of the Spirit in the inner man, and pray for it as we have never prayed before. And God answers our prayer, and the Holy Spirit so strengthens us, and works in us, and so moves in us, that we are able 'to will and to do', and to prepare the place for the Lord Jesus Christ in our hearts. Then He will fulfil His own promise: I will manifest Myself to you; I will come and take up My abode in you; I and the Father will dwell in you.

14
'Rooted in Love'

'That Christ may dwell in your hearts by faith; that
ye, being rooted and grounded in love,'

Ephesians 3:17

We now come to consider the last phrase in this seventeenth
verse, namely, 'that ye, being rooted and grounded in love'. It
might also be translated, 'that ye, having been rooted and
grounded in love'. This is necessary, the Apostle tells us, to enable
us to have some comprehension of the love of Christ. It is still
a part of the great prayer the Apostle is offering for the Ephesian
Christians. As we go forward it is important that we should
remember that the Apostle's concern for these people is that they
may know the Lord Jesus Christ Himself. They are not, primarily,
to seek the blessings that He can give, nor even to seek holiness,
but to seek the Lord Himself. All holiness, sanctification, every
kind of blessing and every condition in the Christian life, is to be
the result of our knowledge of Him as a Person and our communion with Himself.

Such is the essential meaning of 'Christ dwelling in the heart
by faith'. My primary ambition should be, not to be a good man,
not even to be a holy man. There are 'holy men' in other religions,
in Buddhism, and Judaism, for example. The specific truth about
the Christian is that our holiness is the result of our knowledge
of Him, and of our relationship to Him. In a sense, therefore,
we must not even speak about 'the deepening of the spiritual
life'; we should speak of the deepening of our knowledge of Him
and our love of Him. When that happens our spiritual life of
necessity will be deepened. So what the Apostle is saying here is
that if Christ dwells in our hearts the result will be that we shall
be 'rooted and grounded in love'. Take note of the order in

which these matters are mentioned. To vary it is extremely dangerous.

The first result of Christ dwelling in our hearts by faith is that we become 'rooted' and 'grounded' in love. Paul does not say that we must be rooted and grounded in *God's* love. That will come later. Here the emphasis is that we ourselves should be rooted and grounded in love. In other words, love should be the predominating and prevailing element in our lives and conduct and experience. Obviously we have no love in us apart from His love. 'We love Him because He first loved us'; and there is of necessity an element of love in the Christian life from the very beginning. One simply cannot believe that the Son of God came on earth and gave Himself to the death of the Cross for us, and for our sins, without there being an element of grateful love toward Him immediately. The Apostle has already dealt with this aspect of truth in the first and second chapters. Here, in the third chapter, he is concerned about a deeper love, a more permanent love, and he is very specifically speaking about our love to Him, rather than about His love to us. So the subject here is our love to God, our love to the Lord Jesus Christ, our love towards our brethren in the faith, our love of Christian work and activity, indeed our love for everything that pertains to the 'truth as it is in Jesus'.

In order to emphasize that the chief characteristic of the Christian life is to be love, the Apostle uses two pictures, 'rooted' and 'grounded'. The first picture immediately makes one think of a tree; the second makes us think of a building. The Apostle deliberately uses the two comparisons, and I suggest that he does so because of certain similarities in the two pictures and also because of certain dissimilarities. Clearly the leading and the central idea in both pictures is that of permanence. But there is also a subtle distinction between the two. What is common to the two pictures is what a great tree has in common with a great building, namely, the idea of depth and of firmness, of permanence and durability. 'Rooted' means 'deeply rooted'. We must not think of a sapling that would be blown down if a slight gale should happen to rise, but rather of a majestic oak tree whose roots go down into the depths of the earth, spreading in many directions and taking a firm hold of earth and rocks. We must think of a great tree of considerable age and girth, that looks as if it is going to stand for ever. In the other picture we are looking at a great and high building, erected upon a firm and strong foundation. As you stand and look at it you are impressed by this idea of solidity. Two elements – depth and strength – are common to both, and therefore permanence and durability.

At the same time there are clearly certain differences to be noted, otherwise the Apostle would never have used the two pictures. If he merely wanted to emphasize solidity and permanence then a building alone would have been sufficient; but the Apostle pictures a tree as well. When you look at a tree you are not only aware of strength and durability, but also of life and vitality, of energy and growth. And not only so, but there is something about a tree which impresses us in a way that a building cannot do. It conveys the idea of life and vitality and energy. It conveys blessings as the result of its active nature. Such elements are lacking in a building. A building suggests a strength which can withstand the stresses and the strains and all other influences that bear upon it; but there is no life there, no vitality, no possibility of growth. It is fixed, set, durable, permanent. We must therefore examine the two pictures more closely in order that we may grasp the Apostle's teaching.

This is not the only place in which the Apostle puts these two ideas together. Indeed he frequently seems to think in terms of these two pictures whenever he is thinking about the Church. So let us turn to 1 Corinthians 3:9, where we find the Apostle reminding the members of the Church at Corinth, 'You are God's husbandry, you are God's building'. They are God's 'husbandry', God's 'farm'; but also God's building as well. The Apostle also says that he thinks of himself both as a farmer and as a master-builder. The one idea without the other did not seem to be adequate for his purpose in conveying to them certain great truths about the Church and the Christian life. In precisely the same manner he uses the two ideas in order to tell us about the centrality of love in the life of a Christian. One picture alone is not enough.

The first picture is that of being 'rooted' in love. Think again of a great oak tree and its roots. Observe their girth, their strength and how they spread and divide and sub-divide in every direction. Do not think of the little delicate threads you see in other plants or in some sapling; but rather of roots that are virtually trees in and of themselves, and which span and embrace a great mass of earth. If that tree is to be blown over it has to raise that tremendous mass of earth with it. But it cannot be shaken because it has gone down so deeply. And such, according to the Apostle, is to be the condition of the Christian. It is his description of love in the life of the mature Christian. Let us remind ourselves once more that the Apostle is praying for people who were already Christians, who had already believed, who had already been sealed by the Spirit. But they must advance beyond their beginnings, and experience the Christian life in its maturity. And that life should call forth admiration. It should be striking and arresting like a tree, a great tree which as you are walking through a forest suddenly makes you stop and stand and say, How marvellous! How majestic! How wonderful! The Apostle prays that these Ephesian Christians may become such.

The picture therefore conveys the idea that love is the soil in which our Christian life is set and in which it grows. The nutriment and nourishment, and all that helps to build us up and make us strong Christians comes from the soil of love. We are to be rooted in it. The tree receives very much of its nutriment in that way. It gets various chemicals from the soil, and also its moisture and various other things. Its needs are met through this network of roots; nourishment is drawn up into the trunk, and out into the branches and the leaves. In this way the life of the tree is maintained. So the ground and the soil of our Christian life is to be love, says the Apostle. Love is that which alone builds up the Christian life and really makes it like the life of Christ Himself. As Christians we are meant to be like Him; we are to be 'conformed to the image of God's Son' (Rom 8:29). We must ever keep this truth before us. We must cease to think negatively of ourselves as being just a little better than we once were or better than someone else. We are to look at Him, we are to be made like Him. In our regeneration we are made anew on that pattern, and we are to become more and more like Him. The only way to become like Him is to be 'rooted' in love. In this way alone shall we become strong and manifest that symmetry and proportion which is ever the most striking characteristic of a majestic tree.

It is only as we are rooted in love that we shall manifest these glories and be a joy and a pleasure and of value to others.

The real strength of the Christian's life is love. We are living in days when love is often regarded as something weak and flabby and sentimental. But love is strong. 'Love is strong as death' (Song of Songs 8:6), indeed it is stronger than death. There is nothing stronger than true love. Here we find the essential difference between true love and mere sentimentality or sentimentalism, which is always weak and maudlin and flabby, and is incapable of action. Love is the grandest and the most powerful influence in the world.

*   *   *

We can emphasize this truth by means of certain contrasts. According to New Testament teaching it is love and not knowledge that makes us strong Christians. This is clearly taught in the eighth chapter of Paul's First Epistle to the Corinthians, where we read the memorable phrase, 'Knowledge puffeth up: but charity (love) edifieth' or builds up (v. 1). This is a most important distinction. Let us remember that it is the great Apostle Paul who says this, a man who was pre-eminently a teacher, the greatest teacher the Church has ever known, the man who was greatly concerned that Christians should have knowledge, and that they should grow in knowledge. It is he of all men who says, 'Knowledge puffeth up, but charity (love) builds up'.

We can state and emphasize this distinction in the following way. There is a sense in which it is true to say that the whole of the First Epistle to the Corinthians is a disquisition on the difference between knowledge and love. The Apostle had written the letter because of divisions, because of sects, because there were many grievous troubles in the Church. He takes these problems up one by one. But a careful reading of the treatment given to the separate individual problems leads to the conclusion that all the troubles had a common origin – the Corinthians were putting knowledge in the place of love. They were making knowledge the supreme thing in the life of the Christian. It was a very gifted church, the Holy Spirit had dispensed many spiritual gifts to them; but they had gone astray because they had forgotten love. If anything is placed in the primary position, or built into the foundation, save love, we are certain to go astray. If we put intellectual knowledge and apprehension first it will probably puff us up and ruin everything. If we put spiritual gifts first it will again puff us up and cause division and schism and ruin everything. Love is the foundation, love is the soil, not knowledge. Knowledge is, of course, absolutely essential; without knowledge there never can be any growth. But knowledge in the truly Christian sense is never merely intellectual. This is so, and that because it is the knowledge of a Person. The purpose of all doctrine, the value of all instruction, is to bring us to the Person of our Lord and Saviour Jesus Christ.

I emphasize this again because it has been a pitfall to many throughout the centuries in the Church. The pitfall for some professed Christians is not to trouble themselves about knowledge at all; such people are already in a false position. Others can see clearly that we are meant to have knowledge, that the Scripture urges this, so they begin to seek knowledge. The devil then enters in and turns this into something purely intellectual. The result is that they have heads packed full of knowledge and of doctrine, but their hearts are as cold and hard as stones. They are dry, and as unlike a majestic tree as it is possible for man to be. True Christian knowledge is the knowledge of a Person. And because it is knowledge of a Person it leads to love, because He Himself is love. 'God is love'. Christ is love incarnate. So to know God and to know Christ, of necessity leads to love. If the knowledge we claim to have has not led to greater love in our lives we had better examine ourselves very seriously. Knowledge without love becomes what the Scriptures call 'heady' and 'high-minded'. It turns us into authorities; it introduces a censoriousness and hardness which is positively harmful.

We find a repetition of the same teaching in the thirteenth chapter of that same First Epistle to the Corinthians. In verse 2 we read, 'Though I have the gift of prophecy and understand all mysteries, and all knowledge; and though I have all faith, so that I could remove mountains, and have not love, I am nothing'. However great our knowledge may be, if we have not got this love we are useless. Again in verse 8 of that chapter, 'Whether there be prophecies, they shall fail; whether there be tongues, they shall cease; whether there be knowledge, it shall vanish away'. Verse 9 says, 'We know in part and we prophesy in part'. All our knowledge is but partial; at the very best and highest in our life in this world, we see only 'as in a glass darkly'.

Let us realize then that the business of knowledge is to lead us to love. This is always the ultimate test of our Christian life. Our Lord expresses it thus in the Sermon on the Mount: 'Be ye therefore perfect, even as your Father which is in heaven is perfect' (Matt 5:48). The perfection of which He is speaking is love. He says that God sends rain upon the just and the unjust, and causes His sun to shine upon the righteous and the unrighteous alike. God manifests His love in that way and thereby shows us the way in which we too have to love. The Gentiles, says the Lord, love those who love them, but the question is, Can you do good to them that hate you? That is how God loves; and we are to love as God loves. 'Be ye therefore perfect, even as your Father which is in heaven is perfect'. That is the soil, the only nutriment which can build us up and make us strong, and make us look like representatives and reproductions of the life of the Lord Jesus Christ Himself.

A further truth is that it is love alone which can give us real power to live the Christian life and to work and labour in this Christian life. This is frequently emphasized in the Scripture. Ezra in exhorting the people to the work of rebuilding, after the destruction and devastation in Jerusalem, made this striking statement, 'The joy of the Lord is your strength' (Neh 8:10). There is nothing in the world that so energizes us as love. I stress again the difference between love and sentimentality. The sentimental person sits back in his chair and enjoys some fleeting stimulus. He feels very happy for the moment, and then waits for the next stimulus or experience, but he does nothing. Love energizes and sends a man out upon a task, it urges him and drives him out and on.

The Apostle Paul states this same truth in his Epistle to the Galatians, where we find him saying, 'In Jesus Christ neither circumcision availeth anything, nor uncircumcision; but faith which worketh by love' (5:6). He scarcely ever mentions faith without putting love with it. Indeed faith and hope and love go together as a glorious triad. So, in this third chapter of the Epistle to the Ephesians, after writing about Christ dwelling in our hearts by faith, he proceeds immediately to mention love. He does so because faith works by love, faith is energized by love, and the life of faith is a life that is active because of love. And this refers, we remember, to our love of God, of the brethren, and of the work itself.

Let me illustrate what I mean. A man may preach because it is his work, his task, or because he is announced to do so. And he can be energized, as far as he is energized at all, by that alone. But it is hard work, it is a task. But how different when he is energized by love – the love of God and of Christ and the love of souls! 'Faith which worketh by love'.

Let us next look at this theme in a very beautiful and almost idyllic Old Testament representation of it. The point I am making is that it is love that alone really gives power and strength in the Christian life. Knowledge may give a head knowledge, and a purely intellectual apprehension and interest. But what we need is the dynamic that love provides. We see this at work in the Old Testament in the story of Jacob. Having escaped from home and the wrath of his brother Esau he went into his mother's homeland and came into contact with Laban and his family. There he fell in love with Rachael, one of Laban's daughters, and asked that she might become his wife. But he was tricked by Laban and forced to take Rachel's elder sister Leah, and then was given Rachel on condition that he agreed to work seven years for her. Then comes the interesting statement in Genesis: 'And Jacob served seven years for Rachel; and they seemed unto him but a few days, for the love he had to her' (29:20). Seven years seems a long time when you are looking forward to something. A student who has to face a seven years' course of study feels that it is almost endless. Of if you are waiting to receive money that is to come to you in seven years, it seems to be a great length of time. But to Jacob this working and waiting for Rachel for seven years seems to him but a few days. The explanation is his love for Rachel. Love changes everything. It seems to have the power to cancel time. It makes seconds and minutes and hours and days and months and years to appear as something quite artificial and unreal. Love has its own chronology; and this is so because it produces this energy, this power, this capacity, this capability of seeing everything in a new way. It does not count cost, it does not count time, it is a world of its own, and makes everything to appear new.

Again, love is the only true motive for work and activity in the Christian life. Why do we call ourselves Christian? Why do we partake of bread and wine at the Lord's Supper? Why do we believe that Christ died for our sins on the Cross? The reason for it all is that we know that 'God so loved the world, that he gave his only begotten Son'. Love is God's own motive. Why should the eternal, absolute, holy God trouble at all about this world that rebelled against Him and reduced His paradise to a state of chaos? Why did He not destroy it all, and consign it there and then to perdition? It was because of His eternal, self-generating love! This is the motivation in the heart of God. And as you read the story of the Lord Jesus Christ nothing stands out more prominently in all the Gospels than this very same fact. He looked at the crowd, we are told, and He saw them as 'sheep without a shepherd'. How frequently is the word 'compassion' used in connection with Him! 'He had compassion on the multitude'. His deeds of kindness, His miracles, His relieving of the sick and the suffering, was all because of His great heart of love. That gave Him the energy, and provided the motive also; it was the power that led Him on. And in the Christian life we are to be like Him; we are to follow in His steps, we are to be reproductions of Him. Men and women in the world as they look at us should see Him. This, therefore, must be the compelling motive in our Christian life in every respect, in every aspect of it.

As we have said earlier, love should be the motive even for holy living. The real motive for living the holy life should be that it pleases God, and that sin is displeasing to Him. I must not set up my own little standard of holiness and rectitude and my little moral code, and pride myself that I am a man who always keeps his word and lives up to his own code and standard. That is ultimately unChristian. The world acts frequently from such a motive. The only true motive for holy living is that it grieves God and offends Him when I am not holy. My desire must be to please Him; not simply to obey the divine law, but to give joy to God and to the Lord Jesus Christ. That should be the motive in all our actions and activities. We all have to confess that it is not always so. Men who have been very busy in the life of the Church have often been activated by very different motives from this. The motive has far too often been the exaltation of their own name, their own reputation, their own importance, their own success. But that is quite unworthy of our 'high calling'. Our motive must be love.

See this motive as it is exemplified in the Apostle Paul himself. Scripture portrays him as an indefatigable evangelist and preacher who travelled day and night teaching and preaching, who crossed oceans and was subjected to endless cruelties and indignities at the hands of men. Ask him why he behaved thus. In his Second Epistle to the Corinthians he gives his answer: 'The love of Christ constraineth us' (5:14). The love of Christ is in Him. He has seen the situation of mankind in sin as Christ saw it. He knows what Christ has done for him, and this has created a like love in his heart. He is 'rooted in the love of Christ', it is the base of His entire experience. This is what drives him on, this is the motive, and nothing else. This is to be the way in which we too are to represent Him, to bring glory to His Name and to be well-pleasing in His sight.

There is yet one further element in this idea of being rooted in love. It is negative, yet very important, and has been implied in what we have said. There is no ultimate value in all our work, and all our activity, unless it is rooted and grounded in love. That may appear to be too strong or too extreme a statement; but it is not mine, it belongs to the Apostle himself. He tells us: 'Though I speak with the tongues of men and of angels, and have not love, I am become as sounding brass or a tinkling cymbal'. You may be the greatest orator in the world, you may be able to speak in an affecting manner which can move people to admiration and perhaps even to action; but if love does not control what you are saying or doing you are but as sounding brass or a tinkling cymbal. Further, 'Though I have the gift of prophecy and understand all mysteries and all knowledge; and though I have all faith so that I could remove mountains, and have not love, I am nothing. And though I bestow all my goods to feed the poor, and though I give my body to be burned, and have not love, it profiteth me nothing'. That is a shattering and alarming statement, but it is obviously the simple truth. It must be so because the Christian life is a Christ-like life, and everything in Him had its source in love. So must it be with us. The day of judgment will be a revelation, a day of surprises. What appeared to us to be very great may then appear to be nothing at all; and what appeared to us to be trivial will then be seen to be of great value with the arc-light of God's love shed upon it. What a reversal of our judgments and our conceptions we shall find!

This is not the teaching of the Apostle Paul alone. Our blessed Lord and Saviour taught the same truth. According to Him we are to judge an action, not by its size and its outward appearance, but by the motive that produced it, and by the element of love in it. This is the meaning of the story of the 'Widow's mite'. As regards the amount it was but a 'mite', but it was an expression of her heart's love, and was of infinitely greater worth in the sight of God than millions of pounds would have been without love. She gave all that she had, she gave her love, and showed her desire (Mark 12:41–44). The same principle is found in Luke's Gospel which tells of how our Lord went into the house of Simon the Pharisee. Simon did not give Him water to wash His feet, nor did he give Him oil to anoint His head. Simon did not show Him the ordinary, usual civilities. He was a Pharisee who could not quite understand this Person. He was interested up to a point, but he did not know Him, he did not believe in Him, he did not love Him. However he desired Him to come into his house and to sit down at his table. But then a poor woman, a sinner in the city, came and fell at our Lord's feet. She washed His feet with her tears, wiped them with the hairs of her head, and anointed them with ointment (Luke 7:36–50). Her tears were more acceptable in His sight than the precious, expensive ointment which she used. To be anointed by tears from the heart is of infinitely greater value to Him, even though it be only applied to His feet, than to have His head anointed with spikenard or the most costly spices and fragrant perfumes. Nothing is of value in His sight unless it comes out of a heart of love.

The Christian is not a man who is carrying out a task, or labouring merely to perform a duty. He is one who is 'rooted in love'. And, like his Lord, his every motive arises from it. He is also energized by it, constrained by it. He cannot refrain, he cannot but be thus. Because Christ is dwelling in his heart by faith, his faith is rooted in the soil of love, and it is drawing its precious vital nutriment from that source. Thus it becomes a reproduction of the Lord Jesus Christ Himself. May God open our eyes to this! May He give us this love, and 'shed it abroad' in our hearts! May we seek after it above everything else, because all else without it is nothing, and will lead to nothing but loss. May God root us in His love!

15
'Grounded in Love'

'That Christ may dwell in your hearts by faith; that
ye, being rooted and grounded in love,'

Ephesians 3:17

As we continue our study of the phrase 'being rooted and
grounded in love' we remind ourselves that the Apostle's fundamental proposition is that our whole life must be firmly based
upon love; it must draw its life, its strength, its power, its
nutriment, its everything from this Christian principle of love.
If Christ dwells in our hearts then love must be in our hearts, at
the centre of our being. As we have already seen, the Apostle
presents this truth in the form of two pictures, that of a tree and
also that of a building.

We have seen that there are certain things which are common
to the two pictures and yet each one emphasizes certain particulars.
We therefore turn now to those aspects of this matter which are
illustrated by the picture of a building. We are not only to be
rooted in love, but also to be 'grounded' in love, just as a great
building requires a deep and solid foundation. The principle
taught is that the Christian's life and activity must be built upon
love, for love is an essential and inevitable part of the life of all in
whose hearts Christ has taken up His abode.

A number of obvious principles emerge from this particular
picture. The first is, the importance of making sure that the
foundation is well and truly laid. The Apostle speaks of himself
as a 'wise master-builder' – not merely a master-builder, but a
'wise' one (1 Cor 3:10). The hall-mark of a wise master-builder is
that he pays great attention to the foundation. He does not rush
to set up a building; he wants one which will be durable and
lasting; he wants a solid building in which he will be able to dwell

for a lifetime, and others after him. So as a wise master-builder he will pay very great attention to the foundation, he will take time over it, and go to a great deal of trouble concerning it. A wise master-builder never takes anything for granted in the matter of foundations. He wants to know exactly the kind of soil he is dealing with, whether there is too much clay or sand, and the possibility of a shifting and a sliding later on. He goes into these matters with meticulous care. The wise master-builder does not do this work hurriedly, for he realizes that this matter cannot be rushed. The character of the building, in a sense, is going to depend upon it, so the foundation must be well and truly laid.

This is particularly true if the proposal is to put up a very large or a very high building. The larger and higher the building, the more importance attaches to the foundation. If you intend to erect a very light building, a mere wooden shack, a temporary structure, you need not be over-particular about the foundation. But if you intend to set up a massive building, a 'skyscraper', an edifice of great weight, which will have a tremendous number of rooms, then a very firm and solid foundation is an absolute essential, and the more careful you will have to be that it is adequate to stand up to the stresses and strains to which the building will become subject.

This principle is well illustrated in the case of the many buildings in the city of New York. That collection of massive high buildings has been made possible by the fact that the island of Manhattan is more or less solid rock. It would not be possible everywhere. It is not allowed, for instance, in Los Angeles where there is a limit to the height of any building because of the nature of the soil and the subsoil. If you want to set up buildings such as are found in New York you must make certain in every respect that you have an adequate foundation.

This principle is given great prominence in the New Testament. The Apostle is concerned that the Ephesian Christians may reach a great height in experience, that, in fact, they may be filled with 'all the fulness of God'. And he knows that if that is to be realized much time will have to be spent in preparing an adequate foundation. You cannot build to that height hurriedly. If I may mix the metaphors, even as the Apostle himself does by placing rooting and grounding together, let me illustrate this point from the realm of horticulture. I remember once staying in Weston-super-Mare with a man who was an expert in growing sweet-peas. He had won the first prize and the challenge cup several years in succession at the Shows of the Royal Horticultural Society. I happened to be staying with him at the very time when the sweet-peas were in full bloom. I was much impressed by their beauty and aroma and I asked him the obvious question: Was there any one secret above all others which explained success in winning such a coveted prize year after year? And particularly, what was the secret of their remarkable height? He told me that it was quite a simple principle; if you want great height you must dig deeply. The height above the earth, he said, must correspond to the depth below the earth! To ensure any particular height the roots must be as deep as the height you require. That was the secret principle. In the same way there must be a correspondence between the height and the weight of a building and the foundation on which it rests.

That is, surely, the principle which the Apostle is enunciating here. He is preparing the way for 'the breadth and length and depth and height, and to know the love of Christ which passeth knowledge', and 'that ye might be filled with all the fulness of God'. As that is to be the character of the building, he says, do not rush your foundation. Spend time on it, make sure that it will be adequate. Our Lord Himself said this perfectly, once and for ever, in the famous parable concerning the two houses at the end of the Sermon on the Mount. What He emphasizes so strikingly is the vital importance of the foundation. The same parable in Luke's Gospel gives us a detail which is not found in the Sermon as we have it in Matthew. In Luke we read, 'He that heareth my sayings, and doeth them', is 'like a man which built a house and digged deep, and laid the foundation on a rock' (6:48). In Matthew the Lord speaks simply about 'a wise man who built his house upon a rock' (7:24). Luke gives the added information that this particular man 'digged deep' in order to lay the foundation on a rock. The contrast is with the man who built his house upon the sand. This second man desired quick returns. He was only interested in houses, he was not interested in foundations; he wanted a house in which he could live comfortably. He does not trouble about foundations, he builds on the sand. But when the storms and the trials come, his poor house that seemed so wonderful is demolished. The point which is stressed by our Lord is that if you want to live a life corresponding to the Beatitudes, if you really want to be His disciple, you must dig deep and lay a solid foundation upon a rock.

This is the principle which the Apostle is emphasizing here. We have to realize that there are no short cuts in the spiritual life. These things take time. The Apostle does not merely pray for these people that they might be filled with all the fulness of God; he knows that it cannot happen suddenly and without any preparation. We must be strengthened with might by the Spirit in the inner man and proceed to lay a solid foundation. We must dig deeply and then pour in the concrete in order to lay a solid, a massive foundation. We must always bear in mind the weight of the superstructure that is to be erected.

It is at this point we see the contrast presented by the cults. They are essentially different from the Christian experience. With the cults all is so easy, so quick; there is no need for any preparation or foundation. 'Work out your own salvation with fear and trembling', says the Scripture. It is not so with the cults or any system founded upon a false interpretation of the Scripture. Without the strengthening with might by the Spirit of God, without the dwelling of Christ in the heart, without a being rooted and grounded in love, we have no hope of knowing the higher experiences of the Christian life. A familiar hymn tells us, 'Take time to be holy': and that is right. And we must also take time to make sure that our life is based on love. You cannot rush through these things and say, I want that experience here and now. It is only obtained in God's way. There are rules in the construction of the Christian life and experience; and this is one of the most vital of all.

*   *   *

To turn now to the details: what does this foundation mean? How is it to be laid? The first answer is that all relationships in the Christian life must be based upon love. Everything is to be grounded, founded in love. This is true, first of all, of your relationship to God. I shall never know the love of God unless my relationship to Him is one of love. This is quite basic. What is our customary way of thinking about God? Is it theoretical only? Is it intellectual only? How easy it is to think of God only intellectually, and to be arguing about Him, and reading about Him and debating about Him. How glibly have we all done this! How often have we said that God should have done this and that! That is a purely theoretical view of God; there is no love in it. But if our attitude to God is only theoretical and intellectual we have no hope of being 'filled with all the fulness of God' or of really knowing His love and the unsearchable riches of Christ.

So we must continue to ask ourselves about our habitual attitude towards God. Is it one of love? Our Lord tells us that the First Commandment is, 'Thou shalt love the Lord thy God with all thy heart and soul and mind and strength' (Mark 12:30). The Bible exhorts us not only to believe in God but to love Him: it calls for a personal relationship. God is not impersonal. He is not a mere force or the unknown quantity of the philosophic system. The philosophers talk about 'the Absolute' and the Uncaused Cause. That is to make of God a category, not a Person. But God is a Person, and therefore if we are in the Christian relationship to God it will be one of love, inevitably. We must not attempt a further step forward until we are clear about this. Do I love God? Does love govern my way of thinking of Him and my relationship to Him?

In exactly the same way, my attitude to God must not be one of fear or of dread. There must always be, of course, a reverential awe; but that is not 'the fear that hath torment' for 'Perfect love casteth our fear' (1 John 4:18). The relationship of the Christian to God is to be that of a child to his Father. To Christians God is not merely some great power away in the heavens; He is our Father. Paul says that he 'bows his knees unto the Father of the Lord Jesus Christ, of whom the whole family in heaven and earth is named'. We only pray truly when we know that we are speaking to our Father. He loves us and we love Him because He is our Father.

How vital it is that we should take time over these matters! It is not enough that you say your prayers every day. Much more important than to say our prayers, and more important than what we may say and desire in our prayers, is our attitude towards God when we pray to Him. Sometimes simply to bow and to stay in His presence saying nothing is more indicative of the right relationship to Him: 'To gaze and gaze on Thee', as F. W. Faber expresses it. Contemplation of God, adoration and worship are the highest expression of our love to God. What the Apostle prays for these Ephesians is that their whole life should be based on this foundation. There are many who have spent a lifetime in seeking these higher experiences in the Christian life in vain, simply because they have failed to grasp this first principle. They have taken it for granted, they have rushed on, instead of making sure that they truly love God. And we only come to love God as we realize deeply the truth about Him and what He has done for us in His Son.

However we must not stop at loving God; we are also to love one another, we are to 'love the brethren'. This, again, is constantly emphasized in the Scriptures. We may go the complete round of all the meetings and the conventions seeking some particular blessing, some particular 'it', but we will never find it unless our life is grounded in love, that is, unless we love one another. How easy it is to say that we long to 'be filled with all the fulness of God' while neglecting something which is obviously and glaringly wrong in our personal relationships with someone else! This is not a matter of argument, nor even of appeal. It is a question of sheer common-sense. If the foundation is not truly laid you will never erect this great building; it is impossible; we must take time and obey the scriptural injunctions. The Second great Commandment which follows loving the Lord our God with all our heart and soul and mind and strength is 'Thou shalt love thy neighbour as thyself'. Indeed our Lord's teaching goes further and says, 'Love your enemies'. Whatever they may have said about you falsely, and however grievously they have wronged you or maligned you, you are to 'love your enemies'.

Our Lord taught this more clearly than anywhere else in the Sermon on the Mount, as we find it recorded in Matthew's Gospel, where He contrasts His way with every other way. 'Ye have heard that it hath been said, Thou shalt love thy neighbour and hate thine enemy. But I say unto you, Love your enemies, bless them that curse you, do good to them that hate you, and pray for them which despitefully use you and persecute you; that ye may be the children of your Father which is in heaven: for he maketh his sun to rise on the evil and on the good, and sendeth rain on the just and on the unjust. For if ye love them which love you, what reward have ye? do not even the publicans the same? And if ye salute your brethren only, what do ye more than others? do not even the publicans so? Be ye therefore perfect, even as your Father which is in heaven is perfect' (5:43-48). That is the basis of the Christian life. That is the thing that differentiates us from the best non-Christian. The latter loves people who love him, but he does not love his enemies; he hates them as they hate him, and because they hate him. But that is not Christian; anyone can love those who love him, and all are doing so. At the very foundation of the Christian life is this love of our enemies; and until we are on this foundation we are wasting time in seeking any higher experiences. You will never know the breadth and length and depth and height of the love of Christ which passeth knowledge until you are on this foundation. That is the argument of this prayer which Paul offers for the Ephesian Christians.

The Apostle gives noble expression to this in his Epistle to the Philippians: 'Look not every man on his own things, but every man also on the things of others'. Then 'Let this mind be in you which was also in Christ Jesus' (Phil 2:4-5). That 'mind', as the Apostle explains, led our Lord who was in heaven 'in the form of God', and enjoying that status from eternity, to come on earth and humble Himself because He did not regard that status as a prize to be 'clutched at' and 'to be held on to'. He forsook the signs of His glory, and came to this world in the form of a man, in the likeness of sinful flesh. He made Himself a servant, and even humbled Himself to the death of the Cross. He did all that for us, not because we were good and lovely in His sight or because we loved Him. The exact opposite was the case. It was in spite of us, in spite of the fact that we were rebels and 'hateful and hating one another' and hating Him. That is the 'mind' which is to be in us.

This attitude is clearly something that we have to cultivate, and to make sure that we possess. Am I loving my enemies and blessing those that curse me and who say all manner of things falsely against me? I must consider this carefully, and I must not be satisfied until I can honestly say that I love them, and pray that God may have mercy and pity upon them and open their eyes, and bring them to Himself. Until I do so it is idle for me to seek some higher experience. How important the foundation is!

One of the most subtle temptations of the devil is to get us to ignore foundations and to rush on to seek the higher experiences. In reading the biographies of those who have known and rejoiced in the knowledge of the love of Christ you will find that they have known great humblings and indeed humiliations, and that often they have experienced great trials and testings. At times everything in them wanted to react against their enemies with enmity. Some of them had a proud self-righteous spirit which they had to crucify. They had to take the place of death with Christ; and it was only after they had disciplined themselves severely and apparently had lost everything, and had become a doormat for the whole world, that God suddenly revealed Himself to them and filled them with this knowledge of His love, and with His own fulness.

Furthermore, our attitude towards the demands and commandments of the Christian life must also be one of love if we really would have this great building erected. The Christian life fulfils the Commandments. We have to live out the Sermon on the Mount, and obey the 'royal law of love'. All the injunctions found in the New Testament epistles have to be carried out. The Ten Commandments still remain as the pattern of godly living. So we must ask ourselves whether we love the Lord's Commandments. Recall what the Psalmist could say about this even under the Old Dispensation. He could but look forward vaguely to the dispensation in which we live. He lived in the days of shadows and of types. Christ had not come; the Holy Spirit 'had not yet been given'. But he could say, 'Oh, how I love thy law; I love thy commandments above gold' (Psa 119:97, 127). He could say that the law of God was sweeter to him than honey, and the honeycomb (Psa 19:10). 'Great peace have they that love thy law', he says (Psa 119:165). If he could love the law of God in his day, are we doing so in our day as Christians? In his First Epistle the Apostle John says plainly, 'For this is the love of God, that we keep his commandments; and his commandments are not grievous' (5:3).

If you truly desire to know the love of Christ 'that passeth knowledge', and to say that your chief desire is to be 'filled with all the fulness of God', you must face a preliminary question: Do you love God's commandments as found in the Bible? Or do you regard the Christian life as being narrow, and insist on your 'right to enjoy' life in your own way? If so you will never know what it is to be 'filled with all the fulness of God'. The Christian life is specifically narrow in certain respects. Certain prohibitions are quite clear and definite. They are in the Ten Commandments, and they are in the new law of the New Testament. There are certain things which Christians are not to do. If you really want still to live the worldly life you are free to do so, but you have no right to expect to enjoy the great blessings of the Christian life. There are certain things which do not mix with the foundation of this great building. This building must have a solid foundation; so we must dig deep and get down to the solid rock, and make sure that we are on the foundation.

Many Christians seem to regard the Christian life as narrow, irksome and grievous; and they are always fighting against it. But its demands are a part of the very foundation of the Christian life. 'Ye that love the Lord, hate evil', says an Old Testament word (Psa 97:10). So if we find that we are living the Christian life as a matter of duty, and having to force ourselves or compel ourselves, and drive ourselves to do so, there is little purpose in our going any further in this third chapter of Ephesians. A part of the foundation of love is that we desire and love God's law. 'Blessed are they which do hunger and thirst after righteousness, for they shall be filled'. The people who are going to be filled with the Spirit, the people who are going to enjoy the full blessing are those who are hungering and thirsting after righteousness; not after the blessing, but after righteousness. That is a foundational distinction. It is just here, once more, that the Christian life differs from every other type of life. This is where it differs from what was often mistakenly regarded as puritanism in the last century. That was but a kind of legalism. Quite rightly, many have reacted against it in this century but they have gone to the other extreme – to laxity. Christian liberty means that a man loves the law of the Lord and hungers and thirsts after righteousness. Philip Doddridge expresses it perfectly when he says,

> (*I*) *count it my supreme delight*
> *To hear Thy dictates and obey.*

Our last principle is that the foundation always suggests stability. I state it therefore as a principle by emphasizing that our love must not be fitful, must not be variable. It must be stable and constant, as a foundation that never shakes and never moves. We all know what it is to have occasional spasms of Christian love. You may feel this in a service of worship, or when you are singing a hymn, or reading a book, or as you are looking at some beautiful sunset. We know what it is to have occasional flashes of love for God and our Lord. As the result of something that happens to us, or in certain circumstances, we feel that we really love God. But the experience soon vanishes, and the very next day it may seem as if it had never happened; our love comes and goes. That is not a solid foundation, for our life is to be 'grounded' in love, founded on it. Our love is meant to be like God's love. 'Be ye therefore perfect, even as your Father which is in heaven is perfect' (Matt 5:48).

God's perfect love is self-generated; it does not depend on anything outside Himself; it is a love that starts within and goes out to others. That is why God so loved the world that He gave His only begotten Son. It was in spite of what He saw in the world, and certainly not His response to a demand from man. It was His own self-generated love pouring itself out. It starts in Him, and it is based upon itself. Your love and mine must be the same. It will be so when our life is grounded in love. Our love must be so firm and so founded on this foundation that nothing will be able to move it, or shake it, or affect it to the slightest extent. This, all must agree, is the test of a solid foundation. Whenever the rain descends, and the floods come, and the wind blows, the house on the rock stands. The house on the sand falls and is destroyed. If you want a building that will not be shaken in the storm, dig deep and have a solid foundation.

Does our love for other people vary according to their variations? If so, it is not founded on the rock, it is not truly based on this foundation. Shakespeare, as well as Scripture, recognizes this when he says:

> *Love is not love*
> *Which alters when it alteration finds,*
> *Or bends with the remover to remove:*

O, no! it is an ever-fixed mark,
That looks on tempests, and is never shaken.

(Sonnet 116)

The love that alters and varies and changes is human, erotic love, natural love. It is not the 'agape' of the New Testament, this love of God in the heart. This does not change, it remains in spite of men. In that beautiful thirteenth chapter of his First Epistle to the Corinthians the Apostle Paul says, 'Love suffereth long and is kind'. It 'suffers long' because it is on a solid foundation. It also stands up to the stresses. 'It is not easily provoked'. A love which is easily provoked is not deep. 'Love beareth all things, believeth all things, hopeth all things, endureth all things'. Change in others, malice, spite, bitterness, hatred, anything that may happen they make no difference! love stands firm! 'Love never faileth'. Never! Whatever may come against it, the foundation is so deep that love stands as if nothing had happened.

Have you ever been at the seaside in a storm and watched the waves dashing themselves against a mighty cliff or rock? Back they go, and return with redoubled energy. The gale seems to redouble its force and the waves dash themselves against the rock. But it remains immovable as if nothing had happened. 'Love never faileth'. Does our love conform to this description? Can it stand up to the changes in others? Not only so, can it stand up to changing circumstances? Can it stand up to trials and tribulations? Such experiences come; they must come. But our love, if it is deeply grounded, will stand, whatever may be happening. Job in his day was able to say 'Though He slay me, yet will I trust in Him' (13:15).

Consider the way in which Paul and Silas behaved and reacted to their circumstances at Philippi. They were arrested illegally and wrongly, they were scourged until their backs were bleeding with the stripes that they had been given, they were molested, ill-treated, abused, thrown into the innermost prison, and their feet were made fast in the stocks. In a dank, damp cell, with nothing to comfort and to cheer them, when everything seemed to have gone against them, we read that, 'At midnight Paul and Silas prayed and sang praises unto God' (Acts 16:25). There is but one adequate explanation of such a reaction to cruel circumstances, namely, that they were 'rooted and grounded in love'. The Christian thus grounded is able to sing with Anna Waring:

> *In heavenly love abiding,*
> *No change my heart shall fear;*
> *And safe is such confiding,*
> *For nothing changes here;*
> *The storm may roar without me,*
> *My heart may low be laid;*
> *But God is round about me,*
> *And can I be dismayed?*

Nothing but a deep love to God can stand up to the trials and the stresses, the hazards and the strains of life. Belief alone is not enough. Belief is essential, and it can take you a long way. But when the real storms come, belief alone is not enough. Love alone enables us to stand up to the storms. Another hymn-writer, Edward Mote, was able to say with certainty and assurance,

> *When all around my soul gives way,*
> *He then is all my hope and stay.*

When I cannot understand, when my intellect is baffled, and when I cannot explain, love still holds me up. How vitally important it is that we should take time with the foundation and make sure of being 'rooted and grounded in love'. It is only as our lives have this foundation that the Apostle's petition, 'that ye may be able to comprehend with all saints . . . this love of Christ which passeth knowledge', will truly apply to us. So let us make certain that the foundation is truly laid.

16

'Able to Comprehend with all Saints'

'That ye may be able to comprehend with all saints
what is the breadth, and length, and depth, and
height; and to know the love of Christ which passeth
knowledge, that ye might be filled with all the fulness
of God.'

Ephesians 3:18–19

These two verses tell us what the Apostle's real object was in praying for these Ephesian Christians. All the previous petitions prepare for and lead up to this petition. They were essential as preparation, but they are not ends in themselves; they are designed to lead on to this grand objective. We find ourselves, as it were, upon the pinnacle of Christian truth. There is nothing higher than this. God grant us His Spirit that we may consider it aright! We are in a rarefied atmosphere; in a place to which, alas, we are not accustomed. Far too many of us are content to spend our time in the lowlands and the plains amid the mists and the other characteristics of that level of life. So, in the words of the Apostle Peter, it behoves us to 'gird up the loins of our minds and be sober'.

I confess that I approach this great matter with 'fear and trembling'. And it is quite evident in their writings that all who have assayed to deal with it and to expound it have been conscious of the same inadequacy. That is why, on the whole, they give us such little help. In the case of many passages of Scripture there is an abundance of help; the commentators and expositors expand themselves and spread themselves, and have much to say. But it is interesting to note that when we come to a passage such as this they have little to say. This is because of the very nature and character of the truth with which we are dealing. It is obviously a subject which you cannot divide and analyse into neat categories and compartments in a cut-and-dried manner. Someone once said, very truly, that 'you cannot analyse and dissect a fragrance'. Still less can you analyse and dissect love. All you can do is to look at it and to say certain things about it. Above all you have to experience it. And there are experiences which are almost inexpressible because of their exalted nature and character. Such is this statement at which we have arrived. We must start by taking a general look at it. We must familiarize ourselves with it in general before we begin to particularize. Let us, as it were, take our breath again and make sure that we are breathing easily and freely in this rarefied atmosphere.

I begin by making a number of obvious general propositions – propositions which we tend to neglect so constantly in our thinking. The first is that one of the highest attainments in the Christian life is to know the love of Christ. There is much argument among the learned authorities – and it is on this they spend most of their time in connection with this passage – as to what is meant by 'the breadth and length and depth and height'. Some argue that these words do not refer to the love of Christ, and that the 'and' indicates that the Apostle is clearly thinking of something else when he refers to these dimensions, and then proceeds to speak of the love of Christ. But surely that is a very artificial distinction. If it is argued that 'the breadth and length and depth and height' refer to the whole of God's dealings with us, I am prepared to agree, for in this case it is just another way of saying that the four words refer to the love of God and the love of Christ with respect to us. However, that is the theme which the Apostle has been dealing with in the whole of the chapter. He has already spoken about 'the unsearchable riches of Christ' and so on.

I argue, therefore, that here Paul goes on to something even higher. Let us observe that he is not dealing with our love, but with His love to us. He has dealt with our love in the phrase 'being rooted and grounded in love', which, as we have seen, refers to our love to God and to our fellow-men, our love of the Christian life and the law of God. In verses 18 and 19, however, Paul is no longer dealing with our love, although that was first necessary in order to bring us to the realization and knowledge of His love to us.

Another difficulty may arise here. Some may say that you

cannot be a Christian at all without knowing the love of God and of Christ towards you. That is quite true. If you believe that Christ has died for your sins, you must of necessity believe in the love of God and the love of Christ to you. So there are many who think that the Christian begins with a knowledge of that love. But clearly that is not the explanation of what we are dealing with here. The Apostle is writing to people, and praying for people, who are already Christians. He has reminded them in his first chapter, that they have trusted in the Lord after hearing the word of truth, the gospel of their salvation. They have believed the gospel, and have therefore realized something of God's love to them. And yet the Apostle's prayer for them here is that they may go on to comprehend this love with all saints.

How, then, is this experience to be gained? It seems clear that it is a matter of degree. There is a preliminary awareness of the love of God; but compared with that which the Apostle has in mind here, it is, in the words of a hymn, but 'weak and faint'. Indeed, the love we are now contemplating is so much greater than this awareness, that all who have ever had an experience of it are tempted to say that they had never known the love of God before. They feel that they had known of it, and known about it, but had not really known the love itself. That is the difference between the two degrees of knowledge of God's love. We must never fall into the error of imagining that because we are Christians we therefore know all about the love of God. Most of us are but as children paddling at the edge of an ocean; there are abysmal depths in this love of God of which we know nothing. The Apostle is praying that these Ephesians, and we with them, may go out into the depths and the deeps, and discover things which we have never even imagined.

Another preliminary and essential remark is that we are dealing with love, not as a concept, but as the actual love of Christ. It is personal, it refers to personal knowledge of Him and of His love to us. The Apostle John in his First Epistle writes in similar vein saying, 'And we have known and believed the love that God hath to us' (4:16). The end of all our knowledge should be this knowledge of the love of Christ to us. The end and purpose and objective of every doctrine is to bring us to this. It is possible for us to know all doctrine, in a sense, and yet not to know this.

Doctrine is not to be an end in itself. It is, of course, vital and essential, as the Apostle has already made abundantly clear in leading up to this great petition. No man has ever known this love of Christ, to which the Apostle refers here, unless he has been deeply taught and well versed in doctrine. On the other hand it is equally true to say that if you stop at doctrine you still do not know this love of Christ.

What foolish creatures we are! Many of us are not interested in doctrine at all; we are lazy Christians who do not read, do not think, and do not try to delve into the mysteries. We have had a certain experience and we desire no more. Others of us, deploring such an attitude, say that, because the Bible is full of doctrine, we must study it and grapple with it and possess it. So we become absorbed in our interest in doctrine and stop at that. The result is that, as regards this question of the love of Christ, we are no further on than the others because we have made doctrine an end and a terminus. In this way the devil trips and traps us and robs us of our heritage. If your knowledge of the Scriptures and of the doctrines of the gospel of the Lord Jesus Christ has not brought you to this knowledge of the love of Christ, you should be profoundly dissatisfied and disturbed. All biblical doctrine is about this blessed Person; and there is no greater snare in the Christian life than to forget the Person Himself and to live simply on truths concerning Him.

It is for this reason that some of us have always had a feeling that it is dangerous to have examinations on scriptural knowledge. Some of the Reformers held that view, Martin Luther especially. Some of the Puritans also held it. There should never be such a thing as a 'Degree in Scriptural Knowledge'. This is so, not only because it is wrong in and of itself, but also because it tends to encourage this tendency to stop at truths and to miss the Person. We should never study the Bible or anything concerning biblical truth without realizing that we are in His presence, and that it is truth *about Him*. And it should always be done in an atmosphere of worship. Biblical truth is not one subject among others; it is not something that belongs to a syllabus. It is living truth about a living Person. That is why a theological college should be different from every other kind of college; and that is why a religious service is essentially different from every kind of meeting the world can organize. It is always a matter of worship; we are in the presence of a Person.

The Apostle says this in an arresting manner in the third chapter of his Epistle to the Philippians. Although he had advanced so far in the Christian life, and had had many wonderful experiences, he tells them that this was his ambition: 'That I might know him, and the power of his resurrection, and the fellowship of his sufferings, being made conformable unto His death' (v. 10). And he proceeds to say, 'Forgetting those things that are behind, I press forward'. Love cannot be satisfied. Once you know this Person and begin to love Him, you feel that all you have received is not enough, you want more and more. This is what Paul is praying for these Ephesians. He longs for them also to know Christ, because to know Him is to know His love. The more we know Him, the more we shall know His love toward us. These things are indivisible, and cannot be separated.

Thus our first proposition is that this knowledge of the love of Christ is the goal of all our Christian endeavour. How much do we know of this? Is it real to us? Think again of expressions in certain of our hymns such as

> *How sweet the name of Jesus sounds*
> *In a believer's ear!*

and –

> *Jesus, the very thought of Thee*
> *With sweetness fills my breast.*

Is that true of you? You may have believed, and you may be learned in the Bible and in doctrine; but the question to be faced is: Do you really know Him? Do you know His love? This is the ultimate object of all Christian endeavour.

*   *   *

The second proposition is that this experience is something which is possible for all Christians: 'That ye may be able to comprehend with *all* saints . . .' The two words which are used here are important. Take first the word *saint* – 'may be able to comprehend with all saints'. The word *saints* means 'separated ones', 'holy ones'. It is a term which is used in the New Testament for Christians. In other words the term *saints* tells us that this knowledge is only possible to those who believe in the Lord Jesus Christ. That is why the Apostle has already been emphasizing faith – 'that Christ may dwell in your hearts by faith'. This theme of the love of Christ is something of which the man who is not a·Christian has no conception at all. His complete ignorance and incomprehension are explained by what we read in John's Gospel, where we are told that the Lord promises the gift of the Holy Spirit only to those who believe in Him (14:16–17). Referring to 'the Spirit of truth' He says: 'Whom the world cannot receive, because it seeth him not, neither knoweth him; but ye know him, for he dwelleth with you and shall be in you'.

The test of our condition and position is this: Is the word of truth here in this third chapter of Paul's Epistle to the Ephesians strange to you? Does it seem remote and irrelevant to you in this modern world with its terrifying problems? Is that your reaction to it? If that is so, you are proclaiming exactly where you belong. The world cannot receive the Holy Spirit because it does not know Him. And because it cannot receive the Holy Spirit it knows nothing about this love of Christ. It is only those who are 'strengthened with might by his Spirit in the inner man' who can begin to understand these things. It is truth for saints only. You may have 'a form of godliness' and of Christianity but that of itself does not suffice.

There is a secret element in this matter. It is a secret that is only enjoyed by the Lord's people. The Bible frequently emphasizes this aspect of truth. In the Book of Revelation, for instance, in the letter to the Church at Pergamos, the Lord Jesus Christ says: 'To him that overcometh will I give to eat of the hidden manna, and will give him a white stone, and in the stone a new name written, which no man knoweth saving he that receiveth it' (2:17). The 'hidden' manna! The white stone with a name written on it that nobody can understand except the recipient! Others can see the lettering but it means nothing to them. None understand it save those who truly receive it. This is a secret love that no one else knows. The picture is that of a great affection between two persons which they have kept between them as a great secret. They are enjoying it, their hearts are ravished by it; but no one else knows anything about it. They are enjoying the very secrecy of it, in a sense. Such is the character of this love to which the Apostle refers. The world knows nothing about it; it is only for the saints, only for those who have been separated from the world and brought into the kingdom of God's dear Son. To the saints it is given to enjoy the secrets and to feast on the hidden manna. 'I have food to eat', our Lord said to His own disciples on one occasion, 'that ye know not of'. The hidden manna! The secret name! 'The love of Jesus what it is, none but His loved ones know'.

I hasten to add that this benefit is for *all* the saints. I repeat this because I am aware of the subtle danger of our holding on to certain relics of that completely false Roman Catholic teaching, which says that only certain Christians are 'saints'. In the Roman Catholic Church Christians are not accounted saints, unless they have been canonized. They are very exceptional and unusual people and are called 'Saint so-and-so'. But according to the Scriptures all Christians are saints. The Apostle writes, for example, to 'all that be in Rome beloved of God, called to be saints', and similarly to other churches. All Christians are saints, separated people. So this knowledge, therefore, is for *all* saints. If you accept the Catholic notion of piety and of devotional life and Christian experience, you will feel that what the Apostle is saying is very wonderful, but is clearly only possible for those who forsake the world and give up all worldly prospects and become 'religious'. Saints, according to the Catholic teaching, are those who enter a monastery or nunnery and become monks or nuns or hermits, and who take up religion as the sole occupation of their lives. Then after years of effort, and fasting and sweating and praying in isolation, they may have some hope of arriving at this knowledge. But such ideas are a complete denial of what the Apostle is saying here. 'All saints'! Probably most of those at Ephesus, to whom Paul was writing, were slaves. But he prays that they may know this love; he longs for them to enjoy it with all the saints in all the churches throughout the whole world. It is for every individual Christian.

I emphasize this, because I fear that many may feel within themselves that this experience is possible perhaps for a minister, or a full-time Christian worker who has time to spend in his study thinking and praying, but not for someone who has to spend his day in a business or profession and who may have to take work home with him at night. That is the very lie of the devil. We all have the same opportunity and possibility. It is possible for a man to waste as much time in his study as anywhere else. Your mind may be busied with other things even in a monastery. Thank God this is something that is for *all* saints, whatever their position, whatever their situation. We must take the language of the Apostle and the saints of all the centuries and appropriate it, and determine that this must become true in our own experience. To be content with anything short of this is virtually to tell God that we do not believe His Word, and that we are content with what we have, content to remain in the Church as we are. Nothing is so dishonouring to God and His Word as such a state of self-satisfaction, as such contentment to remain but babes in Christ, and to refuse to scale the heights and make for the mountain-top of God's love. *All* saints are to seek this.

*   *   *

The third matter that demands our attention is the discovery of the way to this knowledge. We must discover how we can hope to enjoy this awareness of Christ's love to us. The Apostle's phrase reads, 'Having been rooted and grounded in love, that ye may be able with all saints . . .' Unfortunately the Authorized Version does not bring out the meaning clearly. The Apostle did not say 'that ye may be able', but 'that ye may be fully able'. He deliberately chose a word which has that extra emphasis. We might well translate it by the word *strengthen* – 'that you may be *strengthened* to comprehend'.

In other words the Apostle once more gives the impression that there are difficulties concerning this matter, and that it is not something which can be described as 'quite simple'. He has already prayed that we may be 'strengthened with might by his Spirit in the inner man', and here he repeats the petition. We must be 'strengthened' or 'made fully able'. We need strength and power and ability before we can know the love of Christ. The illustrations which we have already used really solve the problem. We need to be strengthened, we need to be made fully able, by being rooted and grounded in love, because of the weight of God's love which we are going to bear. Love is powerful and weighty. Love is not weak and flabby and sentimental. Love is dynamite, love is power. 'God is love', and His might and majesty and power are in that love. Thus when you feel the love of God you are feeling something of the might of God, and the weight and the eternity of God's glory.

We find constantly in Christian biographies, as I have had occasion to remark several times, that every man who has ever any sort of impression of the love of God has always had a feeling that it is overwhelming, and has doubted whether he would be able to endure it. When Isaiah saw and felt something of it, that was his reaction. John on the Isle of Patmos tells us that he 'fell down as one dead'. The love of God is so great and powerful that a man feels his physical frame beginning to crack beneath it. Many Christian people, when they have suddenly had an awareness of this love of God, have literally fainted and become unconscious.

An instance of this is found in the accounts of the Revival which took place in Wales in 1904–6 and which is associated with a man called Evan Roberts. Evan Roberts had an experience of this nature which not only proved to be the turning point in his life but also a crucial moment in the story of that Revival. He stood up in a meeting in a chapel, and suddenly this love of God so came upon him that he literally fell to the ground. Many present thought that he was actually dead. What had happened was that he had had a realization of this overwhelming love of God. That is why we need to be 'strengthened'.

Have we ever been caused to feel faint by the love of God? Do we know what it is – to use the language of Solomon's Song of Songs – to be 'sick of love' (2:5), to experience its marvellous power to such an extent that our strength seems to leave us, and we are overwhelmed by it?

A further reason why we need to be made able to comprehend it, is that it is love alone that can recognize love. We need to be 'rooted and grounded in love' in order to comprehend this love of God. Love alone recognizes love, love alone understands love; indeed it is love alone that can receive love. This is a realm where intellect almost appears ridiculous. It is useless to put intellect to meet love; it is incompetent in this realm. Like attracts like. You must have love in your heart if you are going to know love and experience it. There are people who read the Bible and yet hate God, for there is no love in their hearts. It is love alone that can appreciate love. This principle obtains in many realms. You will not be able to appreciate the most glorious music if you are not musical. There are people who are almost driven mad by the sound of some great symphony because they are devoid of a musical faculty. Likewise people can walk through the finest Art galleries and be bored. They are lacking in an artistic sense.

The same is true in respect of love. There are people who remain utterly unmoved by the most eloquent and moving sermons on the love of God, or by the singing of great hymns on the same theme. It is because they have not been 'rooted and grounded in love'. They have not been made fully able to receive it and to comprehend it. That is why we have had to deal so thoroughly with the preparation. We should thank God for the fact that it is love that enables us to comprehend the love of Christ, for it is this that ensures the possibility of *all* saints knowing it. If it were a matter of intellect it would not be open to all the saints; some would have an advantage over others. The man with the greater brain, the greater intellect and understanding, would have an advantage and would be able to know more of the love of God than a less gifted Christian.

How wonderful is God's salvation and God's provision! Because it is a matter of love and not intellect, the most backward person intellectually is on the same level as the greatest genius. Thank God, we can all love, however small our gifts may be, however sunk we may have been in iniquity at one time before conversion. In a natural sense love is more universal than intellect; and in the Christian life the same holds good. So our blessed Lord was able to say, 'I thank thee, O Father, Lord of heaven and earth, that thou hast hid these things from the wise and prudent and hast revealed them unto babes; even so, Father, for so it seemed good in thy sight' (Matt 11:25–26). Nothing is more glorious in the Christian message and faith than the fact that God has chosen to make this central. Other things are of great value, but at this most central point they fail. Here, He postulates something that is common to all, the capacity for love. So when the Lord enters the soul, and strengthens it with His might, it is rendered capable of knowing and comprehending 'the love of Christ which passeth knowledge'. And this, thank God, applies to *all* saints.

*   *   *

Lastly: 'That ye, having been rooted and grounded in love, may be able to comprehend', says the Apostle. At first sight there seems to be some confusion here. If you are already 'rooted and grounded in love', what more do you need? A great biblical principle is involved at this point. Our Lord on one occasion, when dealing with the question of receiving the truth, uttered these words: 'Whosoever hath, to him shall be given, and he shall have more abundance; but whosoever hath not, from him shall be taken away even that he hath' (Matt 13:12). Here we have a typical example of a biblical paradox. 'Unto him that hath shall be given'. But in our wisdom we ask, If he has, why does he need? It is our ignorance that prompts such a question. The principle is, that the more you have in the Christian life, the more you can receive. So you cannot receive this great and ultimate love of Christ without having love already. It is a process which is progressive, and it is a geometric progression, not an arithmetical progression. The more you have the more you will get. Indeed, if you have nothing you will receive nothing: 'Whosoever hath not, from him shall be taken even that which he seemeth to have' (Luke 8:18). Anyone who says, 'I am a Christian, I am a member of a church, and I do not understand this teaching which suggests that I need to know much more of the love of Christ', is simply proclaiming that he has nothing. On the other hand, if you already have a measure of this love to God and Christ in you, even if it be but little; if you have love to the brethren, and to the law of God and to the Christian way of life; you are in a hopeful condition, and will receive more. And as you continue and have more love in your heart, you will experience yet more of the Lord's love to you. Indeed it will continue to increase in that manner to all eternity. The more we love Him the more we shall come to know His love for us. We may feel at times that no more is possible, but that is not so. Because you have what you have, you will get more. And on and on it will go for ever and for ever. 'Unto him that hath shall be given'.

You do not suddenly reach the summit of knowledge of His

love, so if you desire to reach this mountain-top and to 'know the love of Christ which passeth knowledge' you had better start climbing at once. Forsake the flat plains of the Christian life immediately. Turn your back upon the ordinary level and begin to scale the heights. Every step you take up that mountain will bring to your experience something new and fresh that you have never known before. It is a very high mountain; I would emphasize that still. And the devil will try to discourage you, and sometimes you will feel tired. At times you may feel that you have been walking for days and months and years, and that the summit of the mountain seems further off than ever. You may wonder whether the effort is still worth while. Do not listen to the discouragements of the devil. You are already on the way. Keep on. 'Unto him that hath shall be given, and he shall have more abundance.' At any moment, at the very next step you may well feel something more glorious than you have ever felt before. You will begin to see the sun shining with a radiance that you never saw in the plains. You will begin to feel a sense of exhilaration, and an awareness of a new power. You may not understand it at first; but it is the love of Christ being manifest to you. You will become conscious of increasing strength, and you will redouble your efforts, and go on from height to height and strength to strength. But you will never reach the end. It is the love of Christ which 'passeth knowledge'. It is the mountain of God, and He will lead you on throughout eternity. This is because God is inexhaustible, His love is eternal, His mercies are endless, His love is a 'never-ebbing sea'. But oh, the joy and the wonder and the marvel of knowing this love of Christ which passeth knowledge!

So far we have merely been surveying the situation. We must go on to 'comprehend' and to 'know' more about the dimensions of this love. In the meantime ask yourself the question: Do I really know the love of Christ? Seek it from Him! Go to Him, apply to Him for it! Ask God, 'according to the riches of his glory', to 'strengthen you with might by his Spirit in the inner man, that Christ may dwell in your hearts by faith; that you, being rooted and grounded in love, may be able to comprehend this with all saints . . .' Such a prayer is never offered in vain. Trust yourself to His love. He has loved you with an everlasting love; so leave yourself in His hands. Keep His Commandments, do all the things we have already considered, and keep on in the spirit of the hymn which says:

> *Wrestle and fight and pray,*
> *Tread all the powers of darkness down*
> *And win the well-fought day.*

17

'Breadth, Length, Depth, Height'

'May be able to comprehend with all saints what *is*
the breadth, and length, and depth, and height; and
to know the love of Christ, which passeth knowledge, that ye might be filled with all the fulness of
God.'

Ephesians 3:18–19

We now come to the actual petition which was offered by the
Apostle for the Ephesians. It is that, having been rooted and
grounded in love, they may be fully able to comprehend with all
saints 'what is the breadth, and the length, and the depth, and the
height, and to know the love of Christ, which passeth knowledge'.
We must remind ourselves that we are dealing, not with our love
to God and to Christ and to the brethren, but with His love to us.
So far we have looked at it very generally. We now proceed to
consider it in a more detailed manner. Before we examine the
nature or the character of that knowledge we must consider the
knowledge itself, and find out what can be known of the love of
God. The Apostle sets this before us in an extraordinary manner
in the words I have just quoted.

The terminology used by the Apostle in and of itself suggests
vastness. And there is no doubt that he chose to describe it in
this four-dimensional manner in order to give that very impression. It is interesting to speculate as to why he decided to do
this. I agree with those who say that probably he had still in his
mind what he had been saying at the end of the second chapter,
before he began on the digression which occupies the first
thirteen verses of this chapter. There he had been describing the
Church as 'a holy temple in the Lord', as a great building in which
God takes up His abode and in which He dwells. I am ready to
believe that that was still in his mind, and that as he thought of
the vastness of the Church as an enormous temple, he felt it to

be a good way of describing the love of Christ to His people. It is similar to the breadth, length, depth and height of such a great building.

Whether that is so or not, the Apostle was certainly concerned to bring out the vastness of this love. Indeed in doing so he almost contradicts himself by using a figure of speech which is called oxymoron. He prays that we may 'know' the love of Christ 'which passeth knowledge'. How can you know something which cannot be known? How can you define something which is so great that it cannot be defined? What is the point of talking about measurements if it is immeasurable and eternal? But, of course, there is no contradiction here. What the Apostle is saying is that, though this love of Christ is itself beyond all computation, and can never be truly measured, nevertheless it is our business to learn as much as we can about it, and to receive as much of it as we can possibly contain. So it behoves us to look at this description which he gives of the love of Christ.

We are about to look into something which is so glorious and endless that it will be the theme of contemplation of all the saints, not only in this world, but also in the world which is to come. We shall spend our eternity in gazing upon it, and wondering at it, and in being astounded by it. But it is our business to start upon this here and now in this life. It has ever been one of the characteristics of the greatest saints that they have spent much time in meditating upon the love of Christ to themselves and to all God's people. Nothing has given them greater joy. Indeed this is a characteristic of love at all levels; it delights in thinking not only of the object of its love, but also of the love it receives. Nothing therefore should give greater joy to all God's people than to meditate upon this love of Christ. Indeed, our chief defect as Christians is that we fail to realize Christ's love to us. How often have you thought about this? We spend time thinking about our activities and our problems, but the most important necessity in the Christian life is to know Christ's love to us, and to meditate upon it. This has always been the spring and the source of the greatest activity that has ever been manifested in the long history of the Christian Church. So let us try to look at it in terms of the dimensions which the Apostle uses.

* * *

Have you ever considered the *breadth* of this love? There are several places in Scripture where this particular dimension is put before us in a striking manner. In the Book of Revelation, for instance, we find the words: '. . . and hast redeemed us to God by Thy blood out of every kindred, and tongue and people, and nation'. And again: '. . . and the number of them was ten thousand times ten thousand, and thousands of thousands' (5:9, 11). The Book of Revelation seems to be particularly interested in the breadth of Christ's love. As it gives us the picture of the glorified saints, and of the Son of God with His redeemed, it uses these figures: 'After this I beheld, and lo, a great multitude which no man could number, of all nations and kindreds and people and tongues stood before the throne and before the Lamb' (7:9). One day, in the glory, we shall see that perfectly. But in a discouraging time like this in the history of the Church, what can be more encouraging and more exhilarating than to think of this breadth of the love of the Lord Jesus Christ? As Christians we are but a handful of people in this country today, a mere small percentage. That thought sometimes tends to depress us and to discourage us. The antidote to it is to consider the breadth of Christ's love.

The ultimate cause of the failure of the Jews was that they never grasped this particular dimension. They thought that salvation was only for the Jew. But those of them whose eyes were opened by the Spirit, including the Apostle himself, who was 'a Hebrew of the Hebrews', and had once held this exclusive view, had come to see that that narrow, naturalistic dimension was altogether wrong, and that in Christ there is 'neither Gentile nor Jew, Barbarian nor Scythian, bond nor free' (Col 3:11). Nothing is more encouraging and invigorating than to recollect that even in these days of religious declension there are in the world, in every country, in every continent – though differing in colour, in culture, in background, in almost everything – men and women meeting together regularly to worship God and to thank Him for His dear Son and His great salvation. In the glory we shall all be amazed at this, as we realize what the love of God in Christ has accomplished in spite of sin and hell and the devil.

Ten thousand times ten thousand,
In sparkling raiment bright,
The armies of the ransomed saints
Throng up the steeps of light.
'Tis finished, all is finished,
Their fight with death and sin;
Fling open wide the golden gates,
And let the victors in!

That is the glorious prospect on which we must dwell and meditate.

We have no conception of the greatness of this plan of salvation and of its scope. In Luke's Gospel we are told that certain people came to our Lord one day and asked the question, 'Are there few that be saved?' (13:23). I do not know the precise answer to that question, but I do know that Scripture teaches that we shall be astounded when we see all the redeemed gathered in – the 'fulness of the Gentiles', the 'fulness of Israel', 'all Israel' saved, and the redeemed standing in the presence of their Redeemer. It is not surprising that the Apostle should pray so earnestly that these Ephesians might know this because this changes your entire outlook when you tend to feel depressed, when you are tempted to doubt whether there is any future for the Church seeing that we are but a handful of people. The answer is to look at the breadth of Christ's love, to look ahead, to look into the glory and see the final result of His finished work. Once you begin to realize the breadth of His love you will lift up your head again, your heart will begin to sing once more, and you will realize that you are having the precious privilege of being one humble member in a mighty army, one in this thronging multitude who will spend their eternity in the presence of the Lamb of God, and enjoy Him for ever. The breadth of His love!

*   *   *

But let us attempt to look also at the *length* of His love. I am convinced that the Apostle specified these particular measurements in order to encourage the Ephesians, and us through them, to work this out in our minds. To meditate upon the love of God in an abstract manner is not very profitable. We have to work it out in detail as it has been revealed. The length surely conveys the endless character of the love of Christ. Sometimes we read in Scripture about the 'everlasting' love of God – 'I have loved thee with an everlasting love' (Jer 31:3). Have you ever considered the eternity of Christ's love towards you and towards all the saints? The dimension of length reminds us that this is a love which began in eternity. It was always there. The superiority of the Reformers, the Puritans and the evangelical leaders of the eighteenth century over us is seen in the fact that they were more theologically-minded than we are. We foolishly think that the most important thing is to be practical. We agree that the practical is most important; but the men who have accomplished most in this world have always been theologically-minded. A man who rushes into activity without studying theory is finally seen to be a fool. Think of a man who desires to begin to play with atomic power without knowing something about it!

The great evangelical leaders of the past saw the importance of theology and doctrine, and they spoke and wrote much about what they called the Covenant of Redemption which led in turn to the Covenant of Grace. What they meant was that, before time, before the world and man were ever created, an agreement was entered into between God the Father and God the Son. It was an agreement concerning the salvation of those who were to be saved by the Lord Jesus Christ. The Fall of man was foreseen, everything was known; and the Son, as the Representative of this new humanity, entered into a covenant with His Father that He would save them and redeem them. The Father covenanted with the Son to grant certain privileges and blessings to the people who were now given to the Son.

How important it is to meditate upon such a theme! To do so brings us at once to the realization that the love of Christ to His own began before time, away back in eternity. Christ's love to us did not suddenly come into being, it was there before the beginning of time. Hence we read that our names were 'written in the Lamb's book of life from the foundation of the world' (Rev 13:8; 17:8). This is, to me, one of the most staggering things of all, that I was known by Christ in eternity. I, in particular, and every one of us who belong to Him, in particular. We were known to Him, and our names were written in His book. What a dignity it adds to human life, and to our existence in this world, to know that He has set His heart upon us, that His affections rested upon us even in eternity! That is the beginning – if such a term is possible – of the length of His love towards us. Before time!

But let us look at this dimension of length as it works out in life in this world. The love of Christ for His own is from eternity to eternity. It began in eternity, and it continues in time. We can therefore always be sure that it will never change, that it will never vary, that it will always be the same. 'Jesus Christ the same yesterday, and today, and for ever' (Heb 13:8). And His love is always the same. There are no interruptions in it. This 'length' is an unbroken line. Whatever may happen, it goes on; it is not a variable, it is a constant. It does not suddenly cease, and then start again. 'Thine is an unchanging love'. It is a line, a straight line, it is not variable. It is a love that never gives us up or lets us go; it is a love that never despairs of us.

One of the most perfect expressions of this element of dimension is found in our Lord's own parable of the prodigal son. In spite of the fact that the younger son had been a fool and had gone to the far country, spurning the love that had been shown him in his home, and had wasted his substance on the gaudy and tawdry pleasures of that far country, his father still loved him and was waiting for his return and showered blessings upon him. This is the picture of the love of Christ towards His own – patient, long-suffering, bearing with us, never giving us up. Nothing is more wonderful than to realize that, even when we in our folly turn our backs upon the Lord, and even sin grievously against Him, His love still remains. George Matheson's hymn expresses it perfectly: 'O Love, that wilt not let me go'. It is a love that follows us wherever we may go; it 'will not' let us go. God has said, 'I will never leave thee nor forsake thee'.

How important it is that we should meditate upon this love and contemplate it! It is because we fail to do so that we tend to think at times that He has forgotten us, or that He has left us. When troubles and problems and trials come, and we meet difficulties and disappointments, we tend to ask, 'Where is His love?' The answer is that it is there, always there. The fault is in us, that we cannot see it, and have not meditated upon it, have not realized its eternal character, and have not grasped its dimension of length. The Apostle Paul expresses this truth in these words: 'I am persuaded that neither death nor life, nor angels nor principalities nor powers, nor things present nor things to come, nor height, nor depth nor any other creature, shall be able to separate us from the love of God which is in Christ Jesus our Lord' (Rom 8: 38–39). Nothing can ever cause it to change or to fail. As Augustus Toplady says:

> *Things future, nor things that are now,*
> *Not all things below or above,*
> *Can make Him His purpose forego,*
> *Or sever my soul from His love.*

What comfort, what consolation, what strength it gives; what a stay in times of trial and adversity! If He has set His heart and His affection upon you, they will remain there. Nothing will ever be able to pluck you out of His hand, nothing will ever rob you of that love. Nothing! If hell be let loose, if everything goes against you, nothing will ever cause Him to let you go.

And this will continue even into eternity. It has started in eternity, it manifests itself in time, and it goes on again into eternity. This line is unbroken. The author of the Epistle to the Hebrews states it thus: 'Wherefore' – in other words, because Christ has an eternal priesthood – 'He is able also to save them to the uttermost that come unto God by him, seeing he ever liveth to make intercession for them' (7:25). He will save us 'to the uttermost'. Nothing will be left undone. Whatever may happen, His love for His own will continue until the plan of redemption has been completed. Our Lord is in heaven making intercession for us now, and He will always be there. He is not like the earthly priests of the Old Testament dispensation who went in and out of the Holiest of all. They lived and did their work, and then they died and others had to take their place. 'He ever liveth'; He is always there and always will be. That gives us some idea of the length of His love.

*　　*　　*

But let us look at the *depth* of His love. As we look at each dimension we are tempted to say that it is the most wonderful of all, the truth being that that is true of each one! As we consider the depth we can do nothing better than to read what the Apostle wrote to the Philippians in the second chapter, where he shows that the depth of Christ's love can be seen in two main respects. First, in what He did! How guilty we are of reading hurriedly and perhaps thoughtlessly some of the most staggering words ever penned. In eternity our Lord was 'in the form of God'. He was God the Son in the bosom of the Father from all eternity. But the Apostle tells us that 'He thought it not robbery to be equal with God'. That means that He did not regard His equality with God as a prize to be held on to, to be held on to at all costs. Rather He humbled Himself, He divested Himself of those signs of His eternal glory. And He came into this world of sin and shame in the likeness of man, in the form of a man.

This is entirely beyond understanding; as the Apostle says, it is 'the love of Christ which passeth knowledge'. These are facts. He deliberately did not hold on to what He had a right to hold on to, but rather humbled Himself, and entered into the Virgin's womb, and took unto himself of human nature, and came and lived as a man in this world. Recall what we are told about the poverty and the lowliness of the home into which He was born. Recall what happened to Him while He was in this world, how He performed a menial task; He who was equal with the Father, the Son of God eternal.

Next consider what He suffered at the hands of men, the mis-understanding, the hatred, the malice and the spite. Think of His suffering from weariness and hunger and thirst. Think of men laying cruel hands upon Him, arresting Him and trying Him, mocking Him and jeering at Him, spitting in His most holy face. Think of cruel men condemning Him to death and scourging Him. Look at Him staggering under the weight of the heavy cross on His way to Golgotha. Look at Him nailed upon the tree, and listen to His expressions of agony at the thirst He endured and the pain He suffered. Think of the terrible moment when our sins were laid upon Him. He even lost sight of the face of His Father for the one and only time, and gave up the ghost and died, and was buried and laid in a grave. He, the Author of life, the Creator of everything, lies dead in a grave. Why did He do all this? The astounding answer is, because of His love for you and me; because He loved us. Such is the depth of His love! There is no other explanation.

His love shows yet greater and deeper when we remember that there was nothing in us to call forth such love. 'All we like sheep have gone astray'. We all have 'come short of the glory of God'. In our natural state we all were hateful and hopeless creatures. That we may have some true conception of our actual state and condition, and the depth of His love, let us turn to what Paul tells us about the condition of mankind until the grace of God in Christ laid hold upon us. We find it in the third chapter of his Epistle to the Romans, where we read, 'There is none righteous, no, not one: there is none that understandeth, there is none that seeketh after God. They are all gone out of the way, they are together become unprofitable; there is none that doeth good, no, not one. Their throat is an open sepulchre; with their tongue they have used deceit; the poison of asps is under their lips: whose mouth is full of cursing and bitterness: their feet are swift to shed blood: destruction and misery are in their ways: and the way of peace have they not known: there is no fear of God before their eyes. Now we know that what things soever the law saith, it saith to them who are under the law: that every mouth may be stopped, and all the world may become guilty before God' (vv. 10–19). It was for such people that Christ came, enduring the Cross and despising the shame. The Apostle makes the same point in the fifth chapter of the Epistle to the Romans. Our Lord had said, 'Greater love hath no man than this, that a man lay down his life for his friends'; but says Paul, 'God commendeth His love toward us in that, while we were yet sinners, Christ died for us' and 'If, when we were enemies, we were reconciled unto God by the death of His Son . . .' He did all this for sinners, for His enemies, for those who were vile and full of sin and who had nothing to commend them. That is the measure of the depth of His love. He came from heaven, He went down to the depths and rose again for such people. It is only as we meditate upon these things and realize their truth that we begin to know something about His love.

*   *   *

That brings us, in turn, to the *height* of His love. By this dimension the Apostle expresses God's ultimate and final purpose for us. Or we may say that this is the way in which he describes the height to which God proposes to raise us. Most of us tend to think of salvation only in terms of forgiveness, as if the love of Christ only purchases for us the forgiveness of our sins. Anyone who stops at that has clearly never known anything about the height of the love of Christ. Something of this height is seen in the fact that He died not only that we might be forgiven; He died to make us good. He died not only that our sins might be blotted out, but also that we might be given a new birth; not merely to save us from punishment, but also that we might be made children of God, sons of God, heirs of God, and joint-heirs with Christ. Such is His purpose for us, and all He did had that end in view. Furthermore, having given us this new birth, this new principle of life, He causes to dwell in us the same Holy Spirit that was in Himself. 'God giveth not the Spirit by measure unto Him', we are told (John 3:34). He gives the same Spirit by measure to us. That is the height of His love to us.

But, as the Apostle has already been reminding these Ephesians, His love to us is so great that He has actually joined us to Himself. We are united with Christ, He has made us part of Himself, of His own body. That is why we were 'quickened with Him' and 'raised with Him' and are 'seated in the heavenly places' with Him. In the fifth chapter of the Epistle he goes on to say: 'We are members of his body, of his flesh and of his bones'. It is His love that has done that for us. But we read in the Epistle to the Philippians that He is not only saving us in a spiritual sense, He is even going to save our bodies. He purposes to redeem us entirely, so we look for the coming from heaven of the Saviour, 'who shall change our vile body that it may be fashioned like unto his glorious body, according to the working whereby he is able even to subdue all things unto himself' (3:20-21). Have we realized that Christ will not be satisfied until our very body is glorified as His own body was glorified?

We must go even beyond that, and remember how in His last prayer on earth to His Father, He prayed these words, 'Father, I will that they also whom thou hast given me, be with me where

I am, that they may behold my glory' (John 17:24). Our Lord's love toward us knows no bounds; His desire for us is that we should be with Him and see something of that glory which He has shared with the Father from all eternity. He is not satisfied with purchasing our forgiveness and delivering us from the pollution of this sinful world, He wants us to be there with Him in the glory and to spend our eternity there.

The Apostle John in his first Epistle, describing this height, says: 'Behold, what manner of love the Father hath bestowed upon us, that we should be called the sons of God: therefore the world knoweth us not, because it knew him not. Beloved, now are we the sons of God, and it doth not yet appear what we shall be: but we know that, when he shall appear, we shall be like him; for we shall see him as he is' (3:1-2). A lover always desires that the object of his love should share all his privileges and blessings and enjoyments, and so our Lord desires that we should enjoy something of His eternal glory. He will not be satisfied until, as the Apostle says in the fifth chapter of this Epistle, We shall be 'a glorious church, not having spot or wrinkle, or any such thing, but that it should be holy and without blemish' (v. 27). This is His ambition for the Church and for all whom He loves. We shall be glorified in spirit, in soul, and in body: there will be no fault, no blemish, no wrinkle. We shall be perfect and entire and filled with 'all the fulness of God'. The final word is, 'and so shall we ever be with the Lord' (1 Thess 4:17).

Thus we have tried feebly to catch a glimpse of the love of Christ to us. Have you been feeling sorry for yourself, and somewhat lethargic in a spiritual sense? Have you been regarding worship and prayer as tasks? Have you allowed the world the flesh or the devil to defeat you and to depress you? The one antidote to that is to meditate upon and to contemplate this love of Christ. Have you realized its breadth, its length, its depth, its height? Have you realized who and what you are as a Christian? Have you realized that Jesus is 'the Lover of your soul', that He has set His affection upon you? Have you realized the height of His ambition for you? 'Child of God, shouldst thou repine'? Are we but to shuffle through this world? We should rather respond to John Cennick's exhortation:

Children of the heavenly King,
As ye journey, sweetly sing;
Sing your Saviour's worthy praise,
Glorious in His works and ways.

One great cause of the present condition of the Church is that we do not know Christ's love to us. We spend out time with petty things, and in fussy activities and discussions. Were we to be full of this love and of the knowledge of this love we would be entirely transformed. It is this knowledge that makes us mighty. That is why the Apostle prayed without ceasing that these Ephesians might 'with all saints comprehend what is the breadth and length and the depth and the height, and to know the love of Christ which passeth knowledge'. Oh that we might know it, and grow in it and rejoice in it. Let us follow Cennick as he continues in his hymn:

Shout, ye little flock, and blest,
You on Jesus' throne shall rest;
There your seat is now prepared,
There your kingdom and reward.

Lift your eyes, ye sons of light,
Zion's city is in sight;
There our endless home shall be,
There our Lord we soon shall see.

Fear not, brethren; joyful stand
On the borders of your land;
Christ your Lord, the Father's Son,
Bids you undismayed go on.

And then let us join Cennick in saying –

Lord, obediently we go,
Gladly leaving all below;
Only Thou our Leader be,
And we still will follow Thee.

18
Knowing the Unknowable

'May be able to comprehend with all saints what *is* the breadth, and length, and depth, and height; and to know the love of Christ, which passeth knowledge, that ye might be filled with all the fulness of God.'

Ephesians 3:18–19

Having looked at the breadth and length and depth and height of this knowledge of the love of Christ we must now address ourselves to a consideration of the nature or the character of the knowledge. Our understanding of this will obviously have a very serious effect not only upon our desire for it, but also upon our efforts and endeavours to obtain it. Because they have gone astray in their ideas as to the character of the knowledge many have never known it and never experienced it. The Apostle goes out of his way to help us in this matter by telling us three things about the character of the knowledge. He uses three terms which he clearly chose in a deliberate manner in order that their shades of meaning might become clear to the Ephesians, and to all who should subsequently read the Epistle.

The first word we must look at is the word 'comprehend' – 'That ye may be able to *comprehend* with all saints, . . .' The word means 'to take a firm mental grasp' of a thing, or 'to lay hold of something with the mind'. It describes the process of grasping mentally an idea or a truth. So a better translation here might be, 'that ye may apprehend with all saints the breadth and length and depth and height'.

There are, of course, different types of knowledge, and it is good for us to be able to differentiate between them. We need not go into that in detail, but must content ourselves with saying that the type we are looking at here is what is described as 'conceptual' knowledge, a knowledge of concepts and of ideas.

That is a distinct compartment of knowledge. There is an instinctive, intuitive type of knowledge, and there is this other kind of knowledge in which a concept, an idea, is held before us, and we are able to grasp it, to lay hold upon it, to possess it, and to make it our own. This conceptual type of knowledge applies when we are students of any subject, and trying to learn something about its first principles and its governing ideas. The emphasis is upon the fact that it is a mental process, it is something done with the mind. So the Apostle is praying, in the first place, that the Ephesian Christians may lay hold of this love of Christ with their minds.

At once we are confronted by what appears to be a contradiction; not only a contradiction of what I have been saying previously, but also a contradiction of what the Apostle himself has been saying. I have been at great pains to emphasize what Paul is clearly emphasizing, namely, that when you come to the realm of love you do not rely upon the intellect. We saw this when we were dealing with the importance of being 'rooted' and 'grounded' in love, and showing the only way to arrive at this knowledge of the love of Christ. I emphasized that we do not approach love with our mind, with our intellect, and that love alone can comprehend love. But now I am emphasizing the fact that the Apostle has deliberately chosen a word that brings out the mental aspect of this knowledge of the love of Christ.

How do we resolve the apparent contradiction? The answer is that when the Apostle says that he wants the Ephesians to apprehend, to lay hold mentally on the love of Christ, he is not saying that this is a purely intellectual process. He has already made that quite clear. That there is an intellectual element in it does not mean that it is purely intellectual. So Paul is not reversing what he has said previously. What he means is that there is always an intellectual element in love, indeed that intellectual apprehension is always an essential part of love.

There can be no question but that our main difficulty in these matters is that our whole notion of love is seriously defective. We tend to regard love in a sentimental manner, as if it were something purely emotional. The conception of love current in the world today is that it is purely irrational. Generally speaking, it is not love at all, but simply what is called infatuation, and there is no intellectual element in infatuation! But there is always a real intellectual element in love, an element of understanding. Love can give reasons for itself. This is the idea conveyed by the Apostle's use of the word 'comprehend'. At the same time, however, he is not saying that this love is to be apprehended by a pure act of the intellect, but that there is an intellectual element in love which we must never ignore. The Apostle himself elucidates this point in his Epistle to the Philippians, where he says that he is praying for the Philippian Church: 'And this I pray, that your love may abound yet more and more in knowledge and in all judgment; that ye may approve things that are excellent; that ye may be sincere and without offence till the day of Christ' (1:9–10). Note that he is praying that their love may increase in knowledge, and in judgment, and in a sense of discrimination and the ability to differentiate between things that differ.

Love in the New Testament must never be thought of as something intuitive or instinctive, something purely emotional and irrational. Two words are used in the New Testament to describe love – 'eros' and 'agape'. Now the Apostle is not referring here to what we may describe as erotic love. That is purely of the flesh; it is animal and carnal. It is the common prevailing view of love in the world today. The popular newspapers are constantly parading it. Indeed it is one of the main problems of this modern, sex-ridden generation in which we live. There is no more tragic aspect of the world at this present hour than the way in which pleasure and sex mania are debasing the currency of thought as well as leading to great tragedies in the lives of men and women. We are delivered from this evil when we realize the truth of what the Apostle is emphasizing by this word 'comprehend' or 'apprehend'.

In other words, love is something which can be contemplated; indeed we can say that love itself always has a contemplative element in it. If love does not make you think, it is not love; it is a purely physical instinct. Love enjoys ruminating, dwelling upon, looking at, dissecting, analysing and considering. That is an intellectual process involving the conceptual element. So we can say that the Apostle is virtually praying that the Ephesians, together with all saints everywhere, may begin to 'study' the love of Christ. Love is to be studied, and the more you study it the more you enjoy it. This can happen even with secular subjects. We sometimes say, speaking loosely, that we are 'getting to love' a subject. What we mean is that, as the result of our apprehension of the concepts, we are enjoying the subject.

The Apostle says that our first true response to this love is that we begin to lay hold of it with our minds. This is what we are doing when we are considering its breadth and length and depth and height. With our minds we are to dwell upon these dimensions, to talk to ourselves about them, and to meditate upon them. It is not merely a matter of having a feeling. It involves searching through the Scriptures and looking at the manifestation of the love of God objectively and externally. As we apply our minds to it we shall find our love to Christ increasing. It is not a matter of entering into a passive state and hoping that, as you do so, some great feeling will suddenly possess you. You have deliberately to apply your mind to it and try to get hold of the concept, and to obtain a spiritual understanding of the love of Christ.

How often do we meditate upon the love of Christ in the manner that we find in Isaac Watts' great hymn beginning with the words 'When I *survey* the wondrous Cross'? How often do we survey it? Consider the following illustration. You may be staying somewhere in the country, and you hear that not far away a marvellous view is to be obtained, though it will mean that you will have to climb up a mountainside for perhaps an hour or two before you enjoy it. You climb and climb, and finally you stand gazing upon the glorious panorama which stretches out before you. You look at it, and feast your eyes upon it, and drink it in: you 'survey' it. But you have to make the effort; you have to climb the mountain, and having got to the summit you do not merely take a glance at it. Such is the Apostle's meaning at this point in his Epistle. We are to scale the heights to gaze and gaze upon the divine love. It takes time to 'survey' and to meditate on Christ's love. It involves a mental activity, something conceptual.

*   *   *

The Apostle's second word is that we are to *know* the love of Christ 'which passeth knowledge'. This is in many ways a greater word and a stronger word than 'comprehend'. It does not speak of conceptual knowledge but of knowledge which is gained by, and grounded in, personal experience. This is no longer conceptual knowledge, it is now experimental, or experiential knowledge. I am not advancing any theory of my own; if you consult the Greek lexicons in respect of these words you will find that the authorites are agreed in saying what I have just explained. This is the difference between comprehending and knowing. This word 'knowing' as used in the Scriptures is always personal and experimental. Furthermore, the verb 'to know' refers to direct and immediate knowledge which is not the result of contemplation and of meditation; that is to say, it is not mediate, but immediate and direct. It is knowledge in the realm of experience.

We must note carefully the order in which the Apostle uses these two words. It is clear that conceptual knowledge should always come first; and it does come first. But it should lead on to this further experimental knowledge. We are looking now, not primarily at an activity of the mind or of the understanding. A more passive element enters in here. It describes not so much an activity on our part, as an awareness of something that is happening to us, and that is taking place within us. We are no longer looking at the love of Christ externally with a sense of wonder and of amazement; we are now experiencing it, being bathed in it, enveloped by it, being ravished by and filled with it. 'To know' describes our awareness of the fact that Christ loves us; that our Lord is making it plain to us, and telling us, personally, that He loves us with a love that is immeasurable.

Men and women with any spiritual understanding cannot read the New Testament without knowing that Christ obviously loves every Christian. None of us would be Christian at all were it not that Christ had loved us and had given Himself for us. The message of the gospel to us is that 'God so loved the world that he gave his only begotten Son, that whosoever believeth in him should not perish, but have everlasting life'. If I accept the teaching that Christ has taken my sins upon Him and has borne my punishment, it must be obvious to me that He did so because He loved me; it is a proof of His love. I look at this truth as it is stated in the Scriptures, I am aware of it and I believe it; I accept it and I rest upon it. But there is a sense in which it is still all outside me. I believe the concept, I rest upon the concept. How different that is from Christ Himself telling me that He loves me – making it plain and clear to me in an intimate, direct and experimental sense!

We are forced to use analogies at this point. You can be aware of another's love to you by the actions of that person, but what love craves for always is a personal statement. Love always desires a personal word; it is not content with the general manifestations. The Apostle is asserting here that it is possible for Christian people to 'know' the love of Christ in that personal, immediate, direct, experimental, experiential sense. Over and above the conceptual knowledge there is this experimental knowledge. This is such a glorious possibility that the Apostle says that he is bowing his knees before God the Father and praying incessantly that the Ephesian Christians may know it. He knows that they are believers, he has already reminded them of that; they have been 'sealed with the Spirit', and there are many other things which are true of them; but he feels that they do not *know* this love as they should. Not only are they lacking in a conceptual understanding of it, they do not know it in experience as he did; and so his prayer is that they may come to know it in that way.

*   *   *

The third term the Apostle uses in connection with the love of Christ is *passeth knowledge*. It really means 'surpassing knowledge'. I remember a friend once telling me of how he heard a quaint preacher in one of the Southern States of America expounding this term. What the preacher said was very picturesque, and in a sense true, and yet, in another sense it was wrong. The preacher was dealing with the statement of the Apostle in Philippians about 'the peace of God that passeth all understanding' (4:7). What it means, said the preacher, is that in coming down from heaven it passes by the head and goes straight to the heart! We have seen that in a sense he was right; but he was wrong in saying that it had nothing to do with the mind, that it passes by the head. What the Apostle is asserting is that it 'surpasses' it. Not 'by-passes' but 'surpasses'! It transcends it, it excels it. A good translation therefore would be, 'the surpassing knowledge of the love of Christ'; that is to say, though we may come to know it, we shall only know something of it; it is a 'never-ebbing sea', inexhaustible, and unsearchable. It is always much greater than you think it is; though you get more and more of it you are still only starting with it. This is a point at which language fails us completely, and the Apostle has to resort to this oxymoron in order to convey the idea that however much we have already, there is always very much more. So we forget that which is behind, and we press upwards and forwards, always making fresh discoveries. It is a knowledge-surpassing love, this love of Christ!

* * *

Having looked at the terms we have reached a point at which we must ask a question: Is this knowledge that we have been describing really possible for all Christians here and now in this life in this present world; or is this one of the hyperboles in which writers sometimes indulge? Is this simply an example of poetic imagination inflamed by an idea? But such a suggestion is not only insulting to the Apostle Paul, it is also to deny Scripture. Yet it is not surprising that people ask this kind of question because the Apostle's teaching here seems so remote from ordinary Christian experience. But the Apostle affirms that it is open to all Christians, and so he prays that the members of the Church at Ephesus, every one of them, and all saints everywhere, may come to have this knowledge of the love of Christ – the conceptual and the experimental. It is possible in this life and in this world.

The Apostle Peter, writing in his First Epistle to a number of Christian people whom he did not know, and whom he describes as 'strangers scattered abroad', says in referring to the Lord Jesus Christ: 'Whom having not seen, ye love; in whom, though now ye see him not, yet believing, ye rejoice with joy unspeakable and full of glory' (1:8). We also recall what we are told about the manifestations of the Son of God to those who truly know Him especially in the fourteenth chapter of John's Gospel. That portion of Scripture must ever be kept in our minds as the background to this prayer which we are considering. Our Lord says, 'At that day ye shall know that I am in my Father, and ye in me, and I in you'. 'He that loveth me shall be loved of my Father, and I will love him, and will manifest myself to him'. He is going to manifest Himself to the man who already believes in Him (14:20–21). And then in the seventeenth chapter of John's Gospel in verse 23 there is a statement in our Lord's prayer for His own, which is even more astonishing '. . . and that the world may know that thou [the Father] hast sent me, and hast loved them, as thou hast loved me'. Here, it is not a conceptual knowledge of the love of God, but an immediate, direct knowledge of God's love to us. *As* He loved His Son, so He loves us. We are to have that knowledge.

But someone may ask whether this teaching in the Scripture has been verified in the subsequent experiences of God's people in the long story of the Christian Church. The answer is that it has, and that abundantly. There are numerous testimonies to that effect in all the centuries, in all places, and among all types and kinds of people. This experience is not confined only to the apostles and some outstanding saints; but some most humble, unknown people have rejoiced in this conceptual and experimental knowledge of the love of Christ. For example, in a hymn by George Wade Robinson, a Congregational minister of the nineteenth century, we read:

> *Loved with everlasting love,*
> *Led by grace that love to know,*
> *Spirit, breathing from above,*
> *Thou hast taught me it is so.*
> *O this full and perfect peace!*
> *O this transport all divine!*
> *In a love which cannot cease*
> *I am His, and He is mine.*
>
> *Heaven above is softer blue,*
> *Earth around is sweeter green;*
> *Something lives in every hue,*
> *Christless eyes have never seen;*
> *Birds with gladder songs o'erflow,*
> *Flowers with deeper beauties shine,*
> *Since I know, as now I know,*
> *I am His, and He is mine.*

[237]

> *His for ever, only His:*
>   *Who the Lord and me shall part?*
> *Ah, with what a rest of bliss*
>   *Christ can fill the loving heart!*
> *Heaven and earth may fade and flee,*
>   *First-born light in gloom decline;*
> *But while God and I shall be,*
>   *I am His, and He is mine.*

Now, no one could write such words without their being true. It would be almost blasphemy to do so otherwise. It is experience alone which can produce such statements.

Many other hymns could be quoted. In a hymn translated into English from the Welsh of a great eighteenth-century Methodist Father, William Williams, we find the prayer:

> *Speak, I pray Thee, gentle Jesus,*
>   *O how passing sweet Thy words,*
> *Breathing o'er my troubled spirit*
>   *Peace which never earth affords!*
> *All the world's distracting voices*
>   *And enticing tones of ill,*
> *At Thine accents mild, melodious,*
>   *Are subdued, and all is still.*

He had known what it was to hear the voice of this 'gentle Jesus', and when he had temporarily ceased to hear it he longed to hear it again. Nothing else could satisfy him. Can we appropriate this language? Charles Wesley says the same frequently in such words as,

> *Jesus, Lover of my soul,*
> *Let me to Thy bosom fly.*

and . . .

> *Thou, O Christ, art all I want;*
> *More than all in Thee I find.*

But this experience is not confined to the poets. It is found in prose. The following words were written by a man who was by nature and temperament morbid and introspective, and of a sceptical disposition. He had been a Christian for twenty-eight years, and was a teacher, a professor of philosophy. He was far from what could be described as a superficial person capable of being carried away emotionally, but was a man whose business was to analyse and to dissect, and to live in the realm of concepts. But Daniel Steele came to know Christ's love in this experimental sense, and this is how he describes it:

> Almost every week, and sometimes every day, a pressure of His great love comes down upon my heart in such measure as to make my brain throb, and my whole being, soul and body, groans beneath the strain of the almost insupportable plethora of joy. And yet amid this fulness there is a hunger for more, and amid the consuming flame of love, the paradoxical cry is ever on my lips, 'Burn, burn, O Love, within my heart, burn fiercely night and day, till all the dross of earthly loves is burned and burned away.'

Again he says:

> The heavenly Tenant of my soul has changed all this. He has unlocked every apartment of my being and filled and flooded them all with the light of His radiant presence; the vacuum has become a plenum; a spot untouched has been reached, and all its flintiness has been melted in the presence of that universal solvent, 'Love divine, all loves excelling'. I now wish that I had a thousand-heart-power to love and a thousand-tongue-capacity to proclaim Jesus, the One altogether Lovely, the complete Saviour, Who is able also to save to the uttermost them who come to God by Him.

Let me quote also from the life of Edward Payson, a saintly man who lived in the United States of America (1783-1827). Unlike Daniel Steele, he was a strong Calvinist in his theology and in his doctrine. Payson again had been a Christian for a number of years, and had exercised a great ministry, and had been used and blessed of God before he experienced what enabled him to write to a certain clergyman:

> O if ministers only saw the inconceivable glory that is before them, and the preciousness of Christ, they would not be able

to refrain from going about leaping and clapping their hands for joy and exclaiming, 'I'm a minister of Christ, I'm a minister of Christ'! When I read Bunyan's description of the land of Beulah where the sun shines and the birds sing day and night, I used to doubt whether there were such a place. But now my own experience has convinced me of it, and it infinitely transcends all my previous conceptions.

Again, writing to his sister he says:

Were I to adopt the figurative language of Bunyan I might date this letter 'from the land of Beulah', of which I have been for some weeks a happy inhabitant. The Celestial City is full to my view; its glories beam upon me, its breezes fan me, its odours are wafted to me, its sounds strike upon my ear, and its spirit is breathed into my heart. Nothing separates me from it but the River of Death, which now appears but as an insignificant rill that may be crossed at a single step whenever God shall give permission. The Sun of righteousness has been gradually drawing nearer and nearer, appearing larger and brighter as He approached; and now He fills the whole hemisphere, pouring forth a flood of glory in which I seem to float like an insect in the beams of the sun, exulting yet almost trembling, while I gaze on this almost excessive brightness, and wondering with unutterable wonder why God should deign to shine upon a sinful world. A single heart and a single tongue seem altogether inadequate to my wants; I want a whole heart for every separate emotion, and a whole tongue to express that emotion.

And finally:

Christians might avoid much trouble and inconvenience if they would only believe what they profess, that God is able to make them happy without anything else. They imagine that if such a dear friend were to die, or if such blessings were to be removed, they would be miserable, whereas God can make them a thousand times happier without them. To mention my own case, God has been depriving me of one blessing after another [he was on his death-bed when he wrote this], but as each one was removed He has come in and filled its place.

And now, when I am a cripple and not able to move, I am happier than ever I was in my life before or ever expected to be; and if I had believed this twenty years ago I might have been spared much anxiety.

You and I are to apprehend, and to know, with all saints, this love of Christ. This is not an idle fancy; it is a glorious possibility. We should pray unceasingly for ourselves the prayer of Paul for the Ephesians, until with Daniel Steele and Edward Payson we can say with utter honesty that we dwell 'in the land of Beulah', and that Christ personally has made known His personal love to us.

19
The Innermost Circle

'May be able to comprehend with all saints what *is* the breadth, and length, and depth, and height; and to know the love of Christ, which passeth knowledge, that ye might be filled with all the fulness of God.'

Ephesians 3:18–19

We have now reached a point at which we must ask a simple and obvious question. Where do we stand with respect to the Apostle's message? Nothing is more harmful than to consider such teaching as he gives without applying it. We are not meant to have a mere intellectual acquaintance with these things; they are meant to be practical, we are meant to know them. The question we have to face, therefore, is whether we are comprehending this breadth and length and depth and height? Do we know 'the love of Christ, which passeth knowledge'? Probably we would vary considerably in our replies. The saintly Edward Payson, whom I have already quoted, provides us with a practical and convenient way of testing ourselves, by describing various groups or classifications with respect to this matter. He says:

> Suppose professors of religion to be ranged in different concentric circles around Christ as their common centre. Some value the presence of their Saviour so highly that they cannot bear to be at any remove from Him. Even their work they will bring up and do it in the light of His countenance, and while engaged in it will be seen constantly raising their eyes to Him as if fearful of losing one beam of His light.

There he describes the innermost circle of those who live for Him, and even do their work in His presence, and keep on lifting up their eyes to Him, lest they should lose even a single beam of His light. He then describes the next circle, working from within outwards.

> Others, who, to be sure, would not be content to live out of His presence, are yet less wholly absorbed by it than these, and may be seen a little further off, engaged here and there in their various callings, their eyes generally upon their work, but often looking up for the light which they love.

Then, he says, there is a third class:

> A third class, beyond these but yet within the life-giving rays, includes a doubtful multitude, many of whom are so much engaged in their worldly schemes that they may be seen standing sideways to Christ, looking mostly the other way, and only now and then turning their faces towards the light. And yet further out, among the last scattered rays, so distant that it is often doubtful whether they come at all within their influence, is a mixed assemblage of busy ones, some with their backs wholly turned upon the sun, and most of them so careful and troubled about their many things as to spend but little time for their Saviour.

There, I take it, we have a just and accurate analysis. There are Christian people who are to be found in those various circles, in those various positions. Indeed it is possible to be in the third circle which he describes, and yet to be a Christian. This circle contains Christians who seem to spend most of their time with their backs turned towards Christ, and who only very occasionally turn round to seek Him and look to Him. There are many possible gradations between that position and the innermost circle of those to whom Christ is everything and who can say with the Apostle Paul, 'To me to live is Christ, and to die is gain'. The point which I am emphasizing is that those who belong to the outermost circle are Christians, and the Apostle's prayer includes such. It has nothing to do, of course, with people who are not Christians; the Apostle is concerned about the relationship of those who have already believed, as these Ephesians had, and who had experienced much, as these people had done, but who, he still feels, do not know this love of Christ which passeth knowledge.

Payson goes on to say something which is, I think, profoundly true: 'The reason why the men of the world think so little of Christ is that they do not look at Him; their backs being turned to the sun, they can see only their own shadows, and are therefore wholly taken up with themselves; while the true disciple, looking only upward, sees nothing but his Saviour and learns to forget himself'. There we have the key to the Christian life and Christian experience. The one and only way to get rid of self is to look at Christ. You do not get rid of self by going into a monastery and becoming a monk. You do not do so by being a hermit on top of a mountain or by living on a lonely island all on your own. You can be as full of self in such places as you ever were. There is only one way to lose self, and that is, to love Another and to be lost in Him. As Payson says, if you have your back to the sun you are looking at your own shadow the whole time, and thinking about yourself, and looking at yourself and concerned about yourself. There is only one thing to do, namely, to turn round and look at the sun; then you will begin to forget yourself altogether. Nothing is more vital than that we should examine ourselves in this way.

Let us supplement Payson's evidence by introducing another statement, this time by a saintly man of God who lived in Scotland and who died about 1851 at a very early age. This man also held the same doctrinal views as Edward Payson. I add that fact concerning him because there are those who seem to think that these intimate experiences of the Lord Jesus Christ are only to be found among certain people who know little about doctrine and who hold vague, mystical, loose notions and ideas. The Scotsman, whom I am now going to quote, was not only characterized by his fondness for doctrine and theology and learning and understanding, but was, moreover, a brilliant philosopher and thinker. I am referring to W. H. Hewitson. He is not as well known as he should be, but he is one whom we can put into the same category as Robert Murray McCheyne. They lived at the same time and knew one another. This is how Hewitson writes:

Don't you think that in the case of many Christians regeneration is followed by a considerable period of, not darkness, but obscurity, such as that of the understanding in childhood, unfitting the soul to take in a whole Christ and consequently to enjoy a perfect peace? Such Christians live far below their privileges as accredited children of adoption, born to an inheritance not in themselves but in Christ.

It is possible for us to be truly regenerate and yet to be living as paupers, knowing little or nothing about the glorious possibilities. Someone writing about Hewitson describes him thus:

> From the time that he was brought clearly to see Christ as his All in all, his soul was filled with Christ's glory, as a present Saviour and ever-living friend. His communion with Him became more and more like that of one friend with another who are personally near, than of a distant correspondent. His holy ambition was to follow the Lord fully.

Here are two further quotations from Hewitson:

> A blessing it is beyond every other to have an ear deaf to the world's music but all awake to the voice of Him who is the Chief among ten thousand and altogether lovely.

> Blessed it is to be really in Him. No awakened soul should stop short of a realization and experimental enjoyment of union with the Lord. No converted soul should rest satisfied till it think every thought and speak every word in communion with Jesus. This would seem to a carnal professor, or to a child of God who is still to a great extent carnal, a standard far too high, but to have a lower standard is to be ignorant of our standing in Christ, of what we have in Him, of the closeness of our union with Him, and of the character we should maintain to be in keeping with our profession of faith in His name.

I cannot imagine a better way of stating what the Apostle Paul had in mind for the Ephesians.

* * *

In the light of all this, the question is, Where do we stand? Is it not far too true of many of us that we are like people who have been left a great fortune in someone's Will, but who do not seem to realize that that is a fact? It seems too good to be true.

We have been so long accustomed to poverty and to penury, and to struggling to make both ends meet, that though we are told we have been left a fortune, we go on living as if nothing had happened. Or, to vary the picture, we seem to be like people who have received an invitation to attend a great banquet, but who remain standing in the street outside the banqueting hall in the cold and the rain, looking occasionally through the windows at the bright lights within and trying to imagine the nature of the feast which has been prepared.

In the same manner many of us far too frequently say that the standard is too high, that these things are impossible. But what is all-important is that we should examine ourselves in the light of the New Testament teaching. Have we attained to this level? Indeed, let me ask a still more searching question: Are we up to the standard and the level of the Old Testament? We read of a Psalmist saying, 'A day in thy courts is better than a thousand', and 'I had rather be a doorkeeper in the house of my God than to dwell in the tents of wickedness' (Psa 84:10). Is that true of us? Can we say that? To help in this self-examination let us turn to Augustus Toplady. His doctrinal position was militantly Calvinistic, but in these matters he and the Wesleys with their strong Arminian views are agreed. This is how Toplady wrote:

> *Object of my first desire,*
>   *Jesus crucified for me;*
> *All to happiness aspire,*
>   *Only to be found in Thee:*
> *Thee to praise, and Thee to know,*
> *Constitute our bliss below;*
> *Thee to see, and Thee to love,*
> *Constitute our bliss above.*
>
> *Lord, it is not life to live,*
>   *If Thy presence Thou deny;*
> *Lord, if Thou Thy presence give,*
>   *'Tis no longer death to die:*
> *Source and Giver of repose,*
> *Only from Thy smile it flows;*
> *Peace and happiness are Thine;*
> *Mine they are, if Thou art mine.*

Whilst I feel Thy love to me,
  Every object teems with joy;
May I ever walk with Thee,
  For 'tis bliss without alloy:
Let me but Thyself possess,
Total sum of happiness:
Real bliss I then shall prove,
Heaven below and heaven above.

Note the experimental emphasis, and the word 'feel' in the last stanza. There are many who do not hesitate to say (thereby confirming Hewitson's supposition) that all this sets too high a standard; and they go further. They say that all this is nothing but mysticism, an unhealthy state into which throughout the history of the Church certain people have fallen, having turned in upon themselves and become introspective and self-centred. These are people, they say, who spend their time in feeling their spiritual pulse and enjoying experiences, who never do anything practical and are of no value to anyone. Such people, they say, just live on experiences; whereas we are meant, as Christians, to believe and to know the teaching which we have; in other words, just to see the truth externally in the Scriptures and to apply it in our daily lives. We are not meant to know and to talk about immediate and direct experiences, and of loving Christ personally. All that, they say, suggests a fevered imagination, not to say a condition which sometimes even crosses the borderline and becomes psychopathic.

There are, unfortunately, even many evangelical Christians who deny that God has any direct dealings with men today, and who hold feeling and emotion at a discount. They frequently substitute for true emotion a flabby sentimentalism. They are afraid of the power of the Holy Spirit, and so afraid of certain excesses which are sometimes found in mysticism and in certain people who claim to have unusual experiences of the Holy Spirit, that they 'quench the Spirit' and never have any personal knowledge of Christ. Indeed, they often go so far as to deny the possibility of such a knowledge.

This is obviously something with which we must deal, for if we hold this particular view we shall clearly never seek the knowledge of which the Apostle is speaking, and therefore shall never have it. How then do we answer this charge?

There is, of course, a false mysticism. This becomes quite clear in books on the subject and especially in the biographies of certain mystics. Beyond a doubt, there were aberrations in the lives of many of them, and much that was morbid and unhealthy. There is a morbid, introspective, selfish, impractical and useless type of mysticism. But because certain mystics have been guilty of such things we should not allow ourselves to be blinded to that which is a true and healthy mysticism, a mysticism which is taught in the Bible itself. There is always the danger of rejecting a true teaching because we dislike a false presentation of it. There are many people who are outside the Christian Church today for the sole reason, apparently, that they have known a man who was a Christian and a church member, who lived a selfish life and was unkind to his wife and children. They dismiss the whole of Christianity because of one unworthy representative! But that is clearly quite unintelligent, and the same people do not use that same argument in other realms. For instance in the realm of politics they would never say that they could not be Conservatives simply because they knew one worthless man who was an active member of the Conservative party. Likewise with the Labour party. In the realm of politics they do not judge in that way, but they do so with respect to religion. In the same way there are Christian people who use that precise argument, and because of certain excesses in the case of some mystics they dismiss mysticism as a whole. The corrective to such reasoning is to point out that the opposite to false mysticism is not a complete denial of mysticism, but true mysticism. But, above all, we must be governed by the Scriptures, and adhere to what is taught in them.

In this section, which we are examining, we find a true Christian mysticism. It shines elsewhere in such statements as, 'I live, yet not I, but Christ liveth in me' (Gal 2:20), 'I can do all things through Christ which strengtheneth me' (Phil 4:13), 'To me to live is Christ' (Phil 1:21). Paul speaks as a true Christian mystic in such statements. When we find him saying, in Philippians 3:10, 'that I may know him', he is not saying that as yet he has not 'known' Him in this personal sense, and only has an objective faith so far, and that he is hoping one day to get to know Him. It is because he already knows Him that he wants to know Him better; it is the cry of the lover for the loved one. He wants to spend more of his time with Him, he wants to know Him more intimately and completely.

The same teaching is found in the writings of the Apostle John. Sometimes a false distinction is drawn between these two apostles, and it is suggested that Paul is logical and legal and doctrinal, whereas John is mystical. That is an entirely false statement. Both are logical and both are true mystics. But again we must remind ourselves that this teaching is found, perhaps supremely, in the words of our blessed Lord Himself. In the fourteenth chapter of John's Gospel, having told them that He is about to leave them, our Lord says: 'Let not your hearts be troubled. Ye believe in God, believe also in me'. They were troubled when told that He was going to leave them. They had been with Him three years, they had looked into His face, they had seen His miracles, heard His sermons, and could always ask Him questions. But now He is going to leave them, and they feared that they could not possibly continue to live and be happy without Him. His answer was, 'I will come unto you. I will manifest myself to you' (vv. 18, 21, 22). But still more explicitly in the sixteenth chapter we find Him saying, 'It is expedient for you that I go away' (v. 7). It would be good for them that He was going to leave them and to go away from them in the form in which He was then with them, because (as He proceeded to explain) 'if I go not away, the Comforter will not come unto you; but if I go away I will send him unto you'. How can it be expedient for the disciples that He should leave them in the flesh and go away from them in the body? How can that be true if it is not possible for the Christian to know Him immediately and directly? Obviously the supreme blessing is to be with Him, in His presence and in His company. What He is really saying is that after He has gone and has baptized them with the Holy Ghost, He will be more real to them than He was at that moment. And this is what actually happened. They knew Him much better after Pentecost than they knew Him before. He was more real to them, more living to them, more vital to them afterwards than He was in the days of His flesh. His promise was literally fulfilled and verified.

But, beyond that, on the Day of Pentecost, the Apostle Peter tells his listeners: 'The promise is unto you and to your children, and to all that are afar off' (Acts 2:39). Our Lord's promise was not made only to the Apostles. The Apostle Paul was not present on that occasion, but later he had experiences equal to those of any one of the apostles. And as we find, he is now praying for the same blessing to come to the Ephesian Christians, and for 'all saints'. The Lord Jesus Christ is not among us in the flesh now; but in the Spirit He can be much more real, and we can know Him with an intimacy that the disciples and apostles did not enjoy when He was here in the days of His flesh.

The Apostle John summarizes this teaching for us in his First Epistle where he tells those early Christians that he was writing to them, 'that ye also may have fellowship with us; and truly our fellowship is with the Father, and with His Son Jesus Christ' (1:3). John's desire is not merely that they may have fellowship with him and the other apostles. They were enjoying that already in a measure. His deep desire is that they might enter into the fellowship which he and the other apostles were enjoying with the Father and the Son in order that their joy might be full. They already possessed the preliminary joy known by men who believe on the Lord Jesus Christ and who realize that their sins are forgiven; but the Apostle's desire is that their joy 'may be full'. It is the 'perfect peace' to which Augustus Toplady refers. And this is possible to every Christian. It is not a vague mysticism. It must not be thought of in terms of the false mysticism of people who retire out of the world and put on camel-hair shirts and scarify their flesh. That to which Paul refers is possible to all who truly believe the Word of God, and who believe in the Lord Jesus Christ.

This teaching, therefore, cannot, and must not, be rejected on the grounds of some vague objection to mysticism. But we must also deal with criticism about the practical aspect. We are living in days when the practical aspect of Christianity is being emphasized almost exclusively by some Christians. It is the day of activism and of activists. The world has never been so busy in trying to deal with its various problems; and the same is largely true of the Church. The practical, activist type of Christian is suspicious of a teaching which he thinks will make people sit down in isolation and wait for experiences. 'They never do anything else', he says, 'they are not practical Christians; they are not involved in all the usual activities.' Such an argument is based on sheer ignorance, not only of the Scriptures, but also of Church history. For the fact is that the men who have been busy in the service of their Lord and Master, in the long history of the Church, have always been those who have known Him best and who have rejoiced most of all in His love.

Let us start with the supreme example. What was it that made the Lord Jesus Christ Himself do all that He did? He tells us repeatedly that it was that He might glorify His Father. It was for that reason that He came from heaven to earth, endured the contradiction of sinners against Himself, and went steadfastly to Jerusalem and to the Cross. He claims in His high-priestly prayer as recorded in the seventeenth chapter of John's Gospel: 'I have glorified thee on the earth' (v. 4). His one motive was to show His love to His Father and the Father's love to Him.

But the same is seen subsequently in the lives of His people. Examine the case of the apostles and especially Peter, who had been so nervous and so cowardly, so afraid of being put to death, that he even denied his Lord. But after his baptism with the Holy Ghost and after he had really come to know the love of Christ, when the authorities commanded him to stop preaching, he answered them saying, 'We cannot but speak the things which we have seen and heard' (Acts 4:20). Having come to know this love of Christ, Peter had to tell all others about it. The Apostle Paul tells the Corinthians that 'The love of Christ constraineth us' (2 Cor 5:14). He could not refrain, Christ's love was pressing him and urging him on. There was never a busier or more active man that this great Apostle. This was not only because he was an active man by nature, but because the love of Christ was energizing him and giving him a compassion for sinners. Whatever might be happening, whether bonds and imprisonment or freedom, he must go and fulfil this ministry and tell the whole world about the love of God in Christ Jesus.

But this experience is not confined to the Apostles. I have referred previously to Count Zinzendorf, and his statement about 'his one passion'. We read concerning him that one day, while looking at a picture of the crucified Christ, he said, 'Thou hast done that for me; what can I do for Thee?' That is the explanation

of his subsequent career. In many ways he was the founder of
foreign mission work, sending missionaries to Greenland fifty
years before the founding of the London Missionary Society, the
Church Missionary Society, and others. It was his knowledge,
his 'comprehending' of the love of Christ that drove him on, and
many others with him.

Nothing stands out more prominently in the life of George
Whitefield than his consciousness of the love of Christ. He knew
it to an exceptional degree and you will find that it was always
after he had had some exceptional experience of Christ that he
was given unusual enlargement and liberty in his preaching, and
that men and women were broken down and melted before his
holy eloquence and his portrayal of the love of God in Christ
Jesus. Charles Wesley knew it equally well, and so writes:

> *Enlarge, inflame, and fill my heart*
> *With boundless charity divine!*
> *So shall I all my strength exert,*
> *And love them with a zeal like Thine.*

This has been true of God's greatest servants in all ages, in all
centuries, in all places.

Perhaps the greatest danger confronting the Church and
Christian people today, is that instead of realizing that the supreme
need of the moment is this knowledge of the love of Christ, we
spend our time and energy in organizing activities. We have made
of activity an end in itself. We say we must be 'getting busy'.
And in a carnal manner we are attempting to do God's work. But
how little happens! It is not surprising. We are forgetting the
true motive and the energizing power. We should not work as
Christians simply because it is good and right for Christians to
work. The motive is all-important. We must work because of the
love of Christ. We must not work because we decide to do so or
because we are told that now we are converted we must 'get
busy'. Our motive must not be to fill the churches again. That is a
travesty of the New Testament picture and manner, as is the
whole idea of training people to be witnesses and to do personal
evangelism. Everything today has to be organized, and the
impression is given that no Christian can witness without undergoing a course of training.

The answer to this modern idea is to discover what has happened in past centuries, and especially the first. There were no training classes and examinations and diplomas in those times. The secret of the early Christians, the early Protestants, Puritans and Methodists was that they were taught about the love of Christ, and they became filled with a knowledge of it. Once a man has the love of Christ in his heart you need not train him to witness; he will do it. He will know the power, the constraint, the motive; everything is already there. It is a plain lie to suggest that people who regard this knowledge of the love of Christ as the supreme thing are useless, unhealthy mystics. The servants of God who have most adorned the life and the history of the Christian Church have always been men who have realized that this is the most important thing of all, and they have spent hours in prayer seeking His face and enjoying His love. The man who knows the love of Christ in his heart can do more in one hour than the busy type of man can do in a century. God forbid that we should ever make of activity an end in itself. Let us realize that the motive must come first, and that the motive must ever be the love of Christ.

I end with the question which I asked at the beginning: To which of the circles do you belong? Are you pressing your way right into the centre? You may have seen people in a crowd, when the Queen or some other notable person is passing, trying to push themselves forward in order to have a front-line view. The same thing occurs at various games. There are those who always want to be in the front to have the best view. Are we pressing into the innermost circle? Are we seeking the Lord's face? Are we coveting the knowledge of His love? The Apostle prayed for every single member of the Church at Ephesus that he or she 'might be able to comprehend with all saints what is the length and breadth and depth and height, and to know the love of Christ, which passeth knowledge'. How tragic it is that any of us should be living as paupers, out on the cold street, while the banqueting chamber is open and the feast prepared. Let us search for the knowledge of the Lord in the Scriptures and read about it in the lives of the saints throughout the centuries. As we do so, we shall never be content until we are in the innermost circle and looking into His blessed face.

20

Seeking to Comprehend

'May be able to comprehend with all saints what is
the breadth, and length, and depth, and height.'

Ephesians 3:18

It remains for us now to consider the very practical and direct
question as to how we can attain to this knowledge. I assume that
we are now eager and anxious to know it and to experience it.
I am sure that when we arrive in heaven and in the glory we shall
be amazed; not only at what we shall then see and realize, but
still more at our blindness while we were here on earth. Then we
shall see clearly what might have been the case with us. We shall
see what we might have enjoyed. We shall see how we wasted
our time. We shall see how we allowed other things to come
between us and the most marvellous and blessed experience that
can be the lot of any man or woman in this world. And for this
reason I am pressing this matter so urgently upon your
consideration.

I have New Testament authority for saying that it is possible for
Christian people to know something of a sense of shame when
they see Him as He is. The Apostle John in his First Epistle
exhorts the early Christians to press forward in these respects so
that they may 'not be ashamed before him at his coming'. There
is clear teaching of a judgment involving rewards among
believers, so we must consider this matter in the light of that
teaching. The man who thinks that as long as he is forgiven, as
long as he is saved, and as long as he knows that he is going to
heaven, all is well, will discover that in adopting such an attitude
he has been rejecting his Lord's teaching. The Lord meant him
to enjoy so much more, and to use him to help others, and to
use him as a pattern and an example. So, apart from personal

considerations, we must look at this question from the standpoint that the extent to which we are failing to conform to this pattern, is the extent to which we are failing our blessed Lord Himself.

The picture often given in the New Testament is that God is our Father, and that as an earthly father is proud of his children, and likes to look upon them with favour, and to smile at them, and desires everyone to think well of them, so God as our Father in heaven delights in us and desires to show us as 'patterns and examples of His handiwork'. He wants to show His grace to others through us, and by means of us, as we saw when we were studying verse 10. For all these reasons it behoves us to discover how we, with all saints, may come to know this love of Christ which passeth knowledge. There is abundant teaching with respect to this in the New Testament. There is a sense in which the remainder of this Ephesian Epistle deals with this very subject. The Apostle proceeds in the following chapters to deal in detail with a number of matters concerned with conduct and behaviour, and that is one of the best ways of teaching how to attain to this knowledge of the love of Christ.

*   *   *

We can summarize this teaching in a number of principles. The first is to issue a negative, but extremely important warning. This matter must never be thought of in mechanical terms. By this I mean that it must never be assumed that, as long as we do certain things, then, inevitably and automatically, we shall enjoy the blessing. That supposition is never true in the spiritual life. To use an obvious illustration: there is nothing of the slot-machine mechanism in connection with the spiritual life. The cults, on the other hand, are all characterized by that very teaching. They all say in effect that you have but, as it were, to put your coin in the slot and pull out the little drawer, and you will have your piece of chocolate or whatever it is. Such a teaching is foreign to the New Testament, and if we begin to think about these things in such a mechanical manner we are doomed to disappointment.

I must elaborate this because, speaking from my own experience, I know this very danger, and know it to be a snare of the devil. It sometimes works in the following manner. You may be reading the biography of some great saint, for example, one of the people from whose works I have been quoting. There you read about a man who had been a Christian for years but who had never known this love of Christ, and who then tells you how he came to know it. It may have happened in one of many ways. Perhaps he had been seeking for years with nothing happening; then one day, as he was reading a book, almost casually, the whole page seemed to be illumined and he realized that God was speaking to him directly, and he came to know this love of Christ which passeth knowledge. The temptation that comes at that point is to try to discover which book he was reading and then to begin to read that same book, persuading yourself as you do so, that what happened to him is bound to happen to you. So you read the page, but it seems quite dead! The fallacy was to hold a mechanical view. The saint was doing this when he obtained the blessing; so if I do the same I also will obtain the blessing!

Or you read of men who testify that they had read their Bibles many times without ever seeing these things, but suddenly and unexpectedly as they were reading a given chapter the illumination came. But it does not come to you as you read the chapter. The fallacy behind that wrong approach is to forget that we are dealing with personal relationships, and that in the realm of personal relationships mechanical methods not only do not count, but they can even be the greatest possible hindrance. We are not dealing with some 'it' or an experience as such; we are talking about knowing 'the love of Christ which passeth knowledge'. We realize instinctively concerning the love of a human being that it is intensely personal and direct, so we must realize the same here.

We have to start by realizing that this is something which is entirely in God's hands, that He dispenses His blessings as He wills, and when and where, and in His own way. You can guarantee nothing in these matters. I mean that you cannot give any kind of guarantee that if you do 'this' then 'that' must follow. We know that in ordinary human relationships such ideas break down completely. The moment we sense that we are being bribed, or that someone is trying to manipulate us, at once every emotion and every real affection is quelled. This is equally true in the spiritual realm with which we are dealing. That is why it can be said that, while books and manuals on the devout and devotional life are of help and value up to a certain point, they can also be extremely dangerous. The devil can use them to introduce the mechanical notion, and we shall end by being further away from the One whom we are seeking.

*   *   *

Turning to the positive, we find that certain things are taught plainly and clearly in the Scriptures. The first is that there is such a thing as putting yourself in the way of a blessing. We cannot command blessings or 'claim' them. God in His own sovereign will and grace dispenses His blessings. But though we cannot command them, we can do what blind Bartimaeus did. We read that Bartimaeus had heard that the Lord Jesus Christ was going to pass along a certain road, and that he was wise enough to take up his pitch by the side of that road. That is what all of us can do. The Lord walks along certain roads; it is His custom and His habit to pass in certain directions. So all I can do is to tell you how to take up your position along the side of these roads. Put yourself in the way of blessings. I cannot guarantee anything; but I do know that the Scripture exhorts us to do certain things. I also know that every saint who has ever come to the knowledge of Christ's love, in this intimate and personal sense, has generally conformed to these things.

The first step is the one that Paul himself has already mentioned in verse 16. We must pray for ourselves without ceasing, as the Apostle prayed for the Ephesians, that God might 'grant us according to the riches of his glory to be strengthened with might by his Spirit in the inner man'. That is an absolute essential. It is essential – I must repeat myself because we are so prone to forget it – because of the greatness of the knowledge of His love. It is so great that it can almost shatter the human frame, so glorious that one can scarcely contain it. We remember the experiences of the young Isaiah, and the Apostle John on the isle of Patmos. But we also need it for this further reason, that as certainly as we set out in this endeavour we shall become the targets of the concentrated and unusual attacks of the devil.

This again is the universal experience of the saints. No one has ever been tempted in this world by the devil as the Son of God was tempted; and the closer we get to Him the more shall we be tried and tempted. The devil at first does his utmost to prevent anyone from becoming a Christian; but if he fails and we become Christian, his whole endeavour then will be to keep us as babes in Christ, to keep us at the stage of the first principles only, to keep us satisfied with the outermost circle of this realm. The moment we begin to grow and to develop, the devil becomes concerned, because we then become better recommendations for Christ. If we become men, and adult, the devil's kingdom is threatened, so he does his utmost to keep us back, and trains his agents and his powers upon us.

Let me quote the words of one who was a great authority on these matters. In a wonderful phrase he said, 'Baptismal moments are always followed by a temptation in the wilderness'. He refers, of course, to what happened to our Lord Himself when He was baptized by John the Baptist in the Jordan, and was setting out upon His public ministry to do His work as the Messiah. The Holy Ghost descended upon Him in the form of a dove. He is now equipped. He is sealed by the Father, He has been anointed by the Spirit to preach and to carry on the work of redemption. But we read that immediately afterwards He was led of the Spirit into the wilderness to be tempted of the devil for forty days. 'Baptismal moments are always followed by a temptation in the wilderness'. Anyone who has ever endeavoured to walk this road will know how true that is. The more we seek the Lord's face and the knowledge of His love, the more shall we become acquainted with 'the wiles of the devil' and 'the fiery darts of the wicked one'. The devil thereby pays us a great compliment; but we must remember that he is powerful and mighty, and if we go in our own strength and power he will certainly defeat us. We must therefore pray that we may be strengthened with might by His Spirit in the inner man, and also, as the Apostle expresses it in the last chapter of this Epistle, we must 'put on the whole armour of God'. Without it we are doomed to failure. If you seek to be near to Christ the devil will bring out all his reserves against you, and you will become aware of the depths of Satan in a manner you have never even imagined.

Christian people who do not know what it is to be subjected to an onslaught of Satan or to a Satanic attack are but babes in

Christ. He has no need to deal in this manner with the babes; but the moment you begin to grow and become a 'young man', the moment you become strong and know Christ and His love increasingly, you can expect temptation. Thus you find in the lives of all the greatest saints, that side by side with their glorious experiences of the love of Christ there is an awareness at times of a conflict, as if hell were let loose round and about them. It should be clear, therefore, that we are in a realm which is altogether different from the mechanical realm to which the teaching of all the cults belongs, as does all superficial evangelical teaching which assures us that 'it is quite simple'. As the Apostle says later in chapter 6, 'We wrestle not against flesh and blood, but against principalities and powers, against the rulers of the darkness of this world, against spiritual wickedness in the heavenlies' (6:12). We are following in His footsteps who was tempted of the devil in a manner so severe that it is impossible for us to conceive it.

The next vital matter which we must emphasize is that we must learn to seek the Lord Himself. I mean that we must not be content with ideas concerning Him, or with propositions about Him. Once more it is essential that we should emphasize that while doctrines and theology and understanding are absolutely vital to the Christian, it is always wrong to stop at these alone. We must go beyond them and realize that the purpose of all knowledge of doctrine is to bring us to a knowledge of the Person of Christ. As we have seen, 'That I might know Him and the power of His resurrection' was the ambition of the greatest doctrinal, theological teacher and preacher the Church has ever known. Without knowledge of doctrine we may become victims of a false mysticism, or simply remain babes in Christ. In order to be strong, and grow, and become virile and powerful, an understanding of truth is essential to us. But that should lead us to seek a knowledge of the Person Himself.

This is a very subtle matter. All who have ever been concerned about these matters know what snares are at hand. Sometimes a man, in correcting a false subjectivism, goes right over to the other extreme and becomes so entirely objective that he finds his soul and spirit have become dry. But extremes are wrong. The glory of the gospel is that it takes up the whole man, his mind, his heart, his will, indeed, the entire personality. If any one aspect is lacking there is a lack of balance. I emphasize this great danger of being content with ideas and truths about the Lord Jesus Christ instead of knowing the Lord Jesus Christ Himself. You become enamoured of the thoughts, the principles, and the concepts; and you can become so entranced by them that they may come between you and the Person. The very doctrine concerning Him may hide Him from your eyes. Nothing is more tragic than that! Many of us must confess to having been in that condition for years. It is a terrible snare; beware of it. It is as dangerous as false mysticism; it is as dangerous as remaining a babe in Christ.

Again, let me stress that we are to seek the Lord Himself, and not merely experiences which come to us in a general manner in the Christian life. Thank God for experiences of enjoying the reading or the preaching of the Word, experiences that come in meetings for prayer, experiences that come while singing a hymn, or the experiences we know in Christian fellowship, and in many other respects. Thank God for all such general Christian experiences. But while we thank God for them in this particular realm with which we are dealing, we have to realize that even they can be dangerous. This should not discourage us. It is true to say of every level in the Christian life that it has its own peculiar problems. There are many people who have no spiritual experience whatsoever; they have simply accepted certain things with their minds. Clearly that is totally inadequate, but having said that, we proceed to say that we have to be careful about experience. That there are special problems at each stage is true in our ordinary life in this world. The problems of childhood are not identical with the problems of adolescence, and the problems of adolescence are not identical with the problems of middle age; and the problems of middle age are not the problems of old age. On the surface, the teaching appears to be contradicting itself. But that is not so; as we grow older, we are in a different realm, we have arrived at a different stage, and we may have to do something at one stage which appears to be a blank contradiction of what we had to do at an earlier stage. It is precisely the same in the Christian life.

Let me put it yet more simply and directly. Many Christian people live on 'meetings' and not on the Lord Jesus Christ. They may feel disturbed or unhappy in their spiritual experience, and that may well mean that the Holy Spirit is dealing with them. But instead of doing what we are told here, and seeking this knowledge of the Lord, and this love of Him that passeth knowledge, they go to endless rounds of meetings. In the meetings they are made to feel happy, and they go home feeling that all is well. Again they feel miserable; then go to another meeting and the experience is repeated. They may go out every night in the week to some meeting or other, in order to keep themselves in a happy condition. What is happening is that they are living on meetings!

This is not only true in connection with meetings; it can happen also with books. I again plead guilty to this. It is possible to live a kind of second-hand spiritual life on books. It happens in the following manner. Feeling dissatisfied and disturbed, and having a consciousness within that our life is not what it should be, and that there is something much greater possible, we begin to read certain books, for example, the biography of a saint or a book which deals with the higher reaches of the Christian life. We greatly enjoy doing so and we are moved. Though we have not had the experience itself of which we are reading, we feel happier and better. We may do this for years without realizing that we are living on books instead of living on Christ. We can live on other people's experiences which we may hear in a meeting, or read of in books, but have no experience of our own. Because we have a comfortable feeling, and feel a little happier, we are content, and we do not go on to seek the Lord Himself.

Indeed, it is possible for us so to misuse the means of grace as to live on them instead of going on through them to discover the Giver of all grace. How subtle all this is! And it is so because we are still not perfect, and because of the wiles of the devil. The great rule which must never be forgotten is: Seek the Lord Himself. Seek the Person. The Christian life is not simply a matter of adopting a number of ideas; Christianity is not a philosophy, not a collection of thoughts and concepts. Its special glory, and what makes it unique, is that it not only teaches us to apply a teaching, but to get to know a Person, and to walk with Him in the light. It is personal, it is individual. The essence of success in this matter is to keep that ever in the forefront. We must not allow anything, however good and beneficial it may be in itself, to satisfy us in our spiritual life until we can really say, I know Christ Himself.

This is particularly true in the matter of prayer. Prayer really means talking to God, listening to God, and having communion with God. That obviously involves personal relationship. What do we really know of true prayer? We can so easily delude ourselves into thinking that if we get on our knees and think certain good thoughts, or certain good thoughts pass through our minds concerning God, that we are praying. I believe that God in His mercy is prepared even to accept that; but it is not true prayer. 'Our fellowship', says John, 'is with the Father, and with His Son, Jesus Christ'. By 'fellowship' he means knowing and walking with Them.

George Müller of Bristol knew more about prayer than most Christians; and you will find that the first thing he always did when he prayed was to make sure of a realization of the presence of God. He did not present his petitions until he had realized God's presence. This was the secret of that great man of prayer. We talk about Müller's great faith, and of course it was great faith; but the real secret of George Müller was not his great faith but the fact that he knew God and spoke to God as one who knew Him. Realization of the presence of God! You cannot know the love of Christ until you know Christ. That is why the Apostle tells the Philippians that his greatest ambition was 'that I may know him' (3:10). The first thing we have to do is to realize the presence of the Person, to seek the Lord Himself – not His blessings, not thoughts or teachings concerning Him. These things are excellent and we must continue to seek them; but we must not stop at them. We must go through them and use them to seek the blessed Person Himself.

The next principle in connection with this teaching, follows from that in an inevitable manner; it is that we must ever remind ourselves that the Lord Jesus Christ is to dwell with us: being 'strengthened with might by his Spirit in the inner man, that Christ may dwell in your hearts by faith'. What we need to do at this point is to realize that He Himself has said, 'Behold, I stand at the door and knock; if any man hear my voice, and open the door, I will come in to him, and will sup with him, and he with me' (Rev 3:20). When that becomes a fact, Christ is within us. I sometimes think that the realization of this is the most transforming event that can happen to anyone. It is the essence and the secret of sanctification. It is not a matter of trying to obtain something, it is not simply striving to live on a certain moral level; the secret of it all is to realize that He dwells within us, that He is in our hearts. The Apostle not only teaches this about our Lord but also about the Holy Spirit.

How slow we are to learn the great lessons of Scripture! In the sixth chapter of his First Epistle to the Corinthians, the Apostle deals with the very practical problem of sinning in the body. 'Flee fornication', he says (v. 18). But in showing how this is to be done he does not indulge in some vague moral teaching or give a lecture on the medical consequences of sin, or make some general appeal. His method is very different. He says, '*What?* know ye not that your body is the temple of the Holy Ghost which is in you, which ye have of God, and ye are not your own? For ye are bought with a price: therefore glorify God in your body, and in your spirit, which are God's' (vv. 19–20). The way to overcome sin is to realize that the Holy Ghost is dwelling in you, and that your bodies are His temple. The Holy Ghost is involved, as it were, in whatever you do with your body. '*What!*' The whole secret of sanctification, in a sense, is to know how to utter that word '*What!*' So when you are next tempted, when the devil comes and tempts you to sin in any shape or form, stop and say, 'What?' It is unthinkable! It is impossible! The Holy Ghost dwells within me; my body is His temple. Christ is in me.

We must talk to ourselves in that manner and apply the truth to ourselves. It is because we fail to do this that we are as we are, and what we are. We are to go on seeking this Person, and we must realize that He is within us. His Word is true and cannot be broken. I therefore am to live as a man who believes that the Lord Christ dwells within, indeed, who is fully persuaded that He dwells within. 'I am not my own'; He has come to dwell within me. My whole outlook and attitude will be determined by this realization.

Finally, having taken these steps, we must positively and actively seek His love. The Apostle is praying that these Christians may come to know it in its breadth and length and depth and height. Having realized the truth concerning this glorious possibility, we must now seek the Lord Himself, seek to know His love, and apply to Him for this knowledge. I say again, that this has been the universal practice of all those who have ever been able to testify that they have truly known this love. We find it stressed, not only in the New Testament, but in the Old. For instance, a deep longing and desire for the knowledge of God is expressed in many of the Psalms, for example, Psalms 42, 63 and 84; 'As the hart panteth after the water brooks, so panteth my soul after thee, O God. My soul thirsteth for God, for the living God: when shall I come and appear before God?' (42:1-2); 'Thy loving kindness is better than life' (63:3). And again, 'I had rather be a doorkeeper in the house of my God, than to dwell in the tents of wickedness' (84:10). This same desire is expressed well in a hymn in Welsh by William Williams, translated thus:

> *Tell me Thou art mine, O Saviour;*
> *Grant me an assurance clear;*
> *Banish all my dark misgivings,*
> *Still my doubting, calm my fear.*

Were we but to apply in the spiritual life what we know so well, and do, in the natural life, our spiritual condition would be very different. There is nothing that we desire more than to be told that those whom we love, love us. Actions are not sufficient, we like to be told in words. So let us plead with Him to let us know of a surety that He has loved us individually with an everlasting love.

21

Preparing for the Guest

'And to know the love of Christ, which passeth knowledge, that ye might be filled with all the fulness of God.'

Ephesians 3:19

We have seen that according to the teaching of the Scriptures (and it is amply confirmed by all who have experienced richly this knowledge of the love of Christ) that though we cannot claim this great blessing, or argue that because certain things are true of us we already have it, there are nevertheless certain things which can help to put us in the way of the blessing. Bearing all that as a background in our minds, let us proceed at once to the detailed consideration of what we have to do. The overriding and over-ruling principle is to seek the Person – not to seek general blessings, but to seek *Himself*. But there are also certain things which we have to do in detail. I am increasingly convinced that many go through their Christian life in this world without this knowledge simply because they have never moved from the realm of generalities to particulars. You must start with the general, but that must lead to the particular. It is useless to read a book which describes some great experience and to feel that you would give the whole world if you could but have it, if you then do nothing about it. We have to put ourselves in the way of the blessing as blind Bartimaeus did.

The first and obvious rule is to read the Word of God regularly. This Word has been given in order to reveal Him to us. In a sense the central purpose of Scripture is to reveal the Lord Jesus Christ. This is true of the Old Testament as well as the New. We recall how after His resurrection our Lord took two of His confused disciples through the Law and the Prophets and the Book of Psalms in order to show Himself to them in all the

Scriptures (Luke 24:27, 44). He is to be found everywhere in the Scriptures. A well-known hymn reminds us that the Bible is 'The heaven-drawn picture of Christ, the living Word'. He is to be found, not only in the Four Gospels where we see Him in His earthly state of humiliation, but also in the Epistles. They all refer to Him, they are all revelations of Him. So whenever you read the Bible you can find Him if you know how to do so.

It is possible for us to read the Scriptures in an utterly profitless manner. If you only read the Scriptures mechanically because you believe it is right and good to do so, or because you have been told to do so, you will probably derive little benefit. You may have an immediate sense of self-satisfaction and self-righteousness because you have read your portion for the day; but that is not to read the Scriptures. Every bit of intelligence we possess is needed as we read the Scriptures; all our faculties and propensities must be employed. Even that is not enough; we must pray for the illumination and inspiration of the Holy Spirit. Whenever we turn to the Scriptures we must talk to ourselves before we begin to read, otherwise our reading will not profit us. And we should do this, not only with the Bible, but also with other books or textbooks. We may spend hours with an open textbook in front of us looking at the pages and the words, but if we do not concentrate our attention we shall receive no instruction. You can do more in five minutes sometimes when you are really concentrating than in many hours when your mind is wandering and you are not applying yourself.

There is no book which calls for greater application and concentration of all our powers and faculties than the Bible. So we must talk to ourselves and ask ourselves certain questions such as: What do I expect to receive from Scripture? Why am I reading? What is my object? We must not stop at saying it is good to read it because it is God's Word. We must go beyond that and say to ourselves: This is God's Word through which He still speaks to us; it is a living Word. The fact is that God has continued to speak to the saints through His word throughout the centuries. Read their experiences and you will find that many of them, indeed virtually all of them, say that they have had their greatest personal experiences of the love of Christ as they were reading the Scriptures. Suddenly He seems to meet them through a particular word; He comes out of the Book, as it were, and they know that He personally is speaking to them.

And we can know like experiences if we learn how to read the Bible in a thoughtful, meditative manner. But meditation and contemplation are not easy, as we know from experience. To concentrate on what we are reading and to meditate upon it, demands effort and discipline. Contemplation and inward thinking are still more difficult. According to the manuals on the devout life, the ultimate stage in the holy life is that of contemplation. Few attain to it. So if in this matter of knowing the love of Christ we are left to ourselves we should find it to be well-nigh impossible. But God has stooped to our weakness, and He has provided us with the Word, with the pictures, the instruction and the teaching. So we must take full advantage of this and use it in our efforts to seek Him.

When you read the Gospels for instance, remind yourself that they are portraits of Him, showing us what He was like when He was here in this world. Then remind yourself that He is still the same essential Person. We must deliberately apply our minds to the seeking of Him and the knowledge of His love. In other words, we should go to the Scripture with a spirit of great expectation. We should go to it in a state of eagerness, asking, Is He going to speak to me personally, as well as indirectly through the Word? Having looked at the picture, remind yourself that He is still the same, 'Jesus Christ, the same yesterday, and today, and for ever'. That was the wonderful, thrilling discovery that was made by the various apostles who saw Him after His ascension.

There is a description of the risen Lord in the first chapter of the Book of Revelation, where John tells us how, when he was on the Isle of Patmos and Christ appeared to him, he was alarmed until our Lord put His hand upon his shoulder, proving that He is still the same, though He is in glory. We must deliberately remind ourselves of this and not be content with some vague notion of the Lord Jesus Christ. We must realize that He is still a 'Lamb as it had been slain', the One who was dead but is 'alive for evermore'. We must therefore seek Him. The Scriptures have been given in order to help us, and we must apply what we read in them. The great principle is, that true reading of the Bible involves thought, meditation, preparation of ourselves, and above all expectancy, and eager anticipation, a looking for Him, and a readiness to find Him everywhere.

*   *   *

The next essential in this quest is prayer. Earlier I had to emphasize precisely the same principle. We can spend much time in the posture of prayer and yet not really pray. That is why time-tables, though essential to many, can be most dangerous in these matters. Here again, spiritual instruction seems to be contradicting itself, at one time teaching the importance of discipline and regularity and then pointing out the dangers connected with that. The fact is that we need to know ourselves and our needs, and what we must avoid at given stages. We also need pastoral help in this respect. Let me state this in the form of an illustration. In modern scientific farming they have discovered this principle increasingly. If you want to obtain the best crops out of your land it will pay you to make a scientific analysis of your soil. You take a specimen of the soil and send it to the laboratory, and they will tell you whether it is too acid or whether it is too alkaline. You then have to treat it according to the analysis. If you put lime into land that is already too alkaline you will ruin your yield. But if your land is acid, then it needs more alkali. But it is interesting to learn that as you go on with that process you may find that the soil seems to have changed its character altogether. So you cannot say that, because the first specimen was acid, your land will need alkali for ever and ever. You may well reach a point at which it has become too alkaline; and you will then have to give it acid. You appear to be contradicting yourself, but actually you are simply being intelligent. You realize that you are dealing with living processes in the soil and not static inorganic material, and that therefore you have to treat it as it is at any given time. The same applies to the human frame and constitution. You can so correct over-acidity in your constitution that you produce a new disease called alkalosis. You have become too alkaline and you may have to take some acid to redress the balance.

The same principle applies in the realm of the spiritual life. We may begin, mainly because of natural disposition, by being slack and indolent. We realize that we must have a time-table and we adopt one. But quite unconsciously and gradually we become slaves of our time-table, and we need to be told to forget the time-table and experience more of the freedom of the Spirit. Because of our remaining sinfulness we go from one extreme to another. Thus we have to know ourselves, we have to be examining ourselves, and watching ourselves, and making quite sure that we have not lost sight of the grand objective, which is, to known Him and to know His love.

I urge therefore that there is nothing more important in connection with prayer than preliminary meditation and consideration of what we are going to do. This is what the saints have called 'recollection', which really means that you talk to yourself about yourself and what you are doing. Our chief fault is that we do not talk to ourselves as much as we should. We must talk to ourselves about ourselves. There is little purpose in beginning to talk to God and praying unless we realize our own condition. To fail to do so means that we may be going into the presence of God in a completely false state. We may feel that we have been dealt with very harshly and unkindly and indeed cruelly; we are full of self-pity; and we go to God in that condition and ask Him for certain things. Had we stopped to analyse ourselves, and had we spoken to ourselves quite honestly, we would have discovered that we were probably in a thoroughly bad and unworthy state, that we really needed to be whipped spiritually, and that the trouble was essentially in ourselves. Had we done that, how different our prayer would be! Before we begin to pray we must examine ourselves; and, then, having done so, we must remind ourselves of what we are going to do. We must meditate upon this again, and we must realize the possibilities. Above all we must think again of Him, our great High Priest above. With Isaac Watts we must say:

> *With joy we meditate the grace*
> *Of our High Priest above;*
> *His heart is made of tenderness,*
> *It overflows with love.*

To do this, and to realize that it is true for us, will transform our praying. We shall be truly seeking Him, and expecting a living response from Him.

Another important element is that of thanksgiving. When we read a great passage such as this which we are considering, or the experiences of those who have known the love of Christ, our tendency is to feel that this is what we need, that we would give much to possess it, that we must begin to pray for it and to plead for it; and just go on and on doing so. But such an attitude contains a real fallacy. It is like a child who is always making demands and requests of his parents but never shows any appreciation whatsoever. We must realize that God delights to hear our thanksgiving and our praise. Hence the Apostle, in correcting the tendency to anxiety in the Philippians, says, 'In nothing be anxious; but in everything by prayer and supplication with thanksgiving, let your requests be made known unto God' (4:6). Before we ask God for any new and additional blessings and benefits, we should always be careful to thank Him for what we have already received. If you believe that the Lord has died for you, thank Him for doing so. How often have you done so? That is a real test of our faith. If a human being does us a kindness we thank him at once. We say we believe that Christ died for our sins, but how often do we thank Him? The more you thank Him and express your feeble love to Him, the more likely you are to know His love to you in the greater sense to which Paul refers. The more prominent praise and thanksgiving are in our prayer life the more we shall know His love which passeth knowledge.

*   *   *

It should be obvious also that we must try to please Him in all things. This is quite self-evident when expressed in terms of a human analogy. If we love certain persons we instinctively try to please them; and the more we please them the more they will show their love to us. It really is as simple as that. Our Lord Himself states this quite plainly and clearly in John's Gospel: 'He that hath my commandments and keepeth them, he it is that loveth me. And he that loveth me shall be loved of my Father, and I will love him and will manifest myself to him' (14:21). And yet how often do we forget this! We tend to divide our lives into compartments. When reading the Scriptures or some good book, of the life of a saint, I see this wonderful possibility and I want it, and I begin to pray for it urgently and plead for it. But then I meet the hard facts and difficulties and problems of life, and I seem to forget it all. I become irritable, I become hasty, I become unkind and impatient. I revert to thinking on the human level again, and I do things which I should not do. The result is that my prayer is really of but little value.

The Bible is a very practical book, and it would have us see that love is not a vague sentiment. Our Lord tells us to show our love to Him by keeping His commandments. If we really do desire to know Him and His love, then we must do with all our might everything that He has ever told us to do. We are without excuse if we fail to realize this. It is taught in the Sermon on the Mount, in the Epistles, indeed everywhere in the New Testament. Let us therefore be diligent in the keeping of His commandments. Or, to state the matter negatively, let us realize how important it is to avoid displeasing Him. Certain things are quite incompatible with His presence. This is sometimes expressed in a phrase which I abominate. People talk about 'taking Christ with them'. That is quite wrong, for we do not take Him with us. The question is, whether He will accompany us if we do certain things. There are certain things which He did not do in the days of His flesh; and He still will not do them, for they are quite unthinkable in His presence. The Scriptures therefore warn very clearly about the danger of 'grieving the Spirit'. What applies to the Holy Spirit applies equally to the Lord Jesus Christ. That is why it is so important always to be thinking of Him and reminding ourselves that because we are Christians, Christ is in us and the Holy Spirit is in us, wherever we may go, or whatever we may do. If you long for the manifestation of His love, therefore, avoid the doing of things which you know He cannot abide, things which He hates, the things which sent Him to the death of the Cross. Avoid them!

I can illustrate this by a simple illustration which has often helped me personally, and still helps me. It is a simple, almost a ridiculous story of something which happened within the realm of my own experience; and it always reminds me of all I try to say to myself when facing this particular question.

I was brought up as a boy in an agricultural, rural district, where we all knew everything about one another and knew everything that was happening. There was a man in that area, a farmer's son, who was very much in love with a certain young lady, and wanted to marry her. And she was in love with him. But there was one obstacle to be overcome. This poor fellow, like so many others, had one weakness, and that was the tendency when he went to the market town once a week to drink too much. She hated this, so he fought against it. But suddenly he would break out again and fall to the temptation. She would then have nothing to do with him. The whole neighbourhood was watching this as it went on for several years. She made it perfectly plain to him that as long as he touched alcoholic drink she would have nothing to do with him. We all wondered what the outcome would be. What actually happened was that the man so loved her that he forsook drink once and for ever. The result was that they got married and they lived very happily together for many years.

That simple story illustrates the very essence of this matter. The choice confronting the man was, which did he really want the more, this girl whom he loved or the drink and the boon companions on the market day? He had to arrive at a basic decision; and his love for the girl was so great that he gave up the drink once and for ever. So he won her, and she gave her love and herself to him.

There are certain things which the Lord Jesus Christ hates and abominates: so it is a simple matter of logic to argue that if we hold on to such things and indulge in them we really have no right to expect a manifestation of His love. I remind you once more that you can be a Christian without knowing His love in this way; but if you want to be the kind of Christian Paul wanted these Ephesians to be, then you must give up the things He hates, cost what it may. Then you will find that in His own time He will smile upon you and manifest Himself and His love to you.

Each one of us knows individually the thing, or the things, that are standing between us and Him. Let them go! Strike them out! Even though they may be legitimate in and of themselves, if you are aware in your heart that they are a hindrance, they must go. 'If thy right hand offend thee, cut it off and cast it from thee'; 'if thy right eye offend thee, pluck it out and cast it from thee' (Matt 5:29-30). That is the Lord's own teaching in this matter. Please Him positively; and avoid everything that you know is displeasing in His most holy sight. And do this not merely for a limited period, such as Lent; do it for ever.

*   *   *

The fourth principle involved in this matter urges importunity, that is to say, concentration or whole-heartedness. We find it stated in the Book of Jeremiah: 'And ye shall seek me and find me, when ye shall search for me with all your heart' (29:13). That has become familiar in an oratorio, in the words 'If with all your heart ye truly seek me, ye shall surely find me'. The emphasis falls on the phrase, 'with all your heart'. Again in the Book of Psalms we read: 'Unite my heart to fear Thy name' (86:11). The Psalmist is conscious of the difficulty, so he prays God to unite his heart that he may seek Him with the whole of his being. Recall our Lord's teaching concerning the single eye: 'If thine eye be single, thy whole body shall be full of light. But if thine eye be evil, thy whole body shall be full of darkness' (Matt 6:22-23).

Nothing is more important in this realm than having the 'single eye', that is to say, looking in one direction, concentrating, shuttering everything else out of the field of vision; almost a monomania. This has been a great characteristic of the saints of God. Or take the teaching of our Lord, as recorded in Luke's Gospel, about the importunate widow. The unjust judge, who 'feared neither God nor man', is confronted by a widow woman who keeps on coming to the court with her petition. At last the judge, reduced to a state of desperation, decides that he had better grant her request. Go to God with the importunity of that widow, says the Lord Jesus Christ. Who else would have dared to say that? Importunity is essential. We are all ready to start, yet all too ready to be content with an occasional feelir.g, and occasional spasmodic efforts. But we must keep on, and persist, and never give up.

We must become more like the patriarch Jacob at Peniel. Think of him there on that critical night; in a few hours' time he was going to meet Esau. Recall his fear and foreboding. He had sent everything and everyone across the stream, and there he was alone, when suddenly a man came and began to wrestle with him. Jacob, sensing that this was God dealing with him, held on even to the break of day and uttered those immortal words, 'I will not let thee go except thou bless me'. That is the spirit we must cultivate, the spirit of concentration, the spirit of importunity, the spirit that says, 'I will not let Thee go'. As we do so, He will do various things to us. Leave the time element entirely to Him; but – to borrow a word used by the Puritan Thomas Goodwin – 'Sue Him for it', and keep on doing so, as the importunate widow did with the unjust judge.

*   *   *

That brings us to our last principle, which, like all the others, is also most vital. It can be described as responsiveness to the Lord's approaches. We are dealing with very sensitive and very delicate matters. Or, to vary the picture, we are on the mount of God, where the air is very pure and very rarefied, and slight changes are immediately felt. Responsiveness to His approaches means that you look for them, that you wait for them, and expect them. Often we are so busy reading the Scriptures and praying, and doing all we have been considering, that we feel that nothing is happening. But much may be happening, and the trouble is that we are so dull and so unresponsive or so busy, that we are not aware of it.

The Lord may well come at first very quietly and very gently. The Holy Spirit is compared to a dove, the most gentle of all the birds. That is a picture of our blessed Lord also. He does not always manifest the fulness of His love. He may only give you very slight indications of it. Human love can be expressed in just a look. The eye that can look severe can also look tender and loving. A mere slight flicker in the eye can tell us everything and bring us untold joy. Our Lord deals with us in that way. He is our heavenly Lover, and He manifests His love sometimes very faintly; He gives but a slight indication of it. So we should be looking for these things. His love does not come in one stereotyped manner. He has many ways of manifesting His love to us. Be always on the lookout for the slightest manifestation of it! Never 'despise the day of the small things'.

The moment you feel the slightest drawing or indication of His love, act upon it at once, however it may come. You may be reading a book, for instance, and not really thinking very much about this particular matter, when suddenly you become aware of some urge or some call to prayer. The whole essence of wisdom in this matter is to put down your book immediately, no matter how interesting it may be, and begin to pray. Do not decide to finish the chapter and pray afterwards. If you do so, you may well find that the wonderful, glorious moment has gone; and you cannot recapture it. The moment you feel the slightest movement or indication of His love, respond, act, yield to Him immediately. Whatever He calls you to do, do it at once. And as you do so, you will find that He will come more frequently, and the manifestations will be plainer and clearer. And then a day may come when it will be glorious in its might and power. As William Cowper says:

> *Sometimes a light surprises*
> *The Christian while he sings;*
> *It is the Lord who rises*
> *With healing in His wings.*

Let us at the same time give heed to the warning concerning this very matter found in The Song of Solomon in the fifth chapter, in the first six verses:

> I am come into my garden, my sister, my spouse: I have gathered my myrrh with my spice; I have eaten my honeycomb with my honey; I have drunk my wine with my milk: eat, O friends; drink, yea, drink abundantly, O beloved.

There we have the approach of the bridgeroom as he knocks at the door of the bride. But her response is:

> I sleep, but my heart waketh: it is the voice of my beloved that knocketh, saying, Open to me, my sister, my love, my dove, my undefiled: for my head is filled with dew, and my locks with the drops of the night. I have put off my coat; how shall I put it on? I have washed my feet; how shall I defile them?

Her beloved is there, even entreating her to open the door; but she is tired and feels that she cannot be bothered to get up and soil her feet again in opening the door. She desires him, of course, but it does not suit her convenience at that moment to receive him. 'I sleep, but my heart waketh'. She recognizes the voice but she cannot be troubled to rise at that moment. The account continues:

> My beloved put in his hand by the hole of the door, and my bowels were moved for him.

Having seen his hand she says:

> I rose up to open to my beloved; and my hands dropped with
> myrrh, and my fingers with sweet-smelling myrrh, upon the
> handles of the lock.

She thought that she was going to see him and to be ravished by
his love. But this is what we next read:

> I opened to my beloved; but my beloved had withdrawn
> himself, and was gone: my soul failed when he spake: I sought
> him, but I could not find him; I called him, but he gave no
> answer.

The Song proceeds to describe how she sought him. She went out
as she was and walked through the streets. People maltreated her
and she received chastisement and punishment and was ill-used;
but on and on she went, seeking Him. Thank God He did not
leave her for ever. He was simply teaching her this great and
central and all-important lesson, that whenever He makes an
approach it is to be grasped at, to be held on to immediately, with
a ready response. Do not delay it, do not postpone it. Thank Him
for every indication, however faint; run to Him, receive Him, be
responsive to Him. And as we are responsive to Him and His
every approach, He will come more and more to us; and we shall
find ourselves basking in the sunshine of His face, rejoicing in
His embraces, and drinking in His glorious and eternal love.

We find ourselves here in a very delicate and sensitive atmosphere. May God fill us with His Spirit and with wisdom and
understanding, so that we may be alive and alert and sensitive to
His every approach, and never find ourselves being chided by
Him for having refused, or having failed to recognize, one of His
tender approaches. Remember that He is saying to you, 'Behold,
I stand at the door and knock'. God forbid that there should be
so much noise in the house of our souls that we do not hear Him!
God forbid that there should be so much blaring of the world's
noises that we do not hear Him at all, and leave Him standing
outside. Let us be sensitive to Him, let us be ready, let us be ever
listening and longing and waiting for Him. And as we do so, He
will most surely come and manifest Himself to us.

22

'All the Fulness of God'

'And to know the love of Christ, which passeth
knowledge, that ye might be filled with all the fulness
of God.'

Ephesians 3:19

We now approach a phrase, a statement, which has been well and
rightly described by someone as 'the climax of all prayer'. It is
quite certain that nothing higher than this is conceivable, either
in the realm of prayer and petition or in the realm of experience.
We have been following the Apostle and observing how in this
prayer he has been, as it were, climbing a mountain. He has gone
higher and higher, step by step, and here at last he reaches the
summit. His desire for these Ephesian Christians, and his thoughts
concerning them, indeed, his exposition of the Christian faith and
the possibilities of the Christian life in this world, have gone on
from step to step, until he has arrived at this great height.

He was not satisfied with these believers as they were. He
thanks God for the fact that they, who had been pagans, and who
were far away from Christ and without God in the world, have
been 'made nigh'. But he is not satisfied; that is but the
beginning, not the whole of redemption. He had been called and
set apart to 'preach among the Gentiles the unsearchable riches
of Christ', and they still knew little about that. They had the
first principles, the beginnings of the Christian faith, but no more.
That is why he prays for them as he does. He wants them to
realize that there are higher, greater, infinite possibilities; and not
only so, but he wants them to partake of them; he is anxious that
they should enjoy them. So he has planned his prayer to rise from
step to step; and here we arrive at the climax, the acme, the zenith
of it all.

It has been said, and said rightly, that 'the perfection of man consists in his being full of God'. The Apostle is praying here for that perfection. The connection between the various steps in the prayer is important, so we note that the first word in this phrase is 'that'. It means 'in order that'. He desires them to know and to comprehend with all saints what is the breadth, and length, and depth, and height, and to know the love of Christ, which passeth knowledge, *that* ('in order that') they (and we together with them) 'might be filled with all the fulness of God'.

There is no more staggering statement in the whole range of Scripture than this. We are here face to face with the ultimate in experience, with the highest doctrine of all. We must approach it, therefore, with a sense of awe, and a sense of total inadequacy; and yet, thank God, with a sense of keen anticipation. There is no higher privilege in the world than to be looking together at this particular statement. Our natural minds, of course, are totally inadequate to conceive of this fully or to understand it. We have already been reminded several times in this Epistle that the eyes of our understanding must be enlightened by the Holy Spirit if we are to make anything of it. To those Christians who pride themselves on being practical, and to whom nothing matters but the social or political or cultural application of Christianity, this is nothing but an unhealthy consideration of our own inward states and moods and experiences. But those who harbour such feelings are simply confessing that their eyes have not been enlightened; and, as we have seen earlier, they have not realized that, historically, the men who have actually done most in the relief of suffering in this world have been those who have known most about 'the fulness of God'. Let us concentrate our attention on this in order that, under God, we also may become usable, and used of Him in doing something in this world to relieve its pain and its tragedy and its sorrow. The truly practical people, as distinct from mere talkers and theorists, are men and women who, like the Apostle Paul, know something of this fulness. They have been the greatest benefactors the human race has ever known.

*   *   *

As we come to examine this astonishing phrase we are again driven to start with a negative, because of the misunderstanding of those who come to it with blinded, natural eyes. I again emphasize that we are not dealing with a false mysticism. As we have seen, there are false types of mysticism which completely misuse and misunderstand this phrase. There are those, for instance, who talk about the possibility of our being dissolved or lost in God, in the Eternal or Absolute. Some of the eastern religions suggest it. Final salvation means absorption in the Eternal. You lose your individuality, and your personality, you become merged in the Divine and in the Eternal. But that is not what is meant by being 'filled with all the fulness of God'. What is called Pantheism also misunderstands this phrase. Pantheism teaches that God is in everything, and that therefore, in a sense, everything is God. Though differing from each other radically, these two teachings have one thing in common, namely that the distinction between God and man is lost. Such teachings are never found in the Bible, where there is always an essential distinction between God and man. There is none of this 'dissolving into God' or 'God in everything'; such ideas are a complete contradiction of the essential message of the Scriptures, and particularly of the teaching and the writings of the Apostle Paul. He had to contend against this very thing, as we find, for instance, in the second chapter of his Epistle to the Colossians. There were the so-called mystery religions, and various cults and other religions in his day, as there are still, and the Apostle had to fight against them. There was a teaching which spoke of a series of gradations between man and God, and how man could ascend from one level to another. The Apostle reprobates such teachings which he calls 'philosophies', and 'rudiments of the world'.

Others have thought that what we have in this phrase is what is called, in a figure of speech, hyperbole. They virtually suggest that the Apostle was being carried away by his own eloquence. Of course, a man may be carried away by his own eloquence, and by the momentum of his own speech. He may reach a stage where he has almost stopped thinking. That does happen, and a speaker or a writer may be using words and phrases without thinking soberly and seriously about what he is saying. This charge has often been made against the Apostle Paul; but it is an entirely false charge. The more we analyse his statements, the more we find that when he writes a phrase such as this, though his mind is moved by the glory and the transcendence of what he is saying, he has not forgotten the logical connection with what has gone before. He is still building up his case; the logic is still here, the framework has not been abandoned. His climax is still in keeping with, and indeed is the inevitable conclusion of, all that he has been saying hitherto. So it is not mere eloquence, it is not a case of piling statement upon statement, and throwing words upon words thoughtlessly. It is a logical, a clear, and a very precise statement. The Apostle is never guilty of 'art for art's sake'. He never deliberately sets out to be eloquent. His eloquence is incidental, indeed almost accidental. It is the glory of the truth that produces the eloquence. The Apostle was not concerned about literary forms or merely to produce an impression. He was neither a professional rhetorician nor a professional literary man.

The last misinterpretation to which I call attention is that which says that all the Apostle is really praying for is that the Ephesians might receive and enjoy the various blessings which God has to give us, and that when he says 'that ye might be filled with all the fulness of God', he is actually saying, 'that you may be filled with all the various blessings which God can give to the believing Christian'. I reject this suggestion also, and for this reason, that it would be an anti-climax rather than a climax. To refer only to the blessings of the Christian life after talking about Christ dwelling in the heart by faith, and knowing 'the breadth and length and depth and height', and knowing the love of Christ in an immediate and direct manner, would be pathetic. That is something of which the Apostle is never guilty. No! this is the final step in an ascending series. He has here arrived at the summit, he is standing on one of the great peaks of God's plan of redemption, than which there is nothing higher. This statement must not be reduced to the level of general blessing. He means what he says; we can be truly 'filled with all the fulness of God'.

*　　*　　*

What can be more important, therefore, than to know exactly what the Apostle means by this expression? Unfortunately the Authorized Version is somewhat misleading, for it introduces the word 'with' – 'that ye might be filled with all the fulness of God'. It tends to give the impression that it is possible for us human beings to be filled with all that fulness which is God. The Apostle is not saying that, as I must proceed to show. A better translation, as is generally agreed, would be, not 'that ye might be filled *with* all the fulness of God', but 'that ye might be filled *to* or *with respect to* all the fulness of God'. To translate it thus avoids that most unfortunate suggestion.

It is clearly impossible for a human being to contain the whole fulness of God. Yet, historically, there have been fanatics in the Church who, not realizing what they were saying, have actually claimed that for themselves. This has generally led to disastrous consequences. The devil is always waiting either to hold us back and to keep us from the truth, or, when we have entered its realm, to press us forward and make us claim too much, and to become fanatical. Fanaticism means that we have lost the balance of truth and the balance of faith, and it ends in a pathetic and tragic condition, and much harm is done to the Church. To be as God, is, for man, Christian or otherwise, a sheer impossibility. Indeed, it was the original sin of man to listen to the suggestion of the devil that this was a possibility. This is made clear in the third chapter of the Book of Genesis, where we read: 'And the serpent said unto the woman, Ye shall not surely die (if you eat of the fruit): for God doth know that in the day ye eat thereof, then your eyes shall be opened, and ye shall be as gods, knowing good and evil' (v. 5). In other words, the devil was suggesting that God was unfair to the man and the woman; that He was keeping them down, but that if they ate of that fruit they would become as gods, and equal to God.

We can perhaps best deal with the question before us in a theological manner. It has been traditionally the custom in the teaching of Christian doctrine and of theology to say that the attributes of God can be divided into two groups. Certain attributes of God are incommunicable; they cannot be communicated. But certain other attributes of God are communicable. The vital distinction between two groups provides us with the key to the understanding of our phrase, 'that ye might be filled with all the fulness of God'. If it were true to say that the whole of God may dwell in us, then everything that is true of God becomes true to us. But the incommunicable attributes of God make it immediately clear that that cannot happen.

The incommunicable attributes of God are, first, Eternity. God is eternal, 'from everlasting to everlasting'. Obviously that is an attribute which is incommunicable; it is something which belongs to God alone. Another attribute is Immutability. God cannot change. He is eternally the same, 'the Father of lights, with whom is no variableness, neither shadow of turning' (James 1:17). That can never be true of a man. Then there is Omnipresence. God is everywhere. God is in heaven; God is on earth; God is everywhere. The 139th Psalm gives a notable expression of this truth. This attribute again is plainly incommunicable. Then we think of God's Omniscience. God knows everything; there is nothing He does not know. Then comes Omnipotence. There is no limit to the power of God; it is an absolute power without any limit whatsoever. Obviously, again, it is not communicated to man.

Still more marvellous is God's absolute blessedness; He is 'the ever blessed God' (2 Cor 11:31). That leads to His glory. It is something of which we cannot conceive and is the attribute which shines through all the others. God is glorious in majesty and in power. The Bible speaks constantly of 'the glorious God', or 'the glory of God'. It means His perfection, His majesty, His splendour. 'No man hath seen God at any time' (John 1:18), and 'No man can see God and live'. This is because of the splendour of God, His majesty, and His glory. Even Moses when he desired to see God was told that he could not see His face. God told him that he would only be allowed to see His 'back parts' (Exod 33: 20–23). Those who have had a vision of God have generally been overwhelmed. The Apostle John on Patmos 'fell down as dead' (Rev 1:17). That was because of the glory and the majesty of Christ Jesus. All these attributes of God are His essential attributes and they are all obviously incommunicable. So we must never interpret our phrase as saying that God, as He is, can dwell in any human being, even in a powerful man. This is seen most clearly in our Lord's incarnation as explained in the Epistle to the Philippians, where we are told that He 'humbled himself' in order to come in the likeness of men (2:5–9).

The communicable attributes on the other hand can be given to man, and in the grace of God are given to man. One is holiness. God is holy; yet it is He who commands us thus, 'Be ye holy, for

I am holy' (1 Peter 1:16). So holiness is communicable. The same
applies to righteousness, rightness and justice. The central glory
of the Christian salvation is that 'a righteousness from God' is
now given to man through the redemption that is in Christ Jesus.
Other communicable attributes of God are goodness, love, mercy,
compassion, loving-kindness, longsuffering, faithfulness. Paul in
his Epistle to the Galatians sums this up by saying; 'The fruit of
the Spirit is love, joy, peace, longsuffering, gentleness, goodness,
faith, meekness, temperance' (5:22-23). The communicable
attributes of God appear in man as 'the fruit of the Spirit'.

We now begin to understand something of the meaning of this
great phrase. It must not be taken in an absolute sense; and yet
there is a sense in which it must be taken literally. It means not
only the blessings of God, it is actually the communication of
something of the fulness of God Himself. The question that now
arises is, How does this become ours? In what sense does the
Apostle rightly pray that the Ephesians, and all Christians, may
be filled to, 'in respect of', 'all the fulness of God'? It all happens,
we must remember, in and through our Lord and Saviour Jesus
Christ. It has all become possible as the result of His incarnation
and the work which He has done on our behalf. In other words
the fulness of which Paul speaks becomes ours through the indwelling of Christ in our hearts, and our knowledge of His love.

How carefully the Apostle builds up his case and works it out!
He has already prayed that Christ may dwell in our hearts by
faith, because without that, being filled with the fulness of God
is a sheer impossibility. But when Christ actually dwells in our
hearts by faith, and when we begin to know His love, then the
fulness of God begins to enter into us.

Certain parallel Scriptures help to elucidate this statement.
Take once more what our Lord teaches in the fourteenth chapter
of John's Gospel. He says, 'If a man love me, he will keep my
words: and my Father will love him, and we will come unto him
and make our abode with him' (14:23). There we have a similar
statement. Note the various steps – 'If a man love me, he will
keep my words: and my Father will love him, and we (the Father
and the Son) will come unto him and make our abode with him'.
The Father and the Son! This statement is in connection with the
doctrine of the Holy Spirit, the Comforter who was to come. In

John's Gospel we find our Lord prophesying what was going to be possible. Paul says that it is *now* possible. It had happened to him, and he is praying that it might happen to the Ephesians. First of all, he says, we must be strengthened with might by the Spirit in the inner man, then Christ takes up His dwelling in the heart by faith, and then God the Father – the Father to whom he is praying – grants that His fulness may dwell in us. It is the same order as we find in the fourteenth chapter of John's Gospel. Is it not astounding that we, while still in a world such as this, can be thinking of, and looking into, such amazing and glorious truths? We are not discussing abstract theology, this is intensely practical. The Apostle is praying that Christians might know this and experience it.

This becomes possible because of what is true of the Lord Jesus Christ. If Christ dwells in my heart by faith, then the fulness of the Godhead is in me by faith. Let me demonstrate that this is the case. The Apostle, referring to the Lord Jesus Christ, tells us in his Epistle to the Colossians that 'It pleased the Father that in him should all fulness dwell' (1:19). A little later he says concerning Him, 'In whom are hid all the treasures of wisdom and knowledge' (2:3). All God's wisdom and knowledge are hid in Christ. And then he goes yet further, saying: 'For in him dwelleth all the fulness of the Godhead bodily' (2:9).

How feeble is language! How puny is the human mind and understanding! But there is the truth! Look at Jesus of Nazareth. He is apparently a man in the body as all other men are. He is truly in a body; it is not a phantom covering of the flesh, He is as truly man as we are, His body is as real as yours and mine. And yet, 'in him dwelleth all the fulness of the Godhead bodily'. The whole of God was in Him. Or turn to the Epistle to the Hebrews. 'God', says the author, 'who at sundry times and in divers manners spoke in time past unto the fathers through the prophets, hath in these last days spoken unto us by his Son'. Then he describes that Son, Jesus, thus: 'Who, being the brightness of his glory, and the express image of his person . . .' The brightness of God's glory! The effulgence, the express image of His person! It is not only a likeness, but the very thing itself, the effulgence of God's glory and likeness.

The doctrine therefore is, that in our Lord and Saviour Jesus

Christ, 'dwelleth all the fulness of the Godhead bodily'. It follows therefore that if He dwells in our hearts, we also are filled with all the fulness of God. This is God's purpose for us. The Apostle teaches this explicitly in the Epistle to the Romans where he says: 'For whom he did foreknow, he also did predestinate to be conformed to the image of his Son, that he might be the first-born among many brethren' (8:29). We are to be 'conformed to the image of his Son'.

But apart from those other Scriptures the teaching is plain in the fourth chapter of this Epistle to the Ephesians. The Apostle there says that God has given apostles and prophets, evangelists, pastors and teachers, 'for the perfecting of the saints, for the work of the ministry, for the edifying of the body of Christ, till we all come in the unity of the faith and of the knowledge of the Son of God, unto a perfect man, unto the measure of the stature of the fulness of Christ' (11–13). Nothing less! This is essential Christianity. It does not stop at being converted and knowing that your sins are forgiven, and then remaining content with that for the rest of your life; it means entering into and developing unto the measure of the stature of the fulness of Christ. Our minds and all our powers must be exercised if we are to grasp this. If we are content with anything short of it, we are but babes in Christ, and unworthy of this glorious gospel.

Again, in this fourth chapter of the Epistle to the Ephesians, the Apostle tells these Christians that, in the light of all this they must 'put off concerning the former conversation the old man, which is corrupt according to the deceitful lusts'. 'Be renewed', he writes, 'in the spirit of your mind; and put on the new man, which after God is created in righteousness and true holiness', or 'holiness of the truth', God's own holiness. Such is the Apostle's method of teaching holiness. You cannot be holy without knowing your doctrine. Doctrine is the direct key that leads to holiness. It is only as we realize these fundamental truths that we can follow the inevitable logical appeal for conduct and behaviour pleasing to God.

*   *   *

We turn finally to consider how all this works out in practice. The answer is found in the glorious New Testament doctrine of the union of the believer with Christ. We are 'in Christ'; and Christ is 'in us'. Do not try to understand this, for it 'passeth knowledge'. The New Testament tells us that we are joined to Christ, that we are 'in Him'. In the fifth chapter of this same Epistle we find the Apostle saying that we are 'members of his body, of his flesh, and of his bones' (v. 30). This indicates the nature of the union. In order that we may have some idea of how this works, let us turn to some of the most glorious statements that are to be found in the entire Bible. The Apostle John in the prologue of his Gospel writes: 'And of his fulness have all we received, and grace for grace' (v. 16). Our Lord had taught this truth in the days of His flesh, when he said: 'I am the vine, ye are the branches' (John 15:5). Such is the relationship – that of a vine and its branches. This helps us to understand how we can be filled with the fulness of God. Already, in the first chapter of this Epistle to the Ephesians, referring to the Church the Apostle says: 'Which is his body, the fulness of him that filleth all in all' (v. 23).

The fulness of God, therefore, can reside in me in exactly the same way as the fulness of the life of the vine is in every individual branch and twig. The fulness of the vine, the essence, the life, that element in the sap that makes the vine the vine, is in the branches also. All the fulness of the vine is in the branches because of the organic connection, the vital union of all its parts.

Or taking it in terms of the body, the analogy which the Apostle used so frequently, it is true to say that the whole of the fulness of my life and being is in my little finger because of this organic union and relationship of the parts. The various parts of my body are not loosely stuck together; they are all living parts of me, and my blood passes through my little finger as well as through my head. The fulness of my head is in my little finger because of this organic, vital relationship. So I can speak of the fulness of my life being in my finger. There is a sense in which the whole of my life is not in my finger. I can live without my little finger; and yet while this little finger is a part of my body, my life is in it, my fulness is in it.

In other words, in order to understand this great truth concerning God's fulness in us, we must cease to think in terms of quantity, but must rather think in terms of quality. If Christ is in me, then 'all the fulness of the Godhead' is in me in the sense that that quality of life is in me. The amount varies considerably in the same man from time to time; it varies from one Christian to another, yet we all can receive of the fulness.

In this connection I once heard an illustration which I found helpful in showing how we can have the fulness, and yet have more of it. It involved blowing air into a bladder or into a balloon. You blow into it a certain amount of air and you can say that it is full of air; you then blow more air into it and it is still full of air, yet bigger than it was before. It is full of air on both occasions, but it had become bigger than it was at first. Or you can take a bottle and fill it with water in the sea. You can say that that bottle is now full of the sea. But then you can take a great tank and do likewise. The bottle and the tank both have a fulness, but they do not have the same amount. The fulness of the sea is always the same, and the little bottle has the same characteristics of the sea in its fulness as the tank has, though in terms of gallons there is a great difference. Thus it becomes possible for me to 'grow in grace' as well as in 'the knowledge of the Lord'. It does not mean that we are all identical, because we all have the fulness of God. It does not mean that we all have the same gifts. The Apostle goes on in the next chapter to say that there are varieties – some are apostles, some, prophets; some, evangelists; some, pastors; some, teachers; and so on. The gifts differ and the graces differ. But God is always one, and as the fulness of God is in all of us, we are all one, yet not identical in every respect.

Thus you may have two Christians, one of whom has a brilliant intellect, and the other a most ordinary person without any striking gifts. But, thank God, the latter can be filled with the fulness of God in exactly the same way as the former. This fulness does not suddenly turn the ordinary man into a genius; he does not suddenly become a brilliant writer or speaker or preacher or anything else. His gifts remain as they were, as do all his propensities and powers. But because Christ is in him, and because of his relationship to Christ, he is filled with the fulness of God as truly as the other man. What matters is not the quantity, but the quality of our relationship to Christ, and our experience of Christ's love. This lifts it out of the realm of gifts and powers.

I close by reminding you of how our Lord Himself expressed

this in the Sermon on the Mount, when He said, 'Be ye therefore perfect, even as your Father which is in heaven is perfect' (Matt 5:48). He said this when talking about love, about loving your enemies and doing good to them that hate you. God does so, He says, and you should be like Him and do the same. This does not mean that we have suddenly become divine and ceased to be men, we do not become eternal and immutable and absolute and omnipotent and omniscient; but the fulness of God in His communicable attributes enters into us, and we become capable of manifesting and displaying the same love to our enemies as God shows to sinners. This is what we should be seeking; this is why we should be praying this prayer, which Paul prayed for the Ephesians – praying it for ourselves day by day and incessantly, until we attain even unto 'the measure of the stature of the fulness of Christ'.

23

The Fulness Experienced

'And to know the love of Christ, which passeth
knowledge, that ye might be filled with all the fulness
of God.'

Ephesians 3:19

As we continue with this great subject I would particularly
insist upon our remembering that we are dealing with something
which is essentially practical, and not with some kind of vague,
abstract, mystical contemplation. The Apostle who wrote these
words was an evangelist, a teacher, and a pastor; and he was not
concerned to give the Ephesian Christians some mystical delight,
or some interesting metaphysical problem to unravel. He did not
write in order to stimulate them to argue about doctrine; he
wrote his Epistle in order to help them in their daily life and
living. Something essentially practical, a concrete reality, is here
before us. Indeed I assert that there is nothing which is quite as
practical as this. I am prepared to contend that this prayer of the
Apostle for the Ephesians is the most urgently practical matter
for the consideration of the Christian Church at this time.

I fear that it is true to add that the Church does not realize this,
for we have the curious notion that to be practical means to
indulge in activities on our own level. Such is not the New
Testament teaching. If we really desire to do things for God and
for Christ, then, according to the New Testament teaching we do
not begin to act at once, we must first make certain that we are
filled with the fulness of God, and the power that follows of
necessity from that. The Apostle Paul conceivably did more in
and for the Christian Church than any other man who has ever
lived, but let us never forget that he spent three years in Arabia
before he set out on his ministry. He did not begin to act the
moment he was converted. He did not subscribe to the modern

slogan, 'Give the new convert something to do'. Three years in Arabia! But when he came out of Arabia he came filled with the fulness of God and with power. That is the explanation of his mighty activity and the amazing results that attended his ministry.

The same has been repeated many times in the history of other servants of God throughout the centuries. There was never a busier man nor a more active man, in a sense, than John Wesley before May 1738; but he was a complete failure. But then, and as the result of that one experience in Aldersgate Street, London, when his heart was 'strangely warmed', his whole ministry was changed and shortly he became a powerful and mighty evangelist. In this he had followed the New Testament pattern. He came to realize that he lacked power, and especially that he lacked the knowledge of Christ which certain Moravian brethren had; he felt in fact that he must stop preaching; and it was only after he was given an assurance that his sins were forgiven that God used him and employed him in a striking manner.

So I argue that there is nothing more practical than this experience. The truly practical man is not the man who is always bustling and busy and excited and rushing about here and there, but the man who is being used by God the Holy Spirit. Oh that the Church might be brought to realize this! This is the revival the Church needs. It is only when she is revived by the Spirit that she becomes powerful. As long as we continue to trust to our own abilities and activities we shall avail nothing. The Church needs this fulness of God which alone leads to true practical activity.

I came across a statement recently which seemed to me to pin-point the truth about many Christians at this present time. The writer wrote: 'Religion seems to be part of the unexamined and largely unused background of life'. He was referring to those who are still inside the Church. Their religion tends to be in the background of their lives, and not in the foreground, not in the centre. Using what I regard as a very fine illustration, he went on to say: 'To the vast majority it can be compared with the knowledge that in an emergency "999" can be dialled'. Let every man examine himself. Where do these things come in your life? Is Christian truth something you like to have, and to know that it is there if you are taken desperately ill, or some loved one is taken ill, or if you are suddenly confronted by the loss of your income, or when some disaster takes place, or when you are on your death bed? Is it merely something you have in the background of your life? It is not meant to be in such a position.

That is not what the Apostle is praying for the Ephesians in this prayer. The Christian faith is not some reserve on which you can fall back. It is not some emergency station which you can telephone for help in time of trouble. It is not to be 'unexamined' and 'largely unused'. Do we know what it is to be 'strengthened with might by his Spirit in the inner man'? Is Christ 'dwelling in our hearts by faith'? Do we know with all saints the breadth, and the length, and the depth and the height, of this love of Christ which passeth knowledge, that we might be filled with all the fulness of God'? Are we concerned about this? Is this central in our thinking? Where does our Christianity come in our lives? Is it something which we remember only on Sunday morning, and forget even during the remainder of Sunday, let alone weekdays? Is it something of which we are only reminded now and again? Or is it the centre, the 'be all and end all' of our life and existence and activity? Paul is praying that it may become such; that, in fact, we may know all the fulness of God.

*   *   *

But what does this mean in practice? What does it mean experimentally? We have looked at it doctrinally, now let us look at it experimentally and from the practical standpoint. What is true of a man who knows what it is to be filled with all the fulness of God? First of all, it means that God dwells in us in such a way as to control us and all our faculties; indeed, that by a logical inevitability, God controls the whole of our life. He controls our thinking, and our feelings, and our outward actions. Man must be thought of ever in terms of his mind, his heart, and his will. If we are filled with all the fulness of God it means that God is controlling us in the mind, the realm of cognition; in the heart, the feelings, the sensibilities; and in the realm of the will, the outward actions, and all our activities.

This means first and foremost that our thinking is dominated by God, and by the mind of God. There are statements in the Scriptures which indicate very clearly what that means. Take, for instance, the statement in Paul's Epistle to the Romans: 'I beseech you, therefore, brethren, by the mercies of God, that ye present your bodies – your literal, physical bodies – a living sacrifice, holy, acceptable unto God, which is your reasonable service. And be not conformed to this world: but be ye transformed by the renewing of your mind, that ye may prove what is that good, and acceptable, and perfect, will of God' (12:1–2). Note Paul's mention of the 'renewing of the mind'. Our minds are never free. There is no such thing as 'free thought'. That is always an utter impossibility. I know that the Rationalist Press Association claims that the mind of man is free, but that is but the pathetic delusion of man in sin. The mind by nature, and as the result of sin, is always controlled by the world and the outlook of the world. The difference between a man who is not a Christian and a man who is a Christian is that whereas the non-Christian's mind is controlled by the world, the Christian's mind has been 'transformed' and has been 'renewed' by the Holy Spirit. The result is that the Christian man is now able to think in a spiritual manner, whereas formerly he could not do so.

A particularly clear exposition of this truth is found in Paul's First Epistle to the Corinthians. The Apostle explains that the mind of the natural man, 'receiveth not the things of the Spirit of God'. 'They are foolishness unto him and he cannot know them'. He also says: 'For what man knoweth the things of a man, save the spirit of man which is in him? even so the things of God knoweth no man, but the Spirit of God'. The natural man does not receive them and cannot know them 'because they are spiritually discerned'. Then he adds: 'But he that is spiritual judgeth all things, yet he himself is judged of no man. For who hath known the mind of the Lord, that he may instruct him? But we have the mind of Christ' (2:11–16). The Apostle means that if we are filled with all the fulness of God, and if Christ dwells in our hearts by faith, then we 'have the mind of Christ'. This is inevitable, as the Apostle claims.

In other words Paul says that the man who is filled with all the fulness of God is a man who can think spiritually. There is nothing more glorious, nothing more romantic about the Christian life than the way in which it entirely changes a man's type of thinking, indeed his whole mode and method of thinking. Are we clear about the difference between thinking naturally and thinking spiritually? The Christian not only has a new outlook but also a new way and type of thinking. It follows from this, that a good way of testing whether we are Christians, is our reaction to portions of Scripture such as this which we are examining. Do we feel that it is utterly strange, or does it speak to us? The Apostle thought in a spiritual manner, and he writes not in the words of man's thinking or in man's idiom, but according to the Spirit. The terminology is spiritual, indeed everything is spiritual. And, of course, without a renewed, a transformed, mind these things are foolishness to us. But to the man in whom Christ dwells, to the man who has this 'fulness of God' within him, to the man whose mind is now being governed and controlled by God, they are everything, and his greatest delight. This is happily expressed in the well-known hymn of Frances Ridley Havergal,

Take my life, and let it be . . .

In one of its verses she has this expression:

Take my intellect, and use
Every power as Thou shalt choose.

It is very difficult to express these things in words, but the whole mode of thinking is essentially different. It is unlike political or philosophical thinking; it is spiritual in nature. That is why a man who has been gifted with intellect can think spiritually and understand Scripture much more successfully than a man who has a great brain but no spiritual understanding. The Christian faith necessitates an entirely different type and mode of thinking. The new man in Christ has a spiritual sense, a spiritual instinct, which enables him to follow and understand spiritual truth which means nothing to the natural man, the non-Christian.

*   *   *

The second thing brought under control is the emotional part of our being, where feeling dwells. This again is equally inevitable. The man in whom all the fulness of God dwells is controlled by the love of God. This is seen supremely in the case of our Lord Himself, and as He dwells in us, it becomes characteristic of us. He says repeatedly that He had not come into the world to do His own will, He had come to please and to glorify the Father.

And He could say at the end of His earthly course, 'Father, I have glorified thee on the earth' (John 17:4). In other words, when God controls our hearts we have ceased to be governed by self. When the love of God comes in, the love of self goes out. And when the love of self goes out and the love of God comes in, we begin to love others.

One of the most striking examples and illustrations of this is to be found in the case of the martyr Stephen. He was being condemned unjustly and being stoned to death, yet his prayer is, 'Lord, lay not this sin to their charge' (Acts 7:60). He was so much delivered from self that, like his blessed Lord and Master before him, he could pray for his enemies; he could love his enemies and pray God to have mercy upon them. We find the same spirit in the Apostle Paul. In his First Epistle to the Corinthians he says: 'With me it is a very small thing that I should be judged of you, or of man's judgment; yea, I judge not mine own self' (4:3). What a transformation! There was a time when he had been very sensitive to judgment and criticism. He judged others but he hated being judged himself. But all had been changed. Why? Because he was filled with the love of God! The old love of self and concern about self had gone. He was controlled by God and so what concerned him now was not what people said and thought about him, but what they thought about God and the Lord Jesus Christ.

In the same way the will is controlled by God, as are all our actions and activities. Our Lord says of Himself, 'I came down from heaven, not to do mine own will, but the will of him that sent me' (John 6:38). The Son of God did not hold on to His prerogatives; He humbled Himself, He became a servant, He set aside His own will, and all He said and all He did was determined by the will of the Father.

This was also true of the Apostle Paul. In a lyrical passage in the Book of Acts we find him saying farewell to the elders of the Church at Ephesus. He was on his way to Jerusalem and he says, 'I know not the things that shall befall me there: save that the Holy Ghost witnesseth in every city, saying that bonds and afflictions abide me. But none of these things move me, neither count I my life dear unto myself, so that I might finish my course with joy, and the ministry which I have received of the Lord

Jesus, to testify the gospel of the grace of God' (20:22–24). His will was entirely lost in the will of his Lord.

> *Take my will, and make it Thine;*
> *It shall be no longer mine,*

had been his prayer, and it had been answered, it had come to pass. Later in Acts we find an almost exact repetition of what he said at Ephesus. Certain friends were pleading with Paul not to go to Jerusalem, because they knew that there he would be dealt with severely. But Paul answered: 'What mean ye to weep and to break mine heart? for I am ready not to be bound only, but also to die at Jerusalem for the name of the Lord Jesus' (21:13).He had no will of his own, it had become absorbed in that of His Lord; he had surrendered it, it was lost in His. He was entirely governed by the mind and the heart and the will of the Lord Jesus Christ who dwelt in his heart by faith.

All this is the first inevitable result of being 'filled with all the fulness of God'. It is expressed in an incomparable manner in one of Charles Wesley's greatest hymns:

> *Give me the faith which can remove*
> *And sink the mountain to a plain;*
> *Give me the child-like, praying love*
> *Which longs to build Thy house again;*
> *Thy love, let it my heart o'erpower,*
> *Let it my ransomed soul devour.*
>
> *I would the precious time redeem,*
> *And longer live for this alone –*
> *To spend and to be spent for them*
> *Who have not yet my Saviour known;*
> *Fully on these my mission prove,*
> *And only breathe, to breathe Thy love.*
>
> *My talents, gifts, and graces, Lord,*
> *Into Thy blessed hands receive;*
> *And let me live to preach Thy word,*
> *And let me to Thy glory live;*
> *My every sacred moment spend*
> *In publishing the sinners' Friend.*

> *Enlarge, inflame, and fill my heart*
> *With boundless charity divine;*
> *So shall I all my strength exert,*
> *   And love them with a zeal like Thine;*
> *And lead them to Thine open side,*
> *The sheep for whom their Shepherd died.*

Charles Wesley tells us in those moving words what he prayed for himself, and it is but a reflection of what Paul was praying for the Ephesians. When the fulness of God dwells in us, the mind, the heart and the will are subdued by and controlled by the Lord Jesus Christ.

*   *   *

But secondly, a man who is filled with all the fulness of God is a man whose every spiritual aim and instinct is satisfied. The moment we are born again, or regenerated, the moment this new principle of life is put into us, the moment we become partakers of the divine nature, new instincts, new desires, new aims, new objectives come into being. These begin to stir within us; we are anxious to see their fulfilment; and they become increasingly fulfilled and satisfied. For instance, the moment we have this life within us, we begin to have a desire which we had never known before to know God. I do not say to know 'about' God, but to 'know' Him. This is what the Psalmist knew: 'As the hart panteth after the waterbrooks, so panteth my soul after thee, O God. My soul thirsteth for God, for the living God. When shall I come and appear before God'? (42:1-2). Do we know that desire? Is that desire being satisfied? 'That I might know Him', says Paul. 'This is life eternal, that they might know thee, the only true God, and Jesus Christ whom thou hast sent' (John 17:3). Not to know about Him abstractly, theoretically, so that you can talk and argue about Him; but an intimacy, a directness, a true knowledge of God!

This desire, in some degree, must be in every child of God. He is still interested in other forms of knowledge; but they are all secondary to this desire to know the Lord. Similarly there is in him a loving instinct, crying and clamouring for satisfaction. I am referring not only to knowing the love of God and of Christ, but to the fact that a child of God longs to be filled with love

himself. He becomes unhappy if love is absent from his life.
With William Cowper he says:

> *Lord, it is my chief complaint*
> *That my love is weak and faint.*

He longs to love God more truly and to love Christ more. He
wants to be filled with love to his fellowmen and women. And
when he reads 1 Corinthians, chapter 13, he says: I long to be
like that; I want to be filled with this love and to be an exemplifier
of it.

When a man is 'filled with all the fulness of God' he increasingly
conforms to the pattern of love because 'the fruit of the Spirit
[first and foremost] is love' (Gal 5:22). This should be the subject
of our daily meditation. 'Charity (or love) suffereth long, and is
kind; charity envieth not; charity vaunteth not itself, is not
puffed up, doth not behave itself unseemly, seeketh not her own,
is not easily provoked, thinketh no evil; rejoiceth not in iniquity,
but rejoiceth in the truth; beareth all things, believeth all things,
hopeth all things, endureth all things. Charity never faileth'
(1 Cor 13:4-8). If we are truly children of God, we long to be
filled with that love, and increasingly we know something about
it, to our amazement!

Then again, there is the longing for righteousness. Our Lord
has said, 'Blessed are they that do hunger and thirst after
righteousness, for they shall be filled' (Matt 5:6). The child of
God must of necessity be hungering and thirsting for, and longing
after, righteousness. Are you not tired of sinning? Are you not
tired of failing? Are you not tired of going astray? There is an
instinct in the child of God for holiness and for righteousness.
He no longer complains that the Christian life is narrow and
restricting. If you feel that it is, you are confessing that you lack
this instinct of the new-born babe in Christ. If you have to drag
yourself to worship God, you are a very poor child, if indeed a
child at all. Examine yourself. Instinctively the child of God has
a longing, a desire for righteousness and holiness. And we have
the blessed promise that we shall be filled, that the instinct will
be satisfied.

Another instinctive desire is the longing to have power to
serve Him and to glorify His Name. Charles Wesley's hymn

expressed it perfectly; it was his one burning passion. Yet more powerfully Paul tells how he was governed by it. In the Epistle to the Colossians, referring to the Lord Jesus Christ he says: 'Whom we preach, warning every man and teaching every man in all wisdom; that we may present every man perfect in Christ Jesus: whereunto I also labour, striving according to his working, which worketh in me mightily' (1:28-29). The Apostle knew what it was to be moved by the thrilling power of God through the Holy Spirit. Likewise he tells the Corinthians that his speech and his preaching were in demonstration of the Spirit and of power. Do we know anything about this?

I take leave to say in all humility, that there is nothing more blessed under heaven than to know something of the power of the Holy Spirit. I am sorry for those who have never known it as they have preached and tried to expound the Scriptures. There is an almost inexpressible difference between preaching in one's own strength, and preaching in the power of the Spirit. This can happen also in conversation, and in all the activities and endeavours of the Christian. When we are filled with all the fulness of God, all our spiritual instincts and aims are satisfied. The hymn of Johann Caspar Lavater, quoted earlier, and which should be our daily prayer, says it all:

> O Jesus Christ, grow Thou in me
> And all things else recede.

It describes the child of God crying out for the satisfaction of these new instincts and desires.

> Make this poor self grow less and less,
> Be Thou my life and aim.

It shows how he longs to be delivered from the darkness –

> My darkness vanish in Thy light,
> Thy life my death efface.

It expresses the longing to be delivered, to be set free from self and sin, from shame and failure and weakness, and to be 'filled with all the fulness of God'. All these new instincts are satisfied when we are so filled.

Finally, when a man is 'filled with all the fulness of God', every sense of want, of emptiness, and of insufficiency, has gone.

Let me remind you of what our Lord said to the Woman of Samaria. Pointing to Jacob's Well, He said: 'Whosoever drinketh of this water shall thirst again: but whosoever drinketh of the water that I shall give him shall never thirst; but the water that I shall give him shall be in him a well of water springing up into everlasting life' (John 4:13–14). 'Shall *never* thirst'! How can you thirst if you are filled with all the fulness of God?

But our Lord was not content with saying that once only. He repeats it in that same gospel of John, chapter 6, verse 35; 'He that cometh to me shall never hunger; and he that believeth on me shall never thirst' (John 6:35). Are you hungry? Are you thirsty? Are you unhappy? Are you ill at ease? Do you sometimes find yourself not knowing what to do with the next hour? Have you a sense of vagueness and of loss, of emptiness and of purposelessness? If you are, it simply means that you do not keep on going to the Lord Jesus Christ. 'He that cometh unto me' means 'he that keeps on coming to me'. How can you hunger or thirst if life itself, life indeed, life more abundant, is within you?

*　　*　　*

There, then, we have our Lord's promises: Are they true, are they fulfilled in practice in life? The Apostle Paul gives us the answer in his Epistle to the Philippians: 'Not that I speak in respect of want: for I have learned in whatsoever state I am, therewith to be content. I know both how to be abased, and I know how to abound: every where and in all things I am instructed both to be full and to be hungry, both to abound and to suffer need. I can do all things through Christ which strengtheneth me' (4:11–13). The promises are true! Paul is in a state in which he is never hungry and never thirsty. He says later in the same chapter: 'But I have all, and abound' (v. 18). He was in prison when he wrote these words, and in those days prisons were often dank, dark, and unhealthy. Perhaps he was chained to a soldier. But 'I have all, and abound'. 'I am full'. Of course he is! He was filled with all the fulness of God! He waxes yet more bold and says: 'My God shall supply all your need, according to his riches in glory by Christ Jesus' (v. 19). That is what is meant by being 'filled with all the fulness of God'.

Christian people, do we know this enjoyment? This is

Christianity! It was in order to make this possible that the Son of God left heaven, came on earth, and went to the Cross on Calvary's hill. He died not merely that we might be forgiven and saved from hell. He died that we might be 'filled with all the fulness of God' – here in this life! Not when you are dead and have passed into heaven and into glory, but here and now! We shall have it in greater fulness there, but we are to be filled to the brim here and now. That is what Paul was praying for these Ephesians. It is not a vague ideal which he is setting before them; he is praying that they may truly know this, even as he himself knew it.

This is Christianity! To be content with anything less than this is sinful, and dishonouring to the Lord. Do not be content with the mere fact that you believe in Christ, that your sins are forgiven, and that you are a church member. Press on, give yourself neither rest nor peace; offer this prayer for yourself, the whole of it, and go on doing so until you know something of this blessed satisfaction and have realized something of this fulness. Do not think of this as some kind of substance, as an *it*. Do not think in terms of analogies such as pouring a liquid from a jug into a vessel. This is personal, it is God, Christ, dwelling within. Concentrate on the Person, therefore. Go to the Person Himself, act on your faith, and speak to Him; tell Him your wants and needs, wait upon Him, spend your time with Him. He will give you of His fulness, and then you will be able to agree with another hymn-writer, William Tidd Matson. Matson's father was a great man in the political world, and William was a young man of very great ability who was also destined for the political world, and who would undoubtedly have done brilliantly in that realm. But at the age of twenty he had a profound evangelical experience. He was converted and received this new life of God in his soul. He gave up all the glittering and dazzling prospects and became a humble preacher of the gospel. Was he conscious of having made a great sacrifice? No! It was all gain, as he tells us:

> O blessèd life! the heart at rest
> When all without tumultuous seems,
> That trusts a higher will, and deems
> That higher will, not mine, the best.

O blessed life! the mind that sees,
Whatever change the years may bring,
A mercy still in everything
And shining through all mysteries.

O life, how blessèd, how divine!
High life, the earnest of a higher!
Saviour, fulfil my deep desire,
And let this blessèd life be mine.

John Ryland a preacher who lived from 1753 to 1825, and who also knew something of this fulness, expresses it thus:

O Lord, I would delight in Thee
And on Thy care depend;
To Thee in every trouble flee,
My best, my only Friend.

When all created streams are dried
Thy fulness is the same;
May I with this be satisfied
And glory in Thy Name!

No good in creatures can be found
But may be found in Thee;
I must have all things and abound,
While God is God to me.

He that has made my heaven secure
Will here all good provide;
While Christ is rich, can I be poor?
What can I ask beside?

O Lord, I cast my care on Thee;
I triumph and adore;
Henceforth my great concern shall be
To love and please Thee more.

24
The Grand Doxology

'Now unto him that is able to do exceeding
abundantly above all that we ask or think, according
to the power that worketh in us, unto him *be* glory in
the church by Christ Jesus throughout all ages, world
without end. Amen.'

Ephesians: 3:20–21

'Now unto him that is able to do exceeding abundantly above all
that we ask or think, according to the power that worketh in us,
unto him be glory in the church by Christ Jesus throughout all
ages, world without end. Amen'.

With these words, a doxology, the Apostle ends this remarkable
prayer which he has been offering for the Ephesian Christians.
Nothing could be more fitting than this after such a prayer.
Indeed, nothing else would be fitting at all. We have seen how
the Apostle has risen from petition to petition, and from height
to height, until he has reached the climax, the acme, beyond
which nothing is possible. Nothing greater can ever happen to
us than the answer to, and the satisfaction of, the petition that we
may be 'filled with all the fulness of God'. Having asked for that,
having prayed for that, there is nothing more that one can do,
there is no further prayer, there is nothing to do but to praise God.

So the Apostle ends with this doxology, and it is not surprising
that he should have felt this desire to praise God. He has been
praying that the Ephesians may be 'strengthened with might by
his Spirit in the inner man'. That is a great request in and of itself.
He has gone on to pray that Christ 'may dwell in their hearts by
faith', and then that they might 'know the love of Christ which
passeth knowledge', and above all, that they might be 'filled with
all the fulness of God'. And then, as it were, he stops and asks
himself what it is that makes all this possible. There is only one

answer, it is the grace of God. He has already been extolling that grace in the second chapter, which has been reminding the Ephesian Christians that it is God who, in 'His great love wherewith he loved us', has done all this; that it is all because of 'the exceeding riches of his grace', and 'his kindness toward us in Christ Jesus'.

So here, having offered the petitions, Paul realizes that answers to such staggering petitions are only possible because of the grace of God. It is all of grace. There is nothing in man to deserve such blessings, nothing in man to recommend himself. All the blessings we enjoy come to us through the way of salvation which God Himself has provided in and through His only begotten Son, our Lord and Saviour Jesus Christ. The Apostle was so deeply conscious of this, and so moved by realization of it, that his soul and heart seem to be bursting with a desire to praise, and to thank, and to glorify, the God who has made such things possible for men.

I am suggesting that the Apostle ended with this doxology because he could do nothing else. What he had been requesting for these Christians was such a glorious possibility that he involuntarily bursts forth into this great hymn of praise worship, and adoration. His desire is that all the glory be ascribed unto Him who is the Author and the Giver of salvation, and who alone deserves the glory and the honour and the praise.

*   *   *

The question that now arises is, Do we feel impelled to join him? Are we animated by the same feelings and the same thoughts? Having read the various petitions in the prayer, and having arrived at the climax, are we conscious of the inevitability of the doxology? Do we feel, as the Apostle did, this almost unrestrainable desire to praise God and to magnify His grace? Have we been moved and thrilled, as was the Apostle, as we have realized the tremendous possibilities open to us in this present life? It would be very wrong to begin to consider this doxology without facing such questions. Or is it possible that we rather have the feeling that the Apostle has said too much? We believe the gospel, and we are Christians, and we believe that all is by faith; but when he begins to talk about Christ dwelling in our hearts and our knowing this love of Christ and of being filled with all the fulness of God, then do we suspect that he has gone too far, that he is beside himself and has become the victim of his own eloquence? Do we feel that these things are possible only for very exceptional people such as the Apostle himself, or for those who are called 'saints' who have segregated themselves from the world and gone off into monasteries? Do we feel that they are beyond the reach of the ordinary Christian, so-called, and certainly not possible for us?

We are in one of these two positions. If we have caught a glimpse of these things and seen the possibility, we must feel the desire to offer the doxology and to join the Apostle in it. But if we are doubtful and hesitant, we shall be debating and arguing with ourselves and wondering whether this is not some strange sort of mysticism. The doxology tests us and our profession of the Christian faith.

This is not something which can be considered purely objectively. Do we join the Apostle wholeheartedly and feel this doxology welling up within us? I fear that many of us merit the rebuke God administered to the children of Israel of old in the 81st Psalm, when He reminds them of what He would have done for them but for their unbelief. He says: 'O Israel, if thou wilt hearken unto me'. There is no end to what He will do for them if they will but listen. 'Open thy mouth wide and I will fill it'. 'Oh that my people had hearkened unto me, and Israel had walked in my ways!' (vv. 8, 10, 13). But they had not hearkened; they were afraid of the enemy, and they lacked the faith to receive these promises. They felt that they were too great; they staggered in unbelief. They did not believe the Word of God, they did not believe the promises, and so they wandered and meandered in their journey as the record tells us, doubtful and hesitant and fearful, often sitting in their tents and commiserating with themselves. What a sorry figure they cut! It was all due to the fact that they could not believe the promises because they felt that they were too good to be true. What is our position with respect to them? What is our reaction to the petitions which the Apostle has been offering one after another, and which lead to the great climax about our being 'filled with all the fulness of God'?

I find myself speculating as to whether the Apostle had a feeling that some of the Ephesians might have such thoughts within them. I raise that question for the reason that he couches his expressions in this doxology in such a way as to answer such a possible difficulty. The Apostle was always a teacher and a pastor. Even in a doxology such as this, where he is ascribing praise and glory to God, there is an exhortation. He deals with a possible lack of faith, a possible staggering in unbelief, so he says: 'Now unto him that is able to do exceeding abundantly above all that we ask or think, according to the power that worketh in us, unto him be glory'. He might have said, 'Now unto him, the God who promises so much, be all the glory in the church by Christ Jesus'; but he deliberately adds the others expressions. So as the Apostle praises God, he at the same time encourages us to pray and to praise, and teaches us how to do so.

Are you doubtful about these things? Do you really believe that Christ can dwell in your heart by faith? Is He dwelling in your heart by faith? Have you been able to 'comprehend with all saints what is the breadth and the length and the depth and the height', and have you known 'the love of Christ which passeth knowledge'? Have you felt it, have you experienced it, have you known it in an experimental manner? You may believe it, you may have accepted it by faith, but there is the deeper question of our experiential knowledge of these things. We have seen that the word 'know' carries an experimental emphasis; it is a knowledge of experience. 'The love of Jesus, what it is, none but His loved ones know'. Do we know it in that sense? And do we know something about being 'filled with all the fulness of God' – the satisfaction we have been considering? If we do not 'know' these things, it is because, ultimately, we are ignorant of God, ignorant of the glory and the power of God, ignorant of what He has purposed for us in Christ Jesus. We are ignorant of what He has treasured and stored up for us in the Person of His only-begotten Son in whom 'dwelleth all the fulness of the Godhead bodily', and in whom we are complete.

So let us hearken to the exhortation which is contained in the doxology. The Apostle desires to help us; he stoops to our weakness, he meets us in the place of our ignorance and unbelief. He tells us that what we need above everything else is to know the greatness of God's power. We can know that, he tells us, first of all by looking at it objectively, by looking at it in and of itself.

Then he will ask us to look at it subjectively, and finally in terms of the Church.

*　　*　　*

The theme of the greatness of God's power as seen objectively has been in the mind of the Apostle from the end of the first chapter of the Epistle. In that first chapter the Apostle tells the Ephesian believers that he is praying for them without ceasing, and asking that 'the eyes of their understanding may be enlightened'. He prays for this although they have already believed the gospel, and are already saved, and have already been sealed by the Spirit. He prays that they might be enlightened in order that they might know 'what is the hope of his calling, what the riches of the glory of his inheritance in the saints, and what is the exceeding greatness of his power to us-ward who believe'. He then goes on to describe that power in terms of the power that was exerted by God when He raised His own Son from the grave; in other words, in terms of resurrection power. Such is the power which is working in Christians.

In the second chapter he has worked this out experimentally and in detail; and here he comes back to it again. He wants them to know the 'exceeding greatness of his power to us-ward who believe'. If we but knew that power we would never stagger in unbelief under any circumstances whatsoever. He has already defined it, and described and illustrated it, in the power of the resurrection, but here he describes it in a different form. And he does so in most extraordinary language.

Language has never been strained and used to the limit as it is in this doxology. This is so because language is inadequate. The Apostle is now trying to define the indefinable. He is trying to measure the immeasurable. He is trying to put in human terms that which is illimitable – the absolute! See how he piles words one on top of another. The Authorized Version is quite defective here, and does not adequately express the thought. It reads, 'Unto Him that is able to do exceeding abundantly above all that we ask or think'. But what the Apostle actually wrote consists of a superlative added to a superlative. He first of all says, 'Unto him that is able above [or beyond] all things'. We might have thought that that was sufficient, but Paul was not satisfied. He adds, 'exceeding abundantly beyond all that we ask or think.'

So the entire sentence can be translated thus: 'Now unto ḥim who is able above all things to do exceeding abundantly beyond all we can ask or think'. This shows the total inadequacy of language. Our greatest superlatives do not describe the power of God. Add one to another, multiply them, and add them together, and multiply again, and go on doing so 'beyond all things', 'exceeding abundantly beyond all things', and still you have not succeeded in describing it. Is there anything 'beyond all things'? The power of God is exceeding abundant beyond all things.

Thus the Apostle vainly attempts to give us some conception of God's power. He seems to be asking a series of questions, such as, Do you think I am going too far? Do you think I have been carried away by my own rhetoric or eloquence? Do you think I am lost in some mystical state where logic and reason are left behind? Listen, he says, I have been praying to One whose power is eternal and absolute, above all things, One who can do exceeding abundantly beyond our utmost thought. That is the power of which I am thinking and which I long for you to experience.

The Apostle comes down to our level and helps us in our unbelief and doubts and hesitations. Sometimes in our prayers we think that we have been somewhat daring, and that we have asked for something which is quite impossible. The Apostle tells us that we must never harbour such thoughts, because God is able to do exceeding abundantly beyond all that we can ask. John Newton understood this, and that is why he urges us in one of his well-known hymns to stop and think, and to remind ourselves of certain things before we begin to pray. We must not rush with our petitions into the presence of God. We must ask certain questions. To whom am I praying? Who is the Being and what is the truth concerning the Being I am about to address? Newton answers his own question by saying:

> *Thou art coming to a King,*
> *Large petitions with thee bring;*
> *For His grace and power are such,*
> *None can ever ask too much.*

Bring your most daring petitions, bring your most impossible requests, add others to them; let the whole Church join together in their wildest desires and demands! There is no danger of exceeding the limit – 'For his grace and power are such, None can ever ask too much'. His power is beyond all that we can ever ask.

But not only so, God's power is even beyond what we can think. This is not a division without a distinction. There is a difference between what we ask and what we think. We constantly draw this distinction in daily life. We talk about the realm of the possible. 'Politics', we are told, 'is the art of the possible'; that is the limit of its capacity. There are things of which we say that it would be very wonderful if we could have them, but they are beyond the bounds of possibility. Men have thought and written about an ideal, a perfect state, a kind of utopia, but in a world such as this it is unattainable. You must confine yourself to that which is possible. In other words, there is a distinction between what we ask and what we think. We put a limit upon our requests, upon our actual petitions, because we know that we are hemmed in and bound by this idea of the possible. But then we like to soar in our minds and imaginations and to think and dream of impossibilities. We have risen to a higher level and though we know that such things cannot happen in this world we can nevertheless conceive of them and think of them. But the Apostle covers that also. God is not only able to do exceeding abundantly beyond all that we can ask; but also beyond all that we can imagine, all that we can think of, all that we can conjure up with our highest and most inspired thoughts and imaginations.

Surely our greatest trouble in the Christian life is our failure to realize that God is not as man. The greatest sin of every Christian, and of the Christian Church in general is to limit the eternal, absolute power of God to the measure of our own minds and concepts and understandings. God's people have always been guilty of this. They have 'limited the Holy One of Israel'. 'If only', God says to them repeatedly. This was the case also when our Lord was here in this world in the days of the flesh. This was His condemnation of the Jews when He uttered the lament, 'O Jerusalem, Jerusalem, which killest the prophets, and stonest them that are sent unto thee; how often would I have gathered thy children together, as a hen doth gather her brood under her wings, but ye would not!' (Luke 13:34). 'Hadst thou but known'!

[308]

God's people have, like Sarah, Abraham's wife, constantly been guilty of failure to believe God and to trust in His power. This is seen in the Old Testament and the New alike. When the archangel Gabriel announced to Mary that she was to give birth to the Son of God, she staggered in her unbelief, and the angel had to reprimand her saying, 'With God nothing shall be impossible' (Luke 1:30–37). By asking 'How shall this be?' she was thinking only in terms of human power, and thereby limiting God.

Recall also the occasion when the disciples were watching our Lord as He dealt with the (so-called) 'rich young ruler', who claimed to have kept God's law from his youth up. To show him his need for repentance the Lord corrected his misunderstanding of the Law. The young man was probably handsome in appearance and well known for his benefactions and his upright moral living; yet he 'went away sorrowful' (Luke 18:18–23). The apostles were astonished and asked our Lord, saying, 'Who then can be saved?' Our Lord looked at them and said, 'With man it is impossible, but not with God, for with God all things are possible'. How constantly are we guilty of limiting the power of God in our petitions and requests for ourselves! Thus when we are told that we can be 'filled with all the fulness of God' we feel that it is not possible.

We are guilty of the same unbelief when we limit our petitions with respect to others. For instance, we may say of a certain man that he is so steeped in sin that nothing can save him. You may be concerned about some dear one who is antagonistic to Christ and blaspheming His name, and have prayed for his or her conversion for years; and you begin to say that there is no point in continuing to do so, and that the psychologists are right after all in speaking about a religious temperament. You feel that it is impossible. The answer still is, 'With God nothing shall be impossible'. He is 'able to do exceeding abundantly above and beyond all that we ask or think'. God's word to us today, as of old, is 'Open thy mouth wide and I will fill it'. Let us remember that, when we are praying to God, the omnipotent, the everlasting and the eternal. Thus has the Apostle invited us to look at the greatness of God's power objectively.

*   *   *

Now let us follow him as he asks us to look at the greatness of God's power subjectively and in the realm of experience. 'Now unto him that is able to do exceeding abundantly above all that we ask or think according to the power that worketh in us'. In the words, 'according to the power that worketh in us', we come to the realm of the subjective. One may hear or read these marvellous descriptions of the power of God and yet feel that it is all remote and far removed from the realm of our daily life and experience. It sounds 'too good to be true', something that cannot actually happen to us. It not only can happen but does happen, says Paul, 'according to the power that worketh in us'. The Apostle is not speaking in a purely academic and theoretical manner, but appealing to our experience. The power of which he is speaking, he avers, is the power which is already working in us. This, in a sense, is a still greater proof of God's power, because it answers all the objections that may arise from our subjective feelings. The Apostle is summing up here most of what he has been saying in this Epistle in the first three chapters. It is as if he were challenging anyone in Ephesus who doubts the power of God, and is tempted to feel that Paul is going too far and asking for the impossible. Hence he says that, in addition to all the external proofs of the power of God, there is another proof, namely, the power that is working in us.

Doubtless the Apostle was in the first instance thinking of himself. We recall how he refers to himself at the beginning of this third chapter, when he says, 'If ye have heard of the dispensation of the grace of God which is given me to you-ward: how that by revelation he made known unto me the mystery'. There he has referred them to his own experience. Does anyone doubt the power of God? Well, if so, says the Apostle, look at me! I was at one time a blasphemer, a persecutor, and an injurious person. I hated Christ with all the intensity of my being; I did my utmost to massacre the members of the Church and to destroy it out of sight. I set out to Damascus one day, breathing out threatenings and slaughter against Christians. Never was a man so opposed to Christianity, never was a man so held by prejudices, national prejudice, prejudice of training, prejudice of religion and of learning, prejudice of self-conceit and self-righteousness. How could such a man as I, Saul of Tarsus, ever become a Christian? But I am a Christian! I am the man who has had the privilege of preaching the gospel to you. How has it come about? There is only one explanation – the power of God!

Nothing but this eternal power of God could have turned the blaspheming, persecuting Pharisee into the Apostle of Christ, yea, the Apostle to the Gentiles. But this had not only been working in Paul, the same power had been working in the Ephesian Christians also. He has already reminded them of this. 'You hath he quickened, who were dead in trespasses and sins; wherein in time past ye walked according to the course of this world, according to the prince of the power of the air, the spirit that now worketh in the children of disobedience: among whom also we all had our conversation in times past in the lusts of our flesh, fulfilling the desires of the flesh and of the mind; and were by nature the children of wrath, even as others'. They were in a completely hopeless condition – spiritually dead! But he adds to the description: 'Wherefore remember, that ye being in time past Gentiles in the flesh . . . that at that time ye were without Christ, being aliens from the commonwealth of Israel, and strangers from the covenants of promise, having no hope, and without God in the world' (2:1-3, 11-12). They were barred out from the blessings which the Jews knew, by a middle wall of partition; they were utterly hopeless, lost, damned. How can such people ever become Christians? How could such people ever become heirs of God? How could such people ever become fellow citizens and heirs with the Jews? To man it was a sheer impossibility; and yet, says the Apostle, you know that it has happened; and you are members of Christ's Church. And it has all happened because of this selfsame power of God. It is that power working in you that alone has enabled you to believe the gospel. You could not of yourselves have believed it; you were dead.

No man can believe the gospel in and of himself; the power of the Spirit alone can lead anyone to belief; without it we are spiritually dead and lost and ruined, and under the wrath of God. But God can quicken the dead! And He had quickened the Ephesians. He had put new life into them; He had raised them up together with Christ, He had caused them to be 'seated in the heavenly places with Christ'. They who had been so far off, and so utterly and entirely hopeless, had been 'made nigh' by the power of God. This had actually taken place in their experience. So the logic of the Apostle's argument is that the God who can do that, can do anything, can do everything. There is no limit to such a power!

Once more we just pause to ask ourselves a question: Have you known this power? Does this particular argument about 'the power that worketh in us' apply to you, and convince you? Have you experienced that power imparting new life to you? Are you aware of the new life thrilling in your being? Are you aware of the power of the Spirit sanctifying you, revealing sin to you, 'bringing to light the hidden things of darkness', explaining the Word to you, creating desires after holiness and righteousness within you? Are you aware of being dealt with by God? Is He moving in you? Do you feel and know that He can keep you from falling? This argument is valueless to all who have never known the source of power. But if you know this power of God working in you, then you must go on; you must be logical and say, The God who has done this for me already, is a God who will do all He has promised! There is no end and no limit to this power; it must be endless and eternal.

The Apostle's argument is that if Christians know this power, they must not stagger in unbelief, or doubt or hesitate when he tells them that they may 'be filled with all the fulness of God'. The power which has brought them from death to life will bring them to know 'the love of Christ which passeth knowledge', and cause them to be 'filled with all the fulness of God'. Thus the Apostle makes them look at the power objectively, and then subjectively.

* * *

Thirdly, and lastly, Paul asks them to look at the greatness of this power as it is seen and manifested in the Church. 'Unto him that is able to do exceeding abundantly above all that we ask or think, according to the power that worketh in us, unto him be glory in the church, by Christ Jesus, throughout all ages, world without end. Amen'. Once more the Apostle is summarizing what he has already been saying. Over and above the arguments provided by the objective proofs of God's power, and our personal and individual experiences of it, there is another powerful argument to bring us to a realization of this power of God. We are to look at the Christian Church.

The Christian Church is a miracle. The Apostle has already drawn attention to this several times in his Epistle. The Ephesians were Gentiles, aliens, outside the commonwealth of Israel, and strangers from the covenants of promise. And there were the Jews – self-righteous, proud, and nationalistic. A middle wall of partition was between them. Reconciliation between Jew and Gentile? It seemed sheer madness; it was not within the realm of practical politics. It was something that could not happen. But it had happened. 'But now in Christ Jesus ye who sometimes were far off are made nigh by the blood of Christ. For he is our peace, who hath made both one, and hath broken down the middle wall of partition between us; having abolished in his flesh the enmity, even the law of commandments contained in ordinances; for to make in himself of twain one new man, so making peace' (2: 13–15). Again, 'Now therefore ye are no more strangers and foreigners, but fellow-citizens with the saints, and of the house-hold of God; and are being built up together upon the foundation of the apostles and prophets, Jesus Christ himself being the chief corner stone' (vv. 19–20). It had happened. Nothing but the power of God could ever have brought about this reconciliation, could ever have produced the Church, the one body, and enabled us to say, 'For through him we both have access by one Spirit unto the Father'.

Nothing so shows the power and the glory of God as the Christian Church. The Apostle has reminded us of that by saying: 'To the intent that now unto the principalities and powers in heavenly places might be known by the church the manifold wisdom of God' (3:10). And the wisdom is displayed through the power. The Apostle had already used this argument in the first chapter when he prays that the Ephesians might know 'the exceeding greatness of his power to us-ward who believe'. This is, he says, the 'power which he (the Father) wrought in Christ when he raised him from the dead, and set him at his own right hand in the heavenly places, far above all principality, and power, and might, and dominion, and every name that is named, not only in this world, but also in that which is to come: and hath put all things under his feet, and gave him to be the head over all things to the church, which is his body, the fulness of him that filleth all in all' (vv. 19–23). Paul is but repeating that here, as he so delights to do everywhere.

Nothing gives such glory to God as the Christian Church. God manifested His power when He created the world out of nothing; when He said, 'Let there be light' and there was light! The mountains, the rivers and the raging sea, lightning and thunder, all proclaim His glory. 'The heavens declare the glory of God; and the firmament showeth his handiwork' (Psa 19:1). But there is nothing that so proclaims the glory of God as the Christian Church, the body of which Christ Himself is the Head. Nothing is so wonderful as the fact that men and women, such as you and I are, men and women who were steeped and lost and dead in sin, should have become members of the body of Christ. Here we have the mightiest display of the glory of God. So it is not surprising that the Apostle says, 'Unto him be glory in the church, by Christ Jesus'. It is all 'by Christ Jesus', and all through Him. We are in Him. We are 'members of his body, of his flesh and of his bones'. The Son glorifies the Father, and the Son is glorified in us. He says so in His prayer to His Father before He suffered: 'I am glorified in them' (John 17:10). He has glorified the Father, and we, being 'in him' and in the Church, also minister to the glory of the Father. What a wonderful picture!

This leads us to the final phrase where the Apostle seems again to be beside himself, and piles adjective upon adjective and superlative upon superlative. Again the Authorized Version is inadequate, with its 'Unto him be glory in the church by Christ Jesus throughout all ages, world without end'. What the Apostle actually wrote should read, 'Unto him be glory in the church by Christ Jesus to all the generations of the age of the ages'. You cannot add to that! 'All the generations'. Of what? 'Of the age of the ages'. What is 'the age of the ages'? There is no age to the ages; it is *the* age of the ages, age upon age upon age, for ever and for ever, an infinite number of ages.

Note what Paul says. The Church will be there for ever and ever. You and I will be there, unto all the generations of the age of the ages. The principalities and powers in the heavenly places will look at us in astonishment and amazement, and seeing us, they will ascribe unto God all the honour and the glory and the majesty and the might and the dominion and the power. It is in us, in the Church, that they see the glory and the wisdom of God as they see it nowhere else. We shall thus be manifesting the glory of God for ever and for ever, 'unto all the generations of the age of the ages'. Such is the power of God. While we are still in this world, it is a power great enough to keep us from falling. Jude's doxology reminds us of, and commends us to, 'him that is able to keep us from falling'. But He is not only able to keep and to hold us, He is also able 'to present us faultless before the presence of his glory with exceeding joy'. It is not surprising that Jude adds, 'To the only wise God our Saviour, be glory and majesty, dominion and power, both now and ever. Amen' (vv. 24–25).

Are you joining in this great doxology? Having looked at the possibilities that are open for you even now in Christ Jesus, and having offered these petitions for yourself, are you saying: 'Let all the glory in earth and heaven and sea, and wherever there are any beings, let all glory and honour be ascribed unto the blessed God, the Father of our Lord and Saviour Jesus Christ, our God, the God of our salvation. Unto him be glory in the church by Christ Jesus, unto all the generations of the age of the ages'? Are you ready to join with Samuel Davies in singing:

> *Great God of wonders, all Thy ways*
> *Are matchless, godlike and divine;*
> *But the fair glories of Thy grace*
> *More godlike and unrivalled shine.*

> *O may this strange, this matchless grace,*
> *This godlike miracle of love,*
> *Fill the wide earth with grateful praise,*
> *And all the angelic hosts above:*
> *Who is a pardoning God like Thee?*
> *Or who has grace so rich and free?*